Hawaii 501

Life as a Darts Pro

Wayne Mardle

with Iain Spragg

VSP

Published by Vision Sports Publishing

WAYNE MARDLE

Darts' great entertainer and the most popular player on the circuit, Wayne Mardle was inspired by dad Billy to pick up his first set of arrows at the age of 10. He won his first tournament on his 13th birthday and went on to lift both the British Teenage and Youth titles. The former England international gave up his day job as an accounts clerk in 2003 to became a full-time professional and is now in the top six of the Professional Darts Corporation rankings. When he's not throwing darts he can usually be found throwing away his winnings on internet poker sites. A three-times semi-finalist, he is yet to be crowned World Champion.

IAIN SPRAGG

Iain is a prolific freelance sports writer and the author of numerous books, including *The Reduced History of Rugby* and *The Jonny Wilkinson Story*. Previously an armchair darts fan, he has recently picked up his arrows and is now manfully trying to raise his three-dart average into double figures in the comfort of his north London local.

TO MY LOVELY WIFEY, DONNA.

How you put up with me, I'll never know.

Vision Sports Publishing
2 Coombe Gardens
London SW20 OQU

www.visionsp.co.uk

Produced in association with
Justyn Barnes Media Ltd

www.justynbarnesmedia.com

The first edition published by
Vision Sports Publishing in 2006

Editor
Justyn Barnes

Design
chicken www.herechickychicky.com

Cover photography
Paul Downes at **Objective Image**
www.objectiveimage.com

Cover styling
Rosie Meckiff

Mega Dart maker
Russell Beck Studio Ltd
www.rbeckstudio.demon.co.uk

Proof-reader
Chris Stone

Printed and bound in the UK by
Cromwell Press

A CIP catalogue record for this book is available from the British Library

ISBN 1-905326-06-8

Contents

Foreword

BY PHIL 'THE POWER' TAYLOR

I first saw Wayne play six years ago at the World Championship at the Lakeside in Frimley Green and it was obvious to me even back then he was something special. I was commentating on one of his matches for the BBC and he was like a breath of fresh air up there on the stage, throwing some great darts and working the crowd. I knew then it wasn't the last time I'd be hearing his name. I wasn't wrong.

He hasn't really changed that much since then. He's still a great player and he's still as daft as a brush. The crowds still love him and he's as naturally charismatic as ever. His shirts are a lot brighter than they were back then, but that's Wayne for you. He's never exactly been the shy and retiring type. Wayne turned professional a few years ago but I think 2005 was the year that he really changed from a boy into a man in the darts world. In the early days he was a bit like Anna Kournikova—looked pretty but never won anything—but he's matured and there's no doubt in my mind that once he gets over the winning line in a major final, more titles will follow.

He's definitely got the talent to be World Champion one day. I'm not planning to let it be at my expense, but lesser players than Wayne have won it in the past and there's no reason why he shouldn't get his hands on the trophy in the future.

Some people call Wayne a show pony but I prefer showman. He certainly loves it up on the stage in front of the cameras, but the important thing is the fans love him. He's great for the game and I hope he never changes. After all, professional darts is about entertainment and drama, and Wayne is undoubtedly a star of the circuit. Without him, darts would be a lot duller.

This book is a year in Wayne's life but it's also about the great game of darts, warts and all, which is important. Like a lot of darts players, I get pissed off with the stereotypes about the game and people's stupid and ill-informed preconceptions about it. This book is a behind-the-scenes look at what life on the circuit is really like for the top pros, how hard we have to work and the sacrifices we make to earn a living. It reveals the glamour and the graft involved in the game, both in front of and away from the television cameras, with honesty and humour. People who knock us should read it before they open their mouths.

I'm not going to spoil the thrilling climax to the book and what happens when Wayne and I come face-to-face at the legendary Circus Tavern. Let's just say it's a cracking end to a cracking read. Enjoy.

PHIL TAYLOR

January 2006

CHAPTER ONE

The end of the Worlds

SATURDAY 1ST JANUARY 2005

Happy New Year. It's just gone midnight and I'm stuck indoors all alone in the spare room of my house near Romford, in beautiful sunny Essex. The spare room is where I practice. My wife Donna has abandoned me to go to a New Year's Eve party down the road at my sister's house and I can hear fireworks going off all over the place outside. I've already had a few vodkas to see the new year in but, believe me, it's anything but a knees-up *chez* Mardle.

I'm on my lonesome because I'm playing in the quarter-finals of the World Championship tonight. I'm up against the world number one Colin Lloyd, a fellow Essex boy and old friend of mine, and I've given my sister's party a miss because I know everyone there is going to be the worse for wear. Tonight is the biggest game of my career and I can't risk being hungover. I don't want to be looking all bleary-eyed for the TV cameras either. I'm not vain but you want to look your best on telly, don't you?

The 'Happy New Year' texts from the family start rolling in after 12 but I carry on practising. I'd have loved to go to the party but you've got to make sacrifices. I've got to be at my best against Colin and if this session gives me an edge, it will make it all worthwhile.

My practice room upstairs is nothing fancy. It's not a box room but it's still only about six foot by six with a little recess in one corner that means I can fit my board. I've got a desk and chair for my laptop (which I couldn't live without), a small fridge, a coffee maker, telly and CD player. Although I've won a few over the years, I don't have any of my darts trophies on show but there is a clock in the shape of a darts board, a map of Britain and a cardboard cut-out of a Hawaiian woman dancing on the walls. And that's about it. I spend a hell of a lot of time in here most days practising and it suits me fine. I suppose you could call it a den full of boy's toys but darts is my full-time job, so I prefer to think of it as my office. It's just that I don't have to clock in and out.

Donna gets home at two. She's not legless but let's just say she's obviously had a good time. Fair play to her because I'd much rather have been with her and the rest of my family than on my own worrying about missing double 20. We have a quick kiss and cuddle to celebrate the New Year and then it's straight off to bed for as good a night's kip as my nerves will allow.

I'm up by nine and I'm really starting to get nervous now. The World Championship is the biggest tournament on the calendar by a distance and it's the one every player wants to win. I've dreamed of being world champion ever since I started playing darts over 20 years ago and although I'm what you'd call a relative youngster on the darts circuit, I believe this could be my year. Like all the other players, I want the title so badly. I reached the semi-finals last year but no-one remembers semi-finalists, do they?

Donna cooks me a full fry-up for breakfast, which has become our silly little match-day ritual during the tournament. It's the same every year—whatever I have for breakfast on the first morning of the competition, I then have to have for breakfast each time I play after that. It all started four years ago and this year it's a full English, which is playing havoc with my waistline. I'm not exactly what you'd call a little fella in the first place but Donna refuses to break with the ritual whether I'm hungry or not and it's not often I risk arguing with her.

I'm playing at four this afternoon. The venue is the Circus Tavern, just outside a little place called Purfleet, in Essex. The Tavern is basically a bit of a dodgy nightclub in the middle of nowhere that most nights has strippers and pole dancers on to be ogled at by Essex poseurs but it gets taken over for two weeks over Christmas every year for the darts. They've been staging the Worlds there for 11 years. In truth, it's not the plushest place you can imagine—it looks like a oversized, dilapidated bungalow in a field—but for some reason, it has a great atmosphere for darts. I absolutely love it and when it's packed to the rafters with 1,200 darts fans you can't beat it. It's also only 15 minutes down the road in the car from my house and I always get great support there because I'm a local lad. It's definitely a "home game" for me there when I play.

I like to get to the Tavern five hours before I'm due on stage so I leave at quarter to 11. I say 'I leave', but I really mean me and Donna because I can't drive, so I'd be going nowhere without her. She used to work for the Inland Revenue but when I turned full-time professional a couple of years ago, she gave up her job and became my driver/personal assistant/agony aunt.

The bar upstairs in the players' room isn't open when we arrive but I don't care. I like to arrive early to soak up the atmosphere, chat to people and slowly psyche myself up. I get nervous waiting for my matches but once I'm inside the Tavern, I'm happy.

The rest of my family—mum Barbara, dad Billy, sister Donna, brother-in-law Perry, niece Ellie and nephew Danny—arrive at two to wish me luck and then I head off to the practice room to warm up. The practice room here is actually part of the players' room but it's around the other corner of the bar and separated off by a black curtain. There are three boards in there and when I arrive Colin's already started his warm-up routine. As I said, I've known Colin for donkey's years, ever since we played in the Essex junior side together, and we're soon chatting away about this and that. We don't mention the match (Christ, it's less than two hours to go) so we just prattle on about nothing and everything as we throw. I don't always talk to opponents before a game—it depends on who it is—but Colin's an old mate and neither of us is going to play silly buggers and ignore each other. I have a few double vodkas to settle my nerves and I'm nearly ready. I don't know a single player who doesn't have a drink before a match. The trick is getting the balance right between being relaxed and horizontal.

An official sticks his head around the curtain at about quarter to four to warn us we're on in ten minutes and the adrenalin is really kicking in now. I give Donna a quick kiss, she wishes me luck and me and Colin are then led downstairs to stand behind the door that all the players make their entrance through. It's nearly time. I'm more excited than nervous but I've still got a shiver going down my spine and I just want to be up on the stage, throwing my darts.

The seconds feel like minutes but finally I hear the MC announce me, my 'walk-on' music starts (the theme from *Hawaii Five–0*), they open the doors and I start to make my way through the crowd. The smell of beer, fags and sweat hits me with a thud but it's all part of the Tavern experience. You always gets mobbed by the crowd because they're so close as you pick your way through and it's an incredible buzz to see my fans all over the place wearing their Hawaiian shirts. I get good support wherever I play and it really gives me a lift to see they've turned up in force again today. Getting the fans behind you is a massive advantage in darts and especially at the Tavern because the crowd is within spitting distance of you. It's such a tight, intimate venue and you can almost feel their breath on the back of your neck when you're on stage. There's no hiding place once you're up there.

The first five sets (it's first to five, each set the best of five legs) fly by and I'm four one down before I know what's happening. Shit. I'm playing like a plonker and Colin keeps going for the jugular. I came back from 3–1 behind in the last round to beat a fella called Paul Williams 4–3 and I was hoping tonight wasn't going to be a repeat performance. Colin's world number one and he doesn't often let positions like this slip. A miracle would be very handy just about now. Some people say I'm the kind of player that needs his back against the wall to produce my best darts but that's crap. If I could win every match four, five, six nil, trust me, I would.

But the tide begins to turn. I nick the sixth set to make it 4–2 but the real turning point comes in the fourth leg of the seventh set. Colin's two legs to one up but misses double 16 for the match, I take out a 25 finish to level it up and then take the next leg.

Four sets to three to Colin but I'm on the charge. I'm the man finishing stronger and me, Colin and the crowd all know it. Darts is a confidence thing, a mind game, and I know Colin's going now. I can see it in his body language and he knows I fancy it because I'm jumping up and down after every shot, giving it the big shoulders, anything I can to let him know I think I'm going to beat him. The pressure's got to him. The next two sets are mine. The crowd is going nuts behind me now and Colin folds. I'm into the semi-finals of the World Championship. What a fucking game.

Afterwards I nip into the portakabin at the side of the Tavern which doubles as the press office during the tournament and give a few quick interviews. Most of the reporters ask how I turned it around when I looked dead and buried and although I make all the right noises about sticking in there, keeping the faith and all that nonsense, I can't answer the question honestly. I've no idea why I played like a twat for five sets and then got it together. I've no idea why Colin looked world class for five sets and then started throwing like an amateur at times. Sometimes it's as much of a mystery to the players as it is to the people watching them play. I do know darts doesn't always make sense and it all adds to the drama, doesn't it?

Once the interviews are done and dusted, I nip back into the players' bar and have a drink with Colin. Believe it or not, we don't talk about the game. It's not the right time for all that so I ask after his long-term girlfriend Deta (who's a former women's world number one) and he asks after Donna.

I'm home by 11 and I have an hour or so playing poker online to unwind (you're going to be hearing a lot about my poker addiction) and then I hit the sack. I'm knackered but happy.

SUNDAY 2ND JANUARY

Semi-final day and I feel tip-top. Start the day with a fry-up of course and then practice all morning in the spare room, a couple of hours on the treble 20s and then I concentrate on the doubles. I feel good and I'm definitely up for it tonight.

My opponent is Mark 'Flash' Dudbridge, one of the up-and-coming faces. Like me, he's in his early 30s which makes him a youngster compared to most of the other pros and there's no doubt he's going to be a big star for years to come. He came up with the 'Flash' nickname himself and to be fair he is quite flash. He's one of those sort of blokes who always walks into a room with a swagger, like he thinks he owns the place. There's just something about the way he carries himself. He has an air of arrogance about him but he's also a good pro who'll do anything to improve his game and you've got to respect that.

I'm on at seven, so I get to the Tavern at two and go through my familiar routine of reading the papers, having a chat with whoever's about, practising and having a little drink or two. I don't chat as much with Mark in the practice room as I did with Colin yesterday because we're not close mates or anything but we do say hello and exchange a bit of small talk. An hour before we start I change into my Hawaiian shirt (I like to leave it late so it's crisp and fresh when I walk on stage) and before I know it, we're heading downstairs. I'm experiencing the same mix of anticipation and anxiety as yesterday but this time the stakes are that bit higher. I'm one game away from the World Championship final and a shot at the title. This is it.

The walk-on is out of this world. The crowd are so up for it and all I can hear is the sound of a thousand odd people chanting "There's only one Wayne Mardle." It's not like I'm an egomaniac, but if that doesn't get you going, then nothing ever will.

The problem is it seems to get Mark going even more than me and, surprise, surprise, I go 4–1 down again in a best of 11 sets match. He's playing well, but after all I've said and done about trying to cut down on my mistakes so I don't have to stage another comeback, I've gone and done it again. I keep telling myself that this is the semi-finals of the World Championships—get your head out of your arse mate!

The crowd are brilliant and do all they can to wake me up. I'm one of those players who would be complete crap if I played in an empty room, I need the atmosphere and the noise and the banter to produce the goods. Some players wilt when they get out onto the stage but I'd be nothing without it. I've been called a showpony because I play up to the crowd and prat about on the stage and, while everyone's entitled to their opinion, I prefer to think of myself as a showman. There's a big difference.

I take three of the next four sets to make it 5–4 and the place is going wild. But Mark is a stubborn bugger and even though I'm breathing down his neck, he keeps up a great standard of darts. This time there's no fairytale ending. He doesn't really give me an opening to get back into the match and hits an 80 finish in the tenth set to win it 6–4. My tournament is over.

Back in the players' room and time to think. That was my second successive semi and I can already hear the critics questioning whether I've got what it takes to go all the way to the final. Have I got the mental strength or even the talent to win the tournament? Am I too busy showing off to the crowd? All I can say is this: if I didn't think I was good enough to be world champion, you wouldn't be reading this book because I wouldn't be a professional darts player. I wouldn't be a darts player at all. I'd still be working as an accounts clerk for the Association of Accounting Technicians in Clerkenwell in London, catching the 8.29 from Romford to Liverpool Street, sitting in exactly the same seat every morning, seeing the same faces every day and never speaking a word to any of them. I'd still be nipping out for a pint at lunchtime, eating cod and chips in our office with the 'Do Not Disturb' sign up and catching the train back home. That was my life for 15 years and it still would be if I didn't believe I could be world champion. I'm only 31 years old and most players hit their peak in their mid to late 30s, so I'll be back for another go.

MONDAY 3RD JANUARY

The world doesn't seem too bad a place this morning. I'm still pissed off but it's done with now and no-one's died, so sod it. I didn't play my best game but Mark took it rather than me handing it to him, so I can't moan on about throwing my chance away. Anyway, I was ranked eighth in the world going into the tournament, so I was only supposed to get to the quarter-finals in the first place. Still, it hurts knowing I was so close to the final.

I can't bring myself to go back to the Tavern for the final so I watch it on the telly at home with wifey. The final is between Mark and Phil 'The Power' Taylor, who's won it 11 times in the past and is generally acknowledged as the most talented man ever to pick up a dart. Phil's the red hot favourite and Mark's going to have to pull a rabbit out of a hat to beat him.

I know it sounds a bit sulky not turning up at the Tavern when it's just down the road but I couldn't stand to hear everyone telling me how unlucky I was, blah, blah, blah and me walking around with a fake smile, trying to look like I wanted to be there.

To be fair, it's a great final. Mark more than does himself justice against Phil and plays superb, but we all know it takes more than superb darts to get over the winning line against Phil. World title number 12 to The Power. 12 titles, 12 TITLES... I only dream of one!

It makes me feel worse seeing Phil win. Don't get me wrong, I've got no problem with Phil and it's not as if I'm best mates with Mark. It's just that I'd have prefered to have gone out to the winner rather than the runner-up. It definitely doesn't make me feel any better realising that, on that form, Phil would probably have beaten me as well.

TUESDAY 4TH JANUARY

Sort out my emails—all 56 of them—from my website (waynemardle.com, folks). Forty eight of them are good luck messages for the World Championship, which shows you how often I check my emails, doesn't it?

The good news is the other eight emails are bookings for exhibitions for the year. I do a lot of exhibitions. They're how I make a decent living out of darts since going full-time and the more bookings, the better. I charge between £450 and £500 for an exhibition, depending on how far I have to travel, and if I can do a 100 in a year, it adds up. Well, you can do the maths. Ninety nine per cent of pros will work for anything while players in the top 20 will charge a minimum of £150 but hope to get more. Phil Taylor can charge a grand for a night's work but he's a special case and when you've won as many world titles as he has, you'd expect to pay a premium. I can charge £500 these days because I've got the profile and I've earned a reputation for putting on a good show.

I did my first exhibition five years ago in a pub called The Never Say Die in Clacton. Keith Porter, who's one of the blokes who calls out the scores at matches, knew the landlord and got us the booking as a pair. We split £300 between us and I've never looked back. I reckon I've got 60-odd exhibitions booked already for this year and fingers crossed there will be a few more on top of that.

I've got the website so people can get in touch to book me and I also flog Hawaiian shirts for anyone who wants one (100 per cent finest polyester and just £22.50!).

People are always asking me how I came to wear the Hawaiian shirts. Well, it all started in 1999, when I was playing on the British Darts Organisation circuit, and I was out in Vegas for the North American Open. A mate of mine found this bright yellow Hawaiian shirt in one of the arcades and as soon as I saw him wearing it, I thought, 'That'll do nicely son.' I'm not what you'd call a snappy dresser normally but I knew a distinctive shirt like that wouldn't do my image any harm and, to be honest, the game was crying out for a bit of colour and character.

I remember the BDO World Championship earlier that year when all the players were introduced to the crowd before the tournament started. We were all up on stage wearing black or white shirts and we looked like a bunch of undertakers or tax inspectors or something. Eye-catching we were not.

So I got myself one of the yellow shirts in Vegas and wore it for the first time at the 2000 World Championship. You would not believe the impact it had. Everyone in the crowd was going wild during my first round match and by the time I played in the second round, I reckon a thousand of the fans had gone out and bought their own shirts. There was just this sea of Hawaiian shirts.

I quickly realised I could make some extra dough selling the shirts myself rather than letting other people cash in. I'd turn up for a tournament and blokes would set up stalls to flog all kind of darts-related stuff and they always seemed to sell out of Hawaiian shirts. I was missing out so my darts supplier, B&W Darts, sourced out a massive roll of Hawaiian-patterned cloth for me—it was about 22-foot long—and then they found a tailor in Aldgate in London to make it into 3,000 shirts for me. The thing is, the cloth only came in blue rather than yellow, which is why I don't wear yellow these days because people only want to buy what they see you wearing up on stage, don't they? The shirts were made up at the end of 2003 and now I've only got about 80 left.

I even married Donna in a Hawaiian shirt. We tied the knot in the Flamingo Hotel in Vegas in the summer of 2002 and all 21 guests wore matching Hawaiian shirts with pink flamingos on 'em. Pure class.

I suppose it was inevitable that once I started wearing the shirts that the 'Hawaii 501' nickname would follow. It makes sense, I suppose. It wasn't me who came up with it—the credit has to go to the popular old pro Bobby George, who was commentating on one of my matches at the World Championship in 2000. Cheers for that, Bobby.

Since the heyday of 'The Crafty Cockney' Eric Bristow in the 1980s, any self-respecting darts pro has needed a nickname. I'll tell you the stories behind the other players' nicknames on the circuit when you meet them over the course of these pages.

WEDNESDAY 5TH JANUARY

The Indian Ocean tsunami is all over the news and it puts a lot of things in perspective. It's hard to worry about the trivial things when you see what's happened over there, and the number of people who were killed is just horrific. I lost a game of darts the other day, but those people have lost everything. Enough said.

THURSDAY 6TH JANUARY

Just watched a programme called *Darts Players' Wives* on Sky, which was meant to be a behind-the-scenes look at the some of the players and their other halves on the PDC circuit. They asked me and Donna if we'd be in it and, having just seen the show, Donna did well to keep us out of the frame. She's quite a shy person naturally and she's not the kind of person who likes being in the spotlight, so she told me to turn them down.

Personally, I didn't fancy some film crew following us round 24/7 with a camera in my face anyway. I've done things like that before and they're always on at you to pose for some silly shots, doing something that you'd never do in normal life. It's meant to be reality TV, but what they actually want to film is totally fake. It's all a bit of a con really.

I don't think the show did darts any favours really. It was all a bit tongue-in-cheek and to be honest some of the things said on the programme let me and every other dart player down. Some of it made the game and the players look stupid. And, no names mentioned, but a dust round one of the players' houses in the show wouldn't have gone amiss. You know who you are. If you didn't see it, don't worry, it wasn't must-see TV.

SATURDAY 8TH JANUARY

Fly up to Newcastle today for the North East Budwesier UK Open Regional Final. The tournament is a series of eight regional competitions played all over the country, with the top 142 money-earners qualifying for the finals at Bolton's Reebok stadium in June. As the name (Open) suggests, anyone can pay £50 and enter but all the top names play as well because there are ranking points and money at stake. It's a long slog of a tournament with so many different venues all over the country but there is £30,000 for the winner at the end of the day and the finals are on the telly, which is where everyone wants to be playing their darts.

I'm actually playing in Tyne & Wear rather than Newcastle. It's all the same to me but people up here take that kind of thing seriously, so I thought I'd better point it out for my own safety.

I know it might sound a bit flash to fly but it's a hell of a long drive from Essex and the flights were pretty cheap, so it made sense and saved Donna the hassle of having to take me up there. When you're on the road as much as I am, you'll do anything to avoid yet another boring journey in the car. In the end, it turns out to be a good decision because some of the lads have all sorts of problems getting up there on the roads because of the bad weather.

My first match of the day against Andy Belton is too tight for comfort. Andy's way below me in the world rankings, somewhere down in the 70s I think, and if I'm being honest I'm happy in the end to scrape a 5–4 legs win. Being a top-ranked player in this kind of competition means you're there to be shot at and plenty of the 'big names' get beaten on a regular basis.

In the last 16 I play a guy called Mark Thomson and it's 5–4 to the Mardle again but, with all respect to Mark, I should be beating players of that quality with a bit more to spare. I'm not playing that hot and it catches up on me in the last eight and I get well and truly thumped 5–0 by Gary Welding. Gary's a talented player but he's not in the top 32 in the world and the result is embarrassing. To say I'm pissed off is an understatement. Getting beat to nil is bad enough but it also means

I don't qualify for tomorrow's finals day and I've come all this way for nothing. Gary played well, but I was a disgrace and I feel like a right plonker now. There's nothing worse than missing out on the second day of a two-day tournament. The frustrating thing is I was within a whisker of the World Championship final a week ago and now I can't win a leg against a player who didn't even play at the Tavern this year.

SUNDAY 9TH JANUARY

Back home in Essex after the jaunt to Newcastle and today's the final of the British Darts Organisation World Championship. Now bear with me if you know all this already, but it's worth explaining for those in the dark.

There are two darts organisations: the Professional Darts Corporation (the PDC), who are my lot; and the British Darts Organisation (the BDO). Both have world championships and ranking tournaments through the year and let's just say the two organisations don't exactly see eye to eye.

As far as I'm concerned, all the politics between the PDC and BDO is crap. I'm a darts player and I let other people worry about that sort of nonsense. Court cases and all that rubbish have got nothing to do with me.

Like a lot of the PDC players, I was with the BDO before I switched—I was ranked world number two with them at one stage—and I've got no problem admitting my decision to move was all down to the money.

I'm not a greedy bloke (despite what some of the other lads on the tour will tell you about how much I eat) but the bottom line is the PDC gave me the chance to make enough money to make darts my full-time job. The BDO does a lot of good work for the sport at grassroots level, but it just isn't geared up to making money for the top players. I've always wanted to make a living playing darts and that was never going to happen with the BDO. I want to retire and do nothing when I'm 50. I do it for the dough... and the glory, obviously. Retirement in Vegas—what a plan!

I made the decision to go with the PDC in 2001. The last time I played with the BDO was at the Danish Open, which was a really big ranking tournament. I ended up winning the thing, but by the time I changed my winnings into sterling, I had £606 in my pocket. Take away my travel and accommodation for the weekend and I was £154 in the clear. And I'd just won a big tournament!

It wasn't just me who was feeling the pinch. On the last night of the tournament me and 11 of the other lads went out for a meal and a few drinks. To cut a long story short, when the bill arrived, the other lads all did a runner. I argued about the bill and then did a runner too (bad, I know) and caught up with the rest of them. When they stopped laughing, they all admitted that they only legged it because they were all skint. Everyone had brought £300 with them but even with their prize money, everyone was spent up. God, I miss them days. Not.

Not long after that I got a call from Barry Hearn (who's chairman of the PDC) saying, "Wayne, we want you son". We met up for a chat and he explained what the PDC could do for me and that was that. Everyone thinks I got a massive backhander from Barry. All I can say is that Barry is a very hard man to haggle with. In my mind, I had nothing to lose, though. I'd seen old BDO mates of mine like Kevin Painter and Andy Jenkins switch a couple of years before and make a good living and I thought, 'Why not me?'

My first weekend with the PDC was the Irish Budweiser UK Open Regional in Londonderry. I got beat in the final and went home with £2500, which made my winnings from the Danish Open look like the peanuts they were. Good move, Wayne, good move.

I played six months on the PDC circuit before deciding it was time to finally give it a go as a full-time pro. Jacking in my job was a real wrench because I loved it there, but things at home with Donna were beginning to suffer. With a job and the darts, I was always knackered and never in the house and I thought, enough is enough. I was living two lives and joining the PDC was the solution and, so far, I've got no complaints.

So, I was going to go down to the BDO final. Frimley Green, Surrey, where it's staged, isn't a million miles away from me. It would have been good to see some old mates, but I was worried about the reception I'd get. To be honest, I didn't fancy getting turned away at the door. Last year one of the BDO players, Colin Monk (who has joined the PDC now) invited my mate Andy Jenkins, who plays on the PDC circuit, as his VIP guest but the organisers wouldn't even let him to the players' bar. I say live and let live, but I didn't fancy putting myself in the firing line and decided not to show my face.

Me and Donna watch it on the telly instead. Raymond van Barneveld (you'd never guess he's from Holland) easily beats Martin Adams 6–2 to win his fourth BDO world title. I'm not sure Raymond's a match for Phil Taylor on his day—who is?—but he'd definitely be in the top three of the PDC rankings if he ever switched over.

WEDNESDAY 12TH JANUARY

I'm off over to Holland tomorrow for a week's worth of exhibitions but I have to admit I've got mixed feelings about it. It's seven hard days of shit hotels, long journeys and boredom. And Donna isn't coming with me either, which is a downer. She normally travels with me (maybe she doesn't trust me?), but the Holland gig is really dull except for the exhibitions themselves, so she's going to stay at home. Can't say I blame her.

The Dutch are totally mad for their darts. I think it's because they've got this pub culture, even more than us, where they're always nipping in for a drink after work. And where you've got people in bars, you'll find darts. I'm not complaining—Holland helps me to keep Donna in her shopaholic lifestyle.

THURSDAY 13TH JANUARY

Flew over to Holland from Stansted this morning and I'm in Rotterdam now for tonight's exhibition. I suppose I could have taken the ferry over, which might have been cheaper, but I spend so long travelling as it is that I can't be bothered with any extra hassle.

I don't particularly like flying post September 11 if the truth be told. I'm not worried about the plane blowing up but all the new security measures mean I have to check my darts into the hold rather than carrying them in my hand luggage because they could be used as weapons. That makes me nervous.

I've had the same set of darts for years and I'd be lost without them. I couldn't just pick up another set and hope to play well. It'd be like a snooker player without his own cue or a tennis player using someone else's racquet. It just doesn't bear thinking about. At least in the old days I could keep them close all the time. Now I've got to rely on the baggage handlers getting my suitcase onto the right bloody plane.

I've heard some of the American players actually send their darts by registered post to the venue when they have to fly. That would make me just as nervous because then you're relying on the postman rather than the baggage handlers.

It's hours before the exhibition and I'm finding it tough to be good food-wise. I'm not the biggest of the players on the circuit but I started the year off weighing 17st 7lbs and I'm trying to lose a bit of weight. It's during these boring times when you're stuck in a hotel room that I find it hard to stick to the diet. This week is going to be a big test of my willpower.

There are about 200 people in for the exhibition, which is a good turnout, and they all seem to have a good time. No two exhibitions are exactly the same. Sometimes I work with another pro and we play a few legs, sometimes I'll take on some of the local players and sometimes they want to see a few trick shots and high checkouts. Usually, it's a combination of all three but basically I'll do whatever the organiser wants to make things go with a swing.

I never warm-up for an exhibition because it would feel like I'm short changing the punters. You don't pay good money to go to see a Rolling Stones concert and expect to see them tuning up, do you? I think the same applies to a darts exhibition.

Normally, there's a bit of a Q&A session at the end and I sign whatever the punters put in front of me and chat over a few drinks to anyone who's interested. The pubs and bars who book me pay good money and it's all about entertaining the crowd, so I'm pretty flexible. Give 'em what they want, I say.

After the gig I'm starving and I cave in and get a late-night chicken kebab. Okay, I have salad with it, but so much for my new lifestyle. I'll have to go for a long walk tomorrow.

FRIDAY 14TH JANUARY

Another day, another three-hour journey. I've no idea where we're going and I don't care. It's all the same to me when I'm on the road. Kill time playing pool, snooker and golf on the mobile phone and take a few quid of Russ Bray, the gravel-voiced darts compere, as we pass the handset between us in the back of the car. I let Russ win one just so he doesn't sulk, but I'm still quids in. To be fair, I'm the sulker if I lose, not him.

Like me, Russ earns his extra cash on the road when there are no big tournaments and he does a lot of gigs with me. You need a compere for an exhibition to hold it all together and Russ is an old hand at getting the crowd going and making sure everyone has a good time. Okay, he sounds like someone is sandpapering his tonsils but that's all part of the show and he's superb at what he does.

Russ is an ex-County darts players himself and he got into compering completely by accident. He was at a Hertfordshire County match ten years ago and the caller they booked didn't turn up, so Russ stepped in and was an instant hit. The crowd loved him because his voice has such an unique quality and he's never really looked back. He still throws occasionally but he's complete rubbish these days. Russ is a top bloke to have around though because he's got such enthusiasm for anything and everything and that's not to be sniffed at when you're on the road or stuck in another anonymous hotel, wishing you were somewhere else. It amazes me Russ never complains when we're away because he's got a wife, Sue, and three kids at home but I suppose he needs the cash.

John Part, the two-times world champion, is also in the car. He's doing some of the same exhibitions as me this week, as well as some of his own shows. Without doubt the most intelligent player in the game, John's from Canada and he's a massive sci-fi fan (including *Star Wars*), hence the 'Darth Maple' tag. He spends a lot of time flying between Canada and Europe for tournaments and exhibitions, so he's always reading or watching films. What he doesn't know about most subjects probably isn't worth knowing. The thing with John is you've got to be very careful about getting into a conversation with him because he's very opinionated. You can't just make a point and leave it at that because John will then take an hour explaining to you why you're wrong. He's also loves his cartoons but gets quite obsessive about them. I remember him watching a *Scooby Doo* DVD on a plane once and it was one with Scrappy Doo and John just kept saying "Where did they get the idea for Scrappy Doo from?" over and over again. It really upset him.

I get chatting to an Italian bloke called Salvatore at the exhibition in the evening. Now Italy isn't what you could call a hotbed of darts, but Salvatore tells me he's a big fan because they can watch it on Sky Sports back home. We're not exactly famous over there yet, but it shows the sport is heading in the right direction. Best bit is when he says some of his family live in Sicily and they're all mad for their darts. Can't help but chuckle thinking of the chances of some Mafia blokes in suits and sunglasses, violin cases tucked under their arms, sitting down with their red wine or whatever to watch me throw the arrows.

I don't get round to going for that walk. Settle for 30 sit-ups. Go to bed thinking of Donna and when I'm next going to have the chance to get to a computer and play poker. I think I'm getting withdrawal symptoms... poker, not Donna. Sorry, wifey!

SATURDAY 15TH JANUARY

Amsterdam today and the bad news is we're booked into a crappy little hotel. You know the type—scraggy cats running about the place and all that. I'm none to happy to leave my passport and some of the exhibition money in the room but I don't want to carry all that cash around with me either.

The good news is it's a day off so me, Russ, Russ's son Neil and Suzanne, who's my booking agent in Holland, decide to head into town for a look around (I haven't told Donna about this but I'm sure she'll find out sooner or later...).

Our hotel is only a couple of minutes from the red light district and it isn't long before we're getting approached by touts trying to get us into strip joints and the like, promising us first-class smut and filth. Amsterdam really is a crazy town.

I've got to admit watching all the groups of lads going past the prostitutes windows leaves me a bit uneasy. The main streets seem okay but there's definitely a seedier side to it and I do feel sorry for the girls.

After a while, we all head to a bar for a drink. While we're sitting there I notice a couple of blokes looking over and one of them has obviously recognised me.

"No, it is him."

"Piss off. What's he doing here?"

"It's definitely him."

"Go and ask him."

"I'm telling you, that's Wayne Mardle."

"Nah, Mardle's much fatter than that!"

I don't know whether to be flattered or offended, but I go over to the one who reckoned I was fatter and give it the "Yeah, cheers mate, nice one, thanks for that." Made me laugh afterwards though...

Later in the day, I head off to a place called Deventer in the north of Holland. I'm going to a famous darts shop called Dibo to have my darts repointed. The points of the dart are the sharp metal bits that stick in the board and mine have been getting blunter and shorter as the years have gone by.

I reckon my darts are at least a centimetre shorter than they were through wear and tear and that means they are going into the board right up to the barrel, so I need it sorted.

I've had the same set of darts for 20 years (well I've had the same barrels and tips at least—you have to change the flights and stems more often) and I've not had them altered once, so I'm a bit panicky really. I know it's time to bite the bullet because the length of the points affects how I grip and throw the dart. Short points also mean you limit the entry point of your dart, which basically means you've got less chance of landing all three in the treble.

I get chatting to the guy who owns the shop, Marcel, and he seems to know what he's doing. He also mentions the possibility of some sponsorship, so it makes the trip doubly worthwhile.

SUNDAY 16TH JANUARY

Pick up John Part in Rotterdam and head for a town called Hurdyguryp, in the north of Holland back near where we were two nights ago, for more exhibition work. I say exhibition but in my case tonight it's more of a personal appearance really and I'm a bit nervous about the whole thing.

These guys—10 of them as it turns out—have booked me but I've got to go to one of their houses, not a pub or club. I haven't got a clue who they are, why they want me round the house or what we're going to do. You can see why I'm bricking it a bit. If they've got a shrine to me with candles or anything like that, I'm telling you, I'm gonna leg it!

I'm taking Suzanne's fella Gerald with me as back-up just in case. He's a big strapping German bloke who looks like a bodyguard (which is handy) and I reckon he'd be enough to scare off most nutters. Russ, bless him, would be worse than useless if anything kicked off.

We get to the address (me in the Hawaiian shirt, Gerald trying to look mean and intimidating) and the place looks normal enough, a typical chalet-style Dutch house really, and the lads turn out to be as good as gold. They really are just big dart fans who fancied doing something different. I play them all one leg, have a few beers, a chit-chat and all that sort of thing. But best of all I make even more money on the side at the end of the night.

"Stay for another game, Wayne."

"No problem mate."

"This time we will play you for money."

"Nah, nah, I don't want to take your money."

"But it is more fun to gamble."

"Yes, but I know I'll win."

"So we play for money?"

"Whatever you say..."

I take ten euros off each of them. Hand on heart I wasn't actually going to take the money but they got a bit offended when I tried to refuse, so what could I do? A hundred euros extra. Nice one... and Donna doesn't even have to know!

MONDAY 17TH JANUARY

I'm not happy with my new points at all. I've got the start of the Sky Premier Darts League on Thursday, which is a big deal for me and the other lads because it means more TV exposure, and I still don't feel comfortable with them. My darts are longer than they were a few days ago and they don't feel quite right. Hopefully a couple more exhibitions will break them in. At the moment, it feels like I'm throwing with someone else's arrows. It's like expecting a top snooker player to borrow someone else's cue and then clear the table.

I'm in a place called Helder now, a town in the south of Holland near the Belgian border and I've just had a call from Suzanne saying tonight's venue have tried to cancel because they haven't sold any tickets. She told the landlord he'd have to pay whether I played or not, so they said they'd try and push the tickets.

The hotel is total crap, a glorified pub really, and I'm bored to tears. Can't wait to get home. Do 30 sit-ups just to pass the time.

Funnily enough, the exhibition turns out to be a good one. There's enough people to make it respectable, but best thing about the night is I feel I'm finally getting to grips with the new points. I was moaning about them this morning but now it feels like I've been playing with them for years. I've said before darts is as much a mental as physical game and suddenly everything seems to click.

We also raise a bit of cash for Heart For Darts, which is a charity supported by a lot of the players that pays for medical treatment for people who can't afford it. We get people to sponsor us for the number of 180s or 140s we hit in a night, that sort of thing, as well as raffling off the chance to play a leg against me. A couple blokes put their hands in their pockets and we do alright. Ian Waller, the founder of Heart For Darts, will be pleased.

Have another kebab after the gig. Is there any point in doing those sit-ups? Willpower—if only I had some...

TUESDAY 18TH JANUARY

Jesus Christ, I think I'm going to die! I've been up since four in the morning with diarrhoea, vomiting, the works. I ache, I feel total crap and I can't see myself playing tonight. It was that bloody chicken kebab I had last night—punishment for letting the diet slip again.

I tell Suzanne to warn the landlord who's booked me for tonight that I might not be up to it. I've got a two-hour journey to the digs and I'll see how I feel after that. But right now, I'd have to say there's no chance.

I hate the thought of letting people down. You know people will travel maybe 30 or 40 miles to watch an exhibition and if I can possibly avoid disappointing them, I will. It's not just about the money, I don't want to mess people around.

In the end, I can't play. I'm feeling way too dizzy and spaced out, so I just hide in a dark room of the flat I've rented. The good news is we manage to get Erik Clarys, a Belgian player who won the World Masters about 10 years ago, to stand in for me so they don't have to cancel the evening, which is a relief. It's the first time in the six years

I've been doing exhibitions that I've failed to show.

I've been lucky with illness in my career because it's bloody hard to throw darts when you're feeling total shit. I remember playing Colin Lloyd in the World Championship in 2003 at the Tavern and I was really suffering with a virus or something. I was burning up on the stage and was so rough after the first set I had to go outside, whip my shirt off and lie down on the freezing concrete just to get my body temperature down (the security man on the door didn't know what was going on). I did it again after the fourth set—I was 3–1 down at the time—but it seemed to do the trick because I eventually beat Colin 4–3. As a rule, I'd rather not feel like death warmed up though.

WEDNESDAY 19TH JANUARY

I feel great—100 times better in fact! Thanks for caring...

Pick up John Part again and head to Arnhem for tonight's gig at the town's darts club. First up, we meet up with the organiser, who introduces us to the three gorgeous girls who are going to accompany me, John and Russ for the walk-on. Sorted.

So we get to the venue, we're in the car waiting for the nod and the girls are hanging around outside at the doors, waiting for kick-off. Thing is, they're wearing boob tubes, mini skirts (more like glorified belts) and knee-high leather boots, so when a police car happens to pass by, you don't have to be a genius to realise what the coppers are thinking. They get out of the car and start asking the girls questions. We can see the girls pointing to us in the car, obviously trying to explain what the hell is going on but when one of the coppers comes over, we deny all knowledge. Just try and imagine the copper's Dutch accent.

"Are these girls with you gentlemen?"

"Those girls?"

"Yes sir, those girls."

"They say they are working with you tonight..."

"They might be 'working' tonight but not with us."

"What are you doing here sir?"

"We're here for a darts exhibition officer."

"And the girls?"

"Never seen them before in my life."

Maybe it was a bit cruel but we can't resist it and we're cracking up for ages. Of course, it all gets sorted out but I'm not sure the girls see the funny side.

Inside, it's chaos. As soon as I walk in, it's obvious everyone has been drinking all day. They're all absolutely steaming. Great. The match itself is okay but it's during the Q&A session afterwards things start getting weird and rowdy. At one point, some pissed bloke asks me why the London New Year's Eve fireworks are shit compared to Holland's? What the hell is going on here?

At the end of the night, me and John are having a drink when we get approached by a couple of girls, both 18 if they are a day, and have one of the strangest conversations you can imagine.

"Can we sit here?"

"No problem."

"You're darts players, aren't you?"

"Yes. I'm Wayne, this is John. What do you two do?"

"We're actresses. We're in a Dutch soap opera."

At this point I go to the bar. Suzanne's there and I ask her if she knows the two girls from the telly. She says she's never seen them before in her life. Back to John and the girls...

"So, you're in a soap opera then..."

"Yes, we're quite famous."

"But my friend over there says you're lying. It's all cock and bull, isn't it?"

"Yes, okay, we made it up."

"Why did you do that?"

"Because you're famous and we didn't think you'd want to talk to us unless we were too."

Now you might think we should have been flattered or whatever, but honestly, it scared me because it makes you realise what distorted views other people can have of you. They really thought we were some kind of superstars; I've been called a few things in my time but not that!

Anyway, back home tomorrow. Can't wait.

CHAPTER TWO

Premier feud... and the death of a hamster

THURSDAY 20TH JANUARY

Get up at 4.45am to catch an early flight from Schipol airport to Stansted. Meet Donna at 10 and it's straight into the car (a navy blue Citroen Picasso since you ask) for the drive to Stoke for the Premier League. I'm a bit nervous, as well as excited. It's a new event and also a new format—the best of 12 legs—so no-one really knows what to expect.

There's seven of us in the tournament, the current world top six—Phil Taylor, Colin Lloyd, Peter Manley, John Part, Roland Scholten and little old me—and Mark Dudbridge, who got the 'wild card' place after his performance at the World Championship. Like I said, it's the best of 12 legs for each match and we all play each other twice. The top four after all the round robin stages go through to the semis and then it's a straight knockout competition.

Tonight we're in Stoke but we're going all round the country over the next few months, places like Newcastle, Kidderminster, before the grand final at the end of May.

Flying in from Holland on the same day isn't exactly ideal preparation but the exhibition was booked before Sky announced the dates, so what can you do?

I'm playing Phil 'The Power' Taylor. I think it was the commentator Sid Waddell who coined the nickname a few years ago and it's definitely appropriate because the man is a darts machine.

Phil keeps himself very much to himself on the circuit. He gets on with the other lads okay but you'll never see him in the bar having a beer during a tournament. He's incredibly single-minded and his lifestyle is totally different to the other fellas. I remember chatting to Phil in Las Vegas last year when we were all out there for the Desert Classic tournament. For me, Vegas is a holiday with a tournament thrown in but to Phil is just another day at the office. I asked him what he thought of Vegas and he said, except for his matches, he'd only left his hotel room once during the whole two weeks. He said he had a bag full of clean clothes in the wardrobe because he just hadn't been out. That's Phil Taylor for you but he's won 12 world titles, so he's obviously doing something right.

I play terrible and lose 7–5. To be honest, having been 5–1 down, I'm quite happy to get away with a respectable scoreline but the whole night is a bit of a farce. I knew Phil would get the lion's share of the support because he's a local Stoke lad, but I never expected him to get 99 per cent of it. I'm usually quite popular with the crowds, but I get a hand round the throat and a slap on the back of the head during the walk-on and I could sense everyone willing me to miss when I was throwing. I don't usually let the crowd get to me but I did tonight.

Just to add insult to injury, there's an almighty cock-up with whose throw it is which pisses me off and throws my rhythm.

Normally in darts who throws first in a match (which is a big advantage because you always want a score on the board before your opponent) is decided by who gets closest to the bullseye with one dart in the practice room. But when we start tonight we're told by the referee, Bruce Spendley, that I'm throwing first in the opening six legs, Phil first in the next six. It all sounds a bit weird to me but it's a new competition and that's how they want things to go. So I throw first in the first three legs (I'm 2–1 down); I step up for the fourth leg and hit a treble 20 with my first dart when Bruce leans over to me.

"It's Phil's throw Wayne."

"What?"

"You'll have to take the dart out."

"What are you on about?"

"It's Phil to throw first."

"You told me I'm throwing first in the first six legs."

"We made a mistake."

"You're having me on. I've just hit 60."

"It's you first in the first three legs, Phil for the next three and then alternate throw."

So I take the bloody dart out, turn round in disgust and the camera catches me mouthing "This is a fucking joke!" That'll probably earn me a £100 fine from the PDC.

Still, I have it easy compared to the next pair—my mate Peter Manley and Mark Dudbridge—who have to put up with some unbelievable shit from the fans. Really, it's diabolical stuff with constant shouts of "You fat bastard" and "miss, miss, miss" to Peter, who's a big-boned gentleman (alright, he's massive). The problem is the crowd is mostly 18 to 25-year-old blokes who've been drinking heavily. Bearing in my mind it's meant to be a showpiece, televised event for the sport, I'm not sure the evening does any of us any favours. Hopefully things will improve when we play the next round in Reading.

I think Peter knew it was coming though because he's the player the fans love to hate. He got himself a bit of a reputation back in 2002 when he got to the World Championship final against Phil, who murdered him 7–0. Peter just walked off the stage without even shaking hands and he's been the game's 'baddie' ever since. The fans in Stoke (which is Phil's hometown) obviously haven't forgotten what went on.

Peter's nickname is 'One Dart', which is a reference to his finishing ability (he only needs one dart at the double) but he's quietly been trying to drop the name for a while now because he hasn't been as deadly on the doubles recently. He was turning up for tournaments and people were waving placards like 'One Dart My Arse!', so he's trying to distance himself from it.

He might not be the most popular player on the circuit but he's a good mate of mine. I gave his wife Chrissie away at their wedding in Vegas last year and me and Donna see quite a bit of him and Chrissie socially. The thing with Peter is he's one of the biggest piss-takers in the game. He loves winding people up but he's terrified of being on the receiving end and plays his cards close to his chest.

My favourite story about Peter is when we were all in Vegas for the Desert Classic three years ago. He can't swim and we're all lounging around a pool when Peter turns up and tries to get in the shallow end. He's trying to act cool but he doesn't realise it's actually three metres deep and there are no steps, so he goes flying into the water and starts thrashing about in panic. He looked like a right muppet and we were all rolling about pissing ourselves.

They've got internet access back at the hotel, but not in the rooms so it's another poker-free night. If I don't play soon I might lose the knack. It's my release from darts and I get edgy if I don't play for a while.

I started playing poker online about two-and-a-half years ago. I had a day off from my old job and was messing about on the computer and out of curiosity I had a look at one of the poker sites. I'd seen some of those poker tournaments they show on Sky and before I knew it, I was hooked. I tend to play in tournaments with lots of players rather than the smaller head-to-head games you can enter. When I came in third out of about a thousand people and won $600, I was well and truly bitten by the bug.

I don't play for huge amounts—the tournaments I enter cost

between $30 and $50 to play but I reckon I'm about $1000 up since I started. The longest I've ever played in one sitting is 16 hours but I'm not that bad now. Winning money is nice, but it's as much about switching off as it is the cash.

FRIDAY 21ST JANUARY

A long day ahead. First me and Donna drive back to Essex, basically to unpack my 'Holland suitcase' and then to repack and head off to Eastbourne for the 128 Classic, which is a big tournament for, you guessed it, 128 players.

When we get to the venue—the Winter Gardens—I register for the singles, the pairs (I'm playing with Dutchman Roland 'The Tripod' Scholten) and the mixed pairs, when I'll play with my lovely wifey. Although, she doesn't play much these days, Donna used to be a good player who represented Essex over a hundred times and won a British Open Pairs title.

I met Donna through darts. I was 14 and she was the older woman... well, she was 15. We were both away from home at the Hemsby Darts Festival in Yarmouth. I'd seen her around before in Essex, where we both played on the junior circuit, but I hadn't worked up the bottle to talk to her. So, we were away in Yarmouth and everyone was messing around in their sleeping bags in the chalet and me and Donna ended up face-to-face. I let on I liked her, she let on she fancied my best mate, a bloke called Ian Sarfas, and I thought I'd blown it. I must have a thick skin though because I gave her a ring a few days after we got back to Essex and we've been together ever since. We got married in Las Vegas in July 2002. Funny thing about that weekend in Yarmouth was my voice broke, so I suppose you could say I became a man and met my future wife all in the space of a couple of days.

I haven't got a lot of time to prepare before the pairs and, perhaps predictably, me and Roland play like total tossers and go out in the first round. Well, I play like a tosser anyway. I feel bad because I know I've let Roland down.

As I said, Roland's from Holland and he's a big lad. He's known as The Tripod because, ahem, he's a big boy all over if you know what I mean.

I think Roland's misunderstood because he comes across as all serious but off the board he's one of the funniest guys around and he's always having a laugh. His sense of humour can be quite dry though. He told me story about how he and his girlfriend had spent eight months doing up their house and right at the end of the job, the whole ground floor was flooded by some leak in the pipes. His missus is a bit of a boffin and she had hundreds of books damaged by the water but all Roland could say was "My two books are ruined as well."

Me and Donna win the mixed pairs and pick up a 100 quid each. It's only pocket money to me—I've come for the singles and the ranking points really but Donna's delighted because she's got extra spending money for the weekend.

The smile is soon wiped off her face though when we get to the holiday flat we've rented for the weekend. It's a complete hole. There's no hot water or electric and there's nowhere to park the car. Oh, the glamorous life of a professional darts player...

SATURDAY 22ND JANUARY

Make it through to the quarter-finals of the singles before losing to Ronnie 'The Rocket' Baxter. It's still eight ranking points in the bag, which ain't bad, but I feel like I've wasted the day and I'm pissed off.

Don't get me wrong, Ronnie plays well but I know I can beat him and I didn't really turn up today. Thing is, after the quarter-finals you play on the main stage, which is where I'm at my best, so I've spent the day slogging it out on the 'floor'—32 boards all lined-up alongside each other in one room—only to miss out. I've beaten Ronnie the last three times we've met in a televised match but the floor is his stomping ground and he does the business.

If you only watch darts on telly, you probably think all games are played separately on plush stages but the reality on the circuit is very different. More often than not, the early rounds of tournaments are played in huge rooms like the one in the Winter Gardens in Blackpool, with rows and rows of boards, which we call the 'floor tournaments'.

There are a lot of games to get through in tournaments like this and you have to have scores of people playing at the same time to get anywhere. It's the coalface of the sport—I don't even wear the Hawaiian shirts for these games. Most of the other players are the same—they have their trademark 'match' shirts with their names and nicknames on the back, which they wear for the big games on the telly and the like. It's all part of the image. But for the floor tournaments we all tend to wear T-shirts because they're usually long, 12-hour days and there's no need for a flash shirt. It's like a footballer training in a tracksuit and then playing in his proper kit on the Saturday afternoon.

Anyway, I was watching Ronnie on the floor in an earlier round playing a bloke called Andy Hayfield.

Ronnie's throwing well, hits his double and turns round to shake Andy's hand because he thinks he's won. Andy looks bemused and says, "Nah Ronnie, you're 4–1 up and it's first to five."

Ronnie says, "That makes it five", but Andy's having none of it so they both end up searching through black bin bags for the score sheets from the early legs to see who's right. It all gets sorted out amicably in the end but it shows the glitz of the World Championship or some of the other high-profile tournaments aren't always a true reflection of the circuit.

I didn't think it would be easy against Ronnie, but my preparation was poor and you can't take the piss against players of his quality. My biggest problem was that I stupidly decided to wear a new pair of shoes today and by the time I played Ronnie, my feet were giving me murder. To be honest, it's all down to vanity. I weighed myself this morning and found I'd lost eight pounds, so I thought, 'I'll wear these new shoes because they make me look taller' and I'm going for the tall, slim(mer) look! Yeah, I know, who am I kidding? But I felt tip-top and I thought I'd try and show off a bit. Never again.

Go home. One night in Eastbourne was one too many.

SUNDAY 23RD JANUARY

Spent the night in my own bed last night, which was fantastic, and I treat myself to a proper Sunday dinner with the family. The only downer on the day is my ill-advised attempt to bleed the radiators, which ends with a 12-foot jet of dirty black water going up the white walls in the living room. I'll leave it to Donna next time.

MONDAY 24TH JANUARY

It's Monday, it's January and it's cold. I'm off to Holland again tomorrow, but while it's quiet I may as well explain how I started out in darts.

I picked up my first arrow when I was 10. The family—me, my sister and my mum and dad—were living in Islington, north London at the time and my dad used to play a lot around the area, so it was probably natural that I'd show an interest. By the time I was 11 and we'd moved to Romford, near the dog track, I was playing indoors in my mum and dad's bedroom and I'd already caught the darts bug.

I realised I wanted to be a full-time darts player when I was in my teens. To be precise, it was on 10 May 1986, my 13th birthday—the day I won my first-ever tournament.

Dad took me down to a pub in Romford on Collier Row called the Double Top. It's a restaurant or something these days but back then it was the home of darts in Essex, and every weekend there'd be knockout competitions which attracted good quality players from all over the south east.

I played on the Sunday morning and there were 80-odd players entered, but I kept on winning until I was in the final. I don't know who was more surprised me, dad or the blokes I'd beaten.

I ended up playing a bloke called Tommy Wilson in the final and I slaughtered him. Tommy was a great player (I still see him from time to time on the circuit), but I played blinding and he couldn't live with me. So I land the final double, give it the large one, and go and collect the £50 first prize. That was a lot of dough then. I thought I'd won the pools until my dad came up to me and said, "Give us 20, boy." Turns out he'd agreed with Tommy before the final we'd split it 30 quid for the winner and 20 for the runner-up because they thought I'd lose and dad didn't want me to walk away with nothing. I didn't care though; I was on cloud nine.

I'll always remember something dad said to me afterwards:

"If you can play your best game like that in the biggest game of your life, it can't be bad, can it, son?"

That's always stuck with me and gave me the courage to stick with it all.

I went to school on the Monday morning with 30 quid in my pocket feeling like I'd just won the World Championship and I realised I could go out any night of the week and earn a tenner in the pubs at his lark.

At this time in the mid–80s, the recession was in full swing and the days of me being given whatever I asked for were on hold (God, I had a hard life... not). So when I joined the youth system playing up and down the country for trophies (prize money has only been allowed in the youth game for the last couple of years) I could see that I was pushing my luck, but my mum and dad always stood by me. My dad was a postman, and my mum has worked in insurance, textiles and advertising, but they always supported me to carry on with my dream to be a pro.

I remember winning a TV and video in one tournament and giving it to my sister for a wedding present. I suppose the highlight for me from those days was when I was 16 and I won a tournament at a holiday camp called Highfields. The tournament itself was no big deal but it was £800 for the winner. I remember when I got home I bunged my mum and dad £50 each and I can still see the look on my mum's face when I gave it to her. I think for the first time she realised there was money to be made in darts and I felt good because I'd given something back after everything they'd given up for me.

I went on to win British Teenage and British Youth titles, which were two of the top titles in those days, and it was obvious I was not half bad at the darts lark. Everything just followed on from there.

I got a job as an accounts clerk in London when I left school after a brief stint as a fork-lift driver, joined the BDO, half killed myself juggling my day job with darts and, as I explained earlier, joined the PDC and went full-time. And here I am.

I definitely don't miss the daily commute from Romford. Not once did any of the regulars on the train ever speak to me or anyone else and, to be fair, I never quite had the bottle to try and start up a conversation either. We all just sat there in stoney silence every single day, except for near Christmas when a few brave souls actually nodded to each other. Even then I bet they'd just been to the office party and were half-cut anyway. The journey was even worse in the summer though with all those sweaty armpits. Yep, I don't miss getting on the train one little bit.

TUESDAY 25TH JANUARY

Fly into Schipol airport in the morning, get picked up and head off with Russ Bray to a place called Darle, which is near the Dutch-German border, for the first exhibition of the week. Ten minutes in the hotel to drop off the bags and straight on to the job.

They've sold all 150 tickets, so there's a good atmosphere at the place. Everything goes smoothly, but Russ gets the right hump because the organiser keeps calling him Martin Fitzmaurice, who works for the BDO. Now for those of you who haven't had the pleasure, Martin is probably one of the fattest men on the earth, so Russ, who's a slim jim, isn't best pleased with the bloke for getting it wrong. Makes me laugh though.

WEDNESDAY 26TH JANUARY

Get up nice and early because I know they've got internet access at the hotel and I'm itching for a quick game of poker. I know I don't have much time to spare and I don't want to fork out too much to the hotel for using the line because they always shaft you for it. I still end up playing for an hour and a half though, but only come in third in a 10-player game, so I don't even get my stake back. At least I get my fix.

It's a three-hour journey to a place called 's–Gravenzande, which is near the Hook of Holland on the coast, for tonight's gig. We stop at a service station on the way for a bite to eat and I have my usual Burger King / McDonalds / KFC dilemma but resist the temptation and just have a sandwich. Good boy, Wayne, good boy.

Pick up John Part on the way and we're pleasantly surprised when we check into the hotel they've booked for us. Usually, you expect some crappy dump but we're in the Carlton at 400 Euros a night. Lovely.

The organiser wants to send three tandems to pick me, John and Russ up and take us to the venue (no, really). I'm thinking, it's January, it's freezing cold and it's a 20-minute journey, so I say, "Taxi please."

Once we get there, everything goes well, but for some reason me, John and Russ end the night giving the punters a little bit of a concert with John on the drums, Russ on guitar and me on a sort of organ/piano thing. Now I know we're making an awful racket but everyone else is cheering us on and actually seem to enjoy it. I'm not saying the Dutch have no taste, but back in England we'd have either been shot or lynched for a performance like that.

THURSDAY 27TH JANUARY

Bit of a shitty day really. A day-off, a rare thing indeed, but with Donna back home and me out here, I tend to get a bit pissed off.

A least I do a bit of good business, sorting out a sponsorship deal with Marcel from Dibo darts shop, who I mentioned before. There's a tournament called the Master of Darts series coming up next month in Holland where four of the top PDC names, including yours truly, will play four of the guys from the BDO and I'm going to have some Dibo branding on my shirt. We're only talking a couple of quid, but I'm going to be up there playing anyway.

Spend the evening doing a few sit-ups, eating soup and apples and watching a couple of DVDs—*The Exorcist* (which is shit, by the way. All that fuss about nothing) and *Hell's Kitchen* starring Angelina Jolie. Pretty girl Angelina...

FRIDAY 28TH JANUARY

Hand on heart, I can't tell you where I'm playing tonight. I've no idea where the hell in Holland I am and to be honest I don't really care. I'm missing Donna badly and phoning her makes me feel worse.

The exhibition is alright but it's quiet and I get a bit pissed off being manhandled by the crowd. The Dutch are a very tactile lot and they do like to push and pull you about. And they're all bloody big blokes.

After the darts I get talking to a bloke called Henk at the bar, who is absolutely priceless.

Henk: "You're a good player, but you'll never be world champion."

Me: "Why's that then Henk?"

"You haven't got enough natural talent."

"Talent's the one thing I'm not short of to be fair..."

"You'll never win it; you haven't got what it takes."

"We'll see."

"No really, you're good, but you're not good enough."

Anyway this goes on for about 45 minutes and he just keeps banging on. I need a way out of this conversation or I'll be here all night.

"Do you want a beer, Henk?"

"Yeah, yeah. I'll have a beer with a future world champion."

SATURDAY 29TH JANUARY

A three-hour journey from wherever I was yesterday to a place called Veenendaal. I've been here a few times before and it's the last night of the tour.

Everyone has a good laugh at the exhibition. In fact, they're in stitches when I hit a difficult double, jump up and down like a mad kangaroo to celebrate, trip up over the rope that divides the players from the crowd and go arse over tit and land right on the oche. They all think it's hilarious, I'm in agony!

Before the main part of the night, I play a few legs with some of the local kids and you wouldn't believe how good some of them are. There's this one lad—he's only nine—and he's throwing 60, 45, ton,

60. That might not sound like much, but trust me, for a kid of that age, that's pure class. Mark my words, the way Holland is churning out talented young players these days, they could leave the rest of the world for dead.

Get back to the hotel at 4am. I have a few beers (alright, white wine and sodas...), and because I'm tired and bit tipsy I let my diet defences slip and pig out, so I'm a bit pissed off with myself. Before I go to bed, I pack my bag for the morning and kiss my passport. I'm going home to see my little wifey tomorrow.

SUNDAY 30TH JANUARY

Have a couple of hours to kill at the airport before my flight, so I buy Donna some perfume and get my mum and dad and sister a few packs of cheap fags. Dad doesn't even smoke but he sells them down at his club and makes a couple of quid... oops, I shouldn't have said that, should I?

I've still got time on my hands after the shopping, so I decide to go into the casino to play Blackjack. I leave pretty quickly because no-one else at the table has the first clue how to play—you can't play properly when you're surrounded by morons who don't know when and when not to take a card.

Donna, my sister Donna and my niece Ellie, who's eight, and my nephew Danny, who's 12, meet me back at Stansted. Because me and Donna don't have kids of our own, I've got a lot of time for Ellie and Danny. They're really lovely kids and they know we like to spoil them.

Me and Donna have pretty much decided not to have kids. I'm on the road so much and it wouldn't be fair on Donna or any child stuck at home all the time. It just isn't practical but it does mean Danny and Ellie get a good deal because they're our surrogate kids.

In the car on the way back Donna breaks the news that our pet hamster, Chips (as in casino chips), has got out of his cage and disappeared. We've only had her a year and she's our little mate. I'm really gutted, and, if I'm honest, a bit tearful. Alright, shut it...

TUESDAY 1ST FEBRUARY

A quiet day at home. I've got 57 emails to read but most of them are a load of crap from golf shops trying to flog me stuff. I do like the odd round but I haven't played since October and I definitely don't need any more gear, thank you.

Naturally, I play a bit of poker and win a couple of hundred dollars (you've not lost your touch mate) and spend two hours practising in the spare room. I focus on my doubles today, which have been my undoing recently. The Premier League is coming up in Reading on Thursday and after losing to Phil Taylor last month, I could really do with a win.

It's hard sometimes to keep motivated in practice because it can be monotonous. I try and vary my routines to keep things as fresh as possible but I do feel like I'm going stir crazy at times, throwing dart after dart after dart within the same old four walls. It's part and parcel of the job but it's the most mundane part of being a professional darts player without a doubt.

Like most players I tend to concentrate on treble 20. It's the big score, the shot everyone's looking for and if you're hot on the treble 20s you're in with a shout in any match. At the top level, you've got to be looking for at least one treble every time it's your throw or you just won't score heavily enough. A score of 100 in competition is okay, no great shakes really, but you can't even get that unless you know where the treble is.

After I'm happy with my form on the treble 20, I move to some of the other trebles—mainly 19 and 18—which are also important. Players tend to go for them when they want to even up their score, the treble 20 bed is obscured by their other darts or they're trying to leave themselves a specific finish.

Then it's on to the doubles, which are of course vital. You can hit all the 180s you like but if you can't hit your doubles, you can't win anything. As the old darts saying goes, 'trebles for show, doubles for dough'.

I tend to go clockwise around the board on the doubles, moving on when I'm happy that I'm hitting the previous one regularly. Most players favour double 20 but my favourite is double 18. It's suits me because it's on the right hand side of the board and I'm right-handed, so I don't have to throw across my body. Eighteen always suits me because of the angle my darts hit the board. Some players, like Phil Taylor in particular, throw 'flat' darts, which means they hit the board almost horizontally, whereas my throwing action means the darts have a high arc in flight (it's because I'm a tall fella and I give the dart a little flick with my middle finger as I release) and they come down into the board at a pronounced angle, the flights at least an inch higher than the tips. Eighteen suits because it's a 'big bed' for my darts. As long as I don't miss double 18 low, I can always see the whole bed because my flights are way above it, out of the way and I've still got a clean throw.

Most players favour double 20 because it's in the same corridor as treble 20. It's a straight throw and all they have to is readjust the height of their bread and butter shot at treble 20.

My least favourite double is nine, which is ironic really because if I hit single 18 going for double 18, I then have to go for double nine. Double nine is on the left of the board but except for that, there's no technical reason why I shouldn't like it. It's definitely psychological rather than practical.

Hitting doubles can be my Achilles heel sometimes. I'm usually a heavy scorer in terms of hitting the 180s and 140s but my finishing can let me down. It's an aspect of my game I'm aware of and something the commentators like to mention quite a bit. It's fair comment and it doesn't bother me if people talk about it because I think I'm an honest sort of bloke and it's true. Don't get me wrong, sometimes (lots of times) I can be shit-hot on the doubles but if I'm not firing on all cylinders, it tends to be my doubles rather than my ability to hit ton pluses that deserts me.

People often ask how I (or any other player) can give the treble 20 punishment during a game and then miss a succession of arrows at a double, which is twice as big as a treble after all. There's just no simple answer to that one. For me at least it's because the double represents the climax of the game, the chance to win another leg or set. It's the killer blow, another nail in your opponent's coffin and that brings added pressure. The other reason top players miss is because darts is a sport and sport is unpredictable. Golfers miss makeable putts, Formula One drivers misjudge corners and darts players miss doubles they could hit in their sleep another time.

The other aspect of my game people comment on a lot is the fact my darts can drift into the fives when I'm going for the 20s. There's no denying it's true sometimes but it's not something that really bothers me. Right-handers tend to hit five if they miss 20s and left-handers tend to hit one if they're off target. I know I hit fives more than most right-handers but I also tend to hit more treble 20s than most players, so it's a trade-off really. There's nothing in my action that is fundamentally wrong and if I hit a few more fives than most, so be it. Like I said, another right-hander may never drift into five but odds on they're not going to be giving the treble 20 as much punishment as me, so sod it. I'm an aggressive player and if I drift at times, I drift. I let everyone else worry about it because I don't lose any sleep over it.

WEDNESDAY 2ND FEBRUARY

Arrive in Reading for the Premier League (I'm playing Peter Manley) and me and Donna go out for a nice, quiet meal together, our first in ages. I feel nice and relaxed about tomorrow, which is good, because like in any other sport, the better your preparation, the better your performance.

THURSDAY 3RD FEBRUARY

So much for good preparation. I lose 8–4 to Peter and I'm already bottom of the Premier League table. I'm not saying I deserved to win, but I'm really pissed off because there was a cock-up with the scoring at a crucial moment in the match which rattled me and I never really recovered. This is what happened:

Peter was 4–3 up, threw his darts and it was called 140. Now straightaway I wasn't convinced it was 140. In fact, I was sure he hit

85 but Peter had already taken his darts out off the board in double-quick time and walked back behind me. Now I'm stood at the oche and I saw Gary Woods, the lad who's scoring on my throw, frown at me. Now, I'm wasn't going to throw because by the rules of the game, that would have meant I accepted his score, so I had a word with Gary:

"I think he threw 85" and Gary nodded a "yes" back at me.

I walked back and said to Peter, "You hit 85."

"I might have done."

"I think you did."

"I don't know what I scored, I might have done."

I then had a word with the referee, Freddie Williams, who asked Peter if he was happy to have his score changed to 85. Peter replied he'd be happy with that and after a few minutes confusion it all got sorted out. Except in my head though because Peter's phrase "I don't know what I scored" kept going through in my head. I've never heard a professional player say that in my whole career. A player always knows exactly what he's hit. You're 99 per cent certain standing behind the oche and you always double-check when you take your darts out if there's any doubt. There's just no way you don't know what you've hit. No way at all. And if there's any grey area, you leave the arrows in the board until the referee or caller can have a look. You don't pick out as quick as you can.

I know I shouldn't have let it all affect me but I couldn't get it out of my head. Peter went on to take the leg and by the end of the match, I was chucking the darts at the board as fast as I could because I wanted to get off stage. I was firing them out like a machine gun because I knew I couldn't get any points and I wanted to be somewhere else. It looked bad but I didn't care. I didn't say a word to Peter backstage after the game. I was just too angry.

Having said all that, I've got to be honest with myself now and say I'm really not firing on all cylinders at all at the moment. What's more worrying is that I felt good before the match; the crowd (all 4,000 of them) were fantastic and I even hit a 180 with my first throw, but I still lost. I'm really not happy with my overall game and I know I've got to pick myself up. It's not that I've become a bad player overnight but I just can't seem to find the extra gears at the moment when the pressure's on and I need a big score or a high checkout. I'm playing okay but no better.

What does annoy me is people suggesting my form's suffering because I'm showing off too much on the stage. I was my usual self on the stage against Peter, dancing at the end of my walk-on, pulling a few faces at the crowd and generally trying to enjoy it. That's what I do but I was no more silly against Peter than any other time. OK, I'm not setting the world alight but it's thick to say it's because I'm this show-pony who can't focus on his game when it matters. It's part of my personality to mess about between sets or legs and I can't change who I am. The crowd love it and darts is about entertainment, isn't it? If for a second I thought my chances of winning a game would improve if I went up there all quiet and sombre, I'd do it. The thing is, it won't because it's just not me. I know I show off but at least I'm being honest with myself and the fans. I don't have a persona I take onto stage with me. What you see is what you get.

FRIDAY 4TH FEBRUARY

Travel down from Reading to Portsmouth for the South West Budweiser UK Open Regional final which starts tomorrow and I'm feeling a little better about things. I'm still angry about the way I played last night and the incident with Peter but what's done is done and there's no point crying over spilt milk, is there?

Donna and I have another meal out at lovely Indian restaurant in Portsmouth and have an early night because I've got to be at the Golden Hind pub in town for 10 tomorrow morning in time for a midday start. I'll just have to see how it goes...

SATURDAY 5TH FEBRUARY

I just don't know what's going wrong with my game at the moment. I play reasonably well all day, make it through to the last 16, which is just about respectable but no great shakes, and then I go to pieces and get beat 5–1 by a guy called Andy Smith. Andy's known as 'The Pieman' because he likes a Ginster or four. He's one of the most popular players on the circuit and you'll never hear anyone say a bad word about him. Like all the guys in the last 16, Andy's a good player but I shouldn't be getting beaten 5–1 by anyone at that stage of the tournament. He's below me in the rankings and someone I should be seeing off without too much trouble.

I miss a lot of doubles. I'm throwing with no conviction whatsoever and I'm getting on a real downer about it now. I just don't believe the darts are going to go where I want them at the moment.

The worse thing is I end up having a go at Donna in the car out of frustration and I know that's bang out of order. You now the kind of thing, snapping at your other half for no reason because you're pissed off.

"Where's my phone!"

"I don't know darling."

"Why have you fucking moved it?"

"I haven't touched it sweetheart."

"Well, I can't fucking find it, can I?"

"Wayne. Stop being a twat."

Then there's this stony silence for the next half hour before we look at each other and laugh about it.

Mind you, I'm sure she'd clout me one if I ever really overstepped the mark.

SUNDAY 6TH FEBRUARY

An unscheduled free day because I got knocked out yesterday, so I decide to show my face down at the pub and watch the final. We'd already arranged to drive from Portsmouth straight to Heathrow for a flight to Holland tomorrow for the Master of Darts event, so I thought why not watch the final?

In the end, Andy Smith—the fella who beat me—plays a mate of mine called Andy Jenkins, who's a local Portsmouth lad. Andy's nicknamed 'Rocky' because he's always getting into fights but we all used to know him as 'One Eye' because he used to have a wonky eye. You were never sure whether he was looking at you or someone else when he was talking. We used to take the piss out of him something terrible for it and he'd always come back with "When I've got two eyes, you lot are finished." He had laser treatment for it and it's 90 per cent sorted now, so he gets less stick these days. A top bloke.

Anyway, The Pieman is still in great form and turns Rocky over. At least I lost to the winner then.

MONDAY 7TH FEBRUARY

On the plane to Amsterdam, I read *Mind Games* by Jeff Grout, which discusses why some sports people don't achieve what they think they should and why others do. I find it fascinating. There are interviews with the likes of Nick Faldo and the swimmer Adrian Moorhouse and they talk about their approach to practice. Something Faldo says in particular sticks with me, about how a lot of golfers will go out and hit some balls to hone their swing but they don't actually have a target to aim at. Faldo points out that he's never hit a ball without aiming for something and can't understand how anyone could benefit from just hitting without aiming. Fair point—it's all about being focused in practice, making the most of your time and not just going through the motions. It gives me a few things to think about, but it also leaves me feeling positive.

Land at Schipol airport and get picked up by Suzanne and taken to a lovely hotel in a place called Oldenzaal. The Master of Darts event, taking place at the ExpoCenter in nearby Hengelo, is a really big deal over here. The whole thing has been organised by a Dutch company called P&H Events. They've flogged the broadcast rights to Dutch TV (it's not being shown back home), which is how they're making their dough, and they're hoping it's going to become a regular fixture on the darting calendar.

Although the organisers insist it's not about showing whether the PDC or BDO is top dog, everyone knows that's exactly what it's all about.

It's unusual for the PDC and BDO to turn a blind eye to their players competing in the same tournament but they haven't kicked up a fuss about this. I reckon they were worried about upsetting the lads because it's a big event and it's an extra pay day for everyone involved. Neither organisation would have made any friends if they had tried to put their foot down.

Unfortunately, the opening round of matches don't go well for us PDC boys. Colin Lloyd and Roland Scholten both get beaten and I lose 4–2 to Andy 'The Viking' Fordham.

I come off stage muttering to myself again that I should have won 4–2, but the truth is, I'm still not doing it. When you play against guys of the quality of Andy, you've got to be tip-top or you're going to get done over.

If you don't know Andy, he's a massive mountain of a man who was BDO world champion in 2004. He's the guy who's taking part in that *Celebrity Fit Club* programme on ITV and had trouble doing the 100-metre walk to start with. But to be fair, you can see he's looking much, much better for it. I think he's finally cut down on the 20-odd bottles of beer a day.

There have been a few stories in the papers about darts' drinking culture recently—I think they're even talking about introducing breathalysers during competitions or something—and I've got to admit I'm getting pissed off with some of the press we've been getting.

Let's face it, darts has always had this reputation for heavy drinking and there's no smoke without fire, but it gets me down that people seem to talk about the booze as much as they do about the darts. Take someone like Andy. It pisses me off that you can't read a single bloody interview with Andy without some reference to the fact he drinks so much. He's a great player, but all the attention on him only seems to highlight the negatives and none of the positives. Not all the players are like that, but you trying telling that to someone who's only exposure to darts is the tabloid piss-takes of blokes with massive beer guts. Andy deliberately plays up to the image because he thinks it gives him bragging rights, but it's just stupid.

A lot of people don't understand why players drink either. It's not because we're all alcoholics, it's because it helps steady the hand. There's no other sport that depends so much on a steady hand—if you're shaking up on the stage, you're going to hit nothing. If they came up with some legal substitute tomorrow that had the same effect, trust me, a lot of the players wouldn't touch a drop pre-match (drinking on stage is not allowed at BDO or PDC events). If it was a no-drinking sport, then fine by me, but while it isn't, us players are going to have one or two or three. Like I said, I don't know anyone at all who doesn't have a drink before a match. We are grew up playing under the influence of alcohol and that kind of culture isn't going to change overnight.

Don't get me wrong, I'm no angel but, like a few other players, I definitely drink a lot less than I used to. A few years ago I could have six or seven double vodkas (I've just never been a pints man...) before a match but these days I stick to a couple at most. The older players probably do drink more, but the younger lads definitely drink in moderation. I just don't find I need it as much these days and I think the drinking culture is more a spectator rather than player thing.

Personally, I couldn't drink heavily all the time I'm playing. If I'm doing a week's worth of exhibitions and was pissed every night, I'd soon feel it. I know everyone expects players to drink all the time—the negative image of the sport again—and I do get some funny looks at exhibitions on the nights when I ask for a mineral water or orange juice.

So, yes, I'd vote for alcohol-free tournaments given the choice. We'd all be on a level playing field and I'd be interested to see how it would help darts improve its image and maybe attract more sponsorship, which is always a problem.

I admit the overall standard of the darts the fans would see would drop off initially if everyone was sober at the oche, but maybe by only ten per cent. It would take all the players a couple of tournaments to adjust but I've no doubt the quality of darts would bounce back quickly once everyone got used to it. Who knows, maybe an alcohol ban would raise the bar in the long-term which has got to be good news. There's only one way to find out...

TUESDAY 8TH FEBRUARY

Play a Dutchman called Co Stompe tonight, lose 4–1 and I am well and truly pissed off. The way I'm playing at the moment is just not on. I'm meant to be one of the game's best players but I'm throwing like I'm ranked 30 in the world or something. I struggle to hit my doubles all night and at this level, it was always going to cost me. Co hits his finishes and it's 'night-night Wayne'.

Donna does her best to try and calm me down, saying "it'll all come good soon", but I'm seriously fed up. I've got two matches left—against Tony David and Raymond van Barneveld—and I've got to win them both if I'm going to make the semi-finals.

At least Phil Taylor keeps the PDC's end up, so to speak, beating David 4–0.

WEDNESDAY 9TH FEBRUARY

Wake up with a slight hangover after drowning my sorrows a bit last night. Having too much to drink only makes me more annoyed at myself so I go for a walk in the woods around the hotel to clear my head. Actually, I try to run and I'm going great guns for about 15 minutes until the path I'm on suddenly starts going uphill and I think better of it.

We organise a little game of poker to kill time during the day. There's me, Donna, Georgie 'The Puppy' Noble, who to my mind is the best caller in the world, Rod Harrington, who was the 1999 World Matchplay champion, and Dave 'Stevo' Stephenson, who is Andy Fordham's manager. We all put in 50 euros each and guess what? Donna only goes and beats me in the final. At least the money goes into the Mardle pocket, one way or the other.

In the evening I play Tony David, who was BDO world champion a couple of years ago. In the first four sets there's only one player in it—me—but somehow we're still level at 2–2. After that the wheels come off again and I can't hit a double to save my life and I lose 4–2. This is getting ridiculous.

Afterwards, this guy called Ulfrid pulls me aside and asks if I'll do an interview for a television station called RTL 5, who are covering the event. Obviously I'm pissed off but you've got to do your bit and it would be childish if I'd say no just because I got beat. So, I say yes and we're having this casual chat in the interview room.

Ulfrid: "What's going on, man? You're just not playing..."

Me *[big sigh]*: " I know, I know, I played like a fucking idiot."

He gives me a funny look, but ploughs on anyway.

"Why is that Wayne? Why aren't you playing well, man?"

"I don't know, I just feel a bit pissed off at the moment, just on a bit of a downer, you know."

At this point, he belatedly decides to tell me we're talking live on Dutch TV.

Me: "You're fucking joking!"

Doesn't sound too clever really, does it? Everyone in the players' area is in hysterics when I walk in, calling me an idiot and what have you. I'm glad they find it funny, but for me it's a crap end to a crap day.

THURSDAY 10TH FEBRUARY

A day off spent walking, playing cards (I beat Donna this time to get my revenge) and generally chilling out. I don't go down to Hengelo to watch the darts in the evening even though it's the big one between Phil Taylor and Raymond van Barneveld, the two reigning world champions and definitely the two best players around. Me and Donna decide to watch it in our room, order a bit of room service and relax. Predictably, Phil stuffs Barneveld 4–0.

If you could bottle what Phil's got, you'd make a fortune. Of course, it's talent and it's mental strength but plenty of players have got that. There's something about Phil that sets him apart. I haven't got the answer to what that is but if I've noticed anything watching him and playing against him (I have beaten him, by the way—at the Players Championship in Wales last year) it's that his set-up routine before he throws never, ever, ever changes.

It goes like this: he approaches the oche, looks slowly at the board, very deliberately places dart in hand, raises hand to eye level, cocks his arm and then releases dart.

He's a relatively slow player is Phil (especially compared to me) but that's because he's so meticulous about everything he does. There are slower players around and there are faster but Phil is definitely the most deliberate. It might not sound like that big a deal but he's like a robot in his approach and I'm sure that the complete consistency in his game before he even throws the dart has got to have something to do with his success. Darts is all about small margins and anything you can do give yourself an edge is going to make a difference.

FRIDAY 11TH FEBRUARY

Spend four hours on the practice board in the morning to try and get my rhythm going and arrive at the ExpoCenter at five-ish, ready for my match with Van Barneveld at nine. I'm not feeling great if the truth be told.

Sign a few autographs for about 15 minutes, but I've got to admit there are still plenty of people waiting for me to sign when I call it a day. I do feel bad but the problem is you can't spend two hours signing things for fans before a big match. It's terrible preparation and it's inevitable someone's going to be disappointed. It's a shame but that's the way it is.

The match with Raymond is another disaster. I start brilliantly and before he knows what's hit him, I'm three sets to one up and I need 63 to win the match. I hit the treble 13 with my first dart to leave double 12, hit double nine by mistake to leave double three and miss it by a whisker. Two darts for the match and I miss them both. The momentum of the match is with him now and no prizes for guessing that he makes the most of his good fortune and I end up losing 4–3.

To be fair, I'm not too gutted after the match. For the first time all week I feel I played well. I hit 14 maximums (180s), which is not bad going in a best of seven sets match, and I averaged well into the high 90s, so I'm pretty chuffed despite getting beat again. Phil Taylor regularly averages over a hundred with three darts, but the rest of us are happy with the high 90s.

I have far too many white wines in the bar at the hotel afterwards. I blame the hotel staff, who have looked after us like royalty all week, but shouldn't have sent a bloke over to ask me what I wanted to drink!

We have a bit of a chat, I tell him I like unwooded Australian Chardonnay and he brings me over a bottle. I polish that off in double-quick time and then he brings me another. That's when things get a little hazy...

SATURDAY 12TH FEBRUARY

I know everyone always reckons their own hangovers are the worst in the world but mine definitely beats yours hands down. I feel like shit all day. Mooch about doing nothing much at all apart from sorting out my expenses and playing cards with the usual suspects (Donna wins again... they've started calling her the Ice Maiden).

As for the darts, there was a bit of a fuss during the semi-finals which leaves a bad taste in a few people's mouths. Phil beat Raymond again to reach the final and Raymond stormed off rather than give his TV interview, which was a bit disrespectful to the fans if you ask me. But then he came back, got up on stage and gave a speech during the break of the second semi between Andy Fordham and Roland Scholten. Naughty boy. We wouldn't let that sort of thing happen in the PDC, let me tell you.

SUNDAY 13TH FEBRUARY

Finals day. It's Phil (of course) up against Andy but before they play all eight of us have to do a sort of parade in front of the crowd. I suddenly realise I didn't pack a suit so I borrow a jacket from Rod Harrington. Appropriately, Rod goes by the nickname 'Prince Of Style'. Problem is, Rod's not a small man, but he's not as big as me and the jacket's at least three sizes too small. I think I get away with it by standing behind Raymond, who is definitely a big fella. Hopefully all the Dutch fans were watching him and not me bulging out of a borrowed bit of kit.

As expected, Phil turns Andy over 7–1. Andy plays well, but Phil is just Phil and unless Phil has some sort of breakdown, there's only going to be one winner in that situation. And that's Phil.

Going home tomorrow and I can't wait. It's been a good week but I'm sick of darts now and some of the politics of what people should or shouldn't do, which has been the hot topic of conversation since Raymond's little show. I just want to play.

The thing you've got to understand about darts and the players is there can be a lot of bitching behind the scenes. We all genuinely get on well most of the time but there are times when people get the hump with each other and there's a bit of backbiting and people going into little cliques. I suppose it's natural when you've got so many big blokes crammed into one room or another for a tournament that there's going to be differences of opinion. There's a lot of testosterone in the air and that can cause problems. I've never seen any fights or anything like that but you do get the odd bit of verbals.

What you've got to remember is we're all a threat to each other's livelihoods. There's a limited pot of cash up for grabs at every tournament and everyone has got their eye on getting the lion's share. We can't all come away with a big fat cheque in our pocket, so people always go home disappointed, which is where a lot of the tension can come from. If someone's had a bad run and isn't earning much and then he hears someone else going on about what they've just spent their latest winner's cheque on or whatever, it's going to get under people's skins, isn't it? It's human nature.

The good news is the Master of Darts organisers have already asked me to come back next year, which is a result, and fingers crossed, I'll be coming back as the PDC world champion. I know I've lost every match this week but I still genuinely believe I'll be world champion sooner or later and this year is as good as any other to do it.

Yeah, I know I'm throwing like a prat at the moment but that can all change in one match. The way I see it, I'm still newish to the full-time tour, I've already been in the semis of the World Championship and I'm younger than a lot of the other lads so I've got time on my side. I'm taking nothing for granted but just because I'm on a poor run doesn't mean I've suddenly become a crap player. My confidence has taken a knock to be fair over the last few weeks but I'll be back.

MONDAY 14TH FEBRUARY

First thing we do when we get home is head to the pet shop to buy two Russian hamsters to replace Chips. I suppose you could call them our Valentine's present to each other. We decide to call one Vegas, for obvious reasons, and the other Chops, because he has these massive cheeks.

Spend the rest of the day unpacking and sorting things out at home before sharing a romantic chicken Madras in the evening. "Diet", I hear you say. I say, "Diet, what diet?"

TUESDAY 15TH FEBRUARY

Sky TV invite me and the family to Wimbledon dogs for the day so I take Donna, my mum and my sister over and I do a five-minute stint in front of the camera for them. We have a nice meal, a few complimentary bottles of wine and a top day out all round. Sky found out I'd been involved with the greyhounds since I was about 16 and the family moved near to the track in Romford, so it I feel right at home at Wimbledon. As soon as we settled in Romford, I started going to the track with mates and caught the gambling bug pretty much straight away.

I used to go the Romford track with a mate Georgie Harris, who was my best man at my wedding in Vegas, and at one stage we owned a dog ourselves called Bit Of Bully (after gameshow host Jim Bowen's catchphrase "You can't beat a bit of Bully" on *Bullseye*). We ran the dog over at the track in Crayford and he was quite successful, winning plenty of races, but when we tried him out at Romford, he was complete crap.

WEDNESDAY 16TH FEBRUARY

Back on the road today heading for Taunton for the Premier League. We're playing at a great venue called the Wellsprings Centre but to be honest, I'm still feeling down and dejected about my form and pretty much everything else. I've let my diet slip and I'm not even playing poker at the moment, which is a bad sign. Donna's going to try and book us a week in Tenerife so I can get away from it all and sort my head out. The sooner I get away, and get off the darts treadmill, the better.

THURSDAY 17TH FEBRUARY

Wake up feeling crap and when I get to the venue I know I'm lacking confidence when I warm up. I play John Part in the evening and he thumps me 9–3.

I'd like to be able to tell you about a turning point in the match, to be able to single out something to explain why it's so one-sided, but I can't. I'm never really in the game and the stress is beginning to get to me. I know on the outside I look like the same old Wayne Mardle to everyone else—cocky, full of bravado and all the rest of it—but inside I'm struggling.

I'm worrying about worrying now and all I can see is the negatives rather than the positives. I know there's no need for it, but it's a vicious circle. A few weeks ago I was missing doubles and it was costing me—now, I'm struggling to score heavily enough to even make the chances in the first place. I've got to get my head right and quickly.

I see Peter Manley behind-the-scenes but things aren't right between us since that incident in Reading. He's definitely not as friendly towards me and I'm still unhappy with what went on. We exchange a bit of small talk about the weather and the wives but that's it. We're not at each other throats but it's certainly frosty at the moment. It's a shame, but you can't undo what's been done.

CHAPTER THREE

"Wayne, son, you're throwing rubbish"

FRIDAY 18TH FEBRUARY

Fly out of Gatwick for Tenerife and almost as soon as the plane takes off, I can feel myself unwinding. A whole week away from darts. Bliss. Donna and me watch some film called *Shall We Dance* with Richard Gere and Jennifer Lopez on the flight and I'm ashamed to admit we both cry at the end of it. How sad is that?

We're staying in an apartment in a place called Los Cristianos, which is really peaceful. The weather could be better, but it's still shorts and T-shirt stuff, so can't complain really.

We decide to walk into town for a shufty and I say to Donna, "We've been out for 25 minutes and no-one's recognised me." I'm not an egomaniac, but it's a long-running joke between me and wifey. Of course, two minutes later a bloke from an apartment balcony clocks me.

"Oi, Mardle!"

Here we go.

"Oi, Mardle!"

"Yes, hello mate, you alright?"

"Oi Mardle, you owe me 50 euros."

"How's that then?"

"I put 50 on you to beat John Part last night."

"Okaaay..."

"Yeah, so you owe me 50 euros I reckon."

"You should have told me you were betting on me. If I'd known I'd have made sure I won for you mate."

"Really?"

"What do you think?"

It's only a bit of a laugh and we have a chat after but I hope it's not going to be like this all week. I've come away for a quiet one with the missus.

SUNDAY 20TH FEBRUARY

Feeling nice and relaxed. Donna's happy sunbathing most of the time but I try and keep out of the heat when I can because there's enough fat on my belly to fry an egg if the sun gets on it.

Discover the apartment complex has a darts board near the outdoor pool so I decide to borrow the big brass darts from behind the bar—I deliberately left mine at home—and decide to have a throw. Now don't forget I'm outside with the wind to contend with, the board's older than the hills and I'm throwing with arrows that are heavier than javelins. Still, I only go and hit a 180 with my second throw. You couldn't make it up—as soon as you stop thinking too hard about something, it all just falls into place.

Book a boat trip for tomorrow to watch whales and dolphins then play Donna at tennis. Six one, six love to Wayne, thank you very much. I serve like Goran Ivanisevic and little wifey just can't live with the power.

MONDAY 21ST FEBRUARY

It's pissing down with rain on and off all day and I'm paying the price for the tennis yesterday. I think I've pulled a muscle in my shoulder, which is agony, but decide to take the boat trip anyway. I've never seen a real live whale so it's quite exciting when we see a couple of pilot whales. Okay, they're only about nine-foot long but it's still a treat to see them out in the sea, in their own backyard if you like.

Sadly, that's the highlight of the trip and the wind really picks up later in the afternoon and I swear the boat's going to capsize. There are people everywhere being sick and I start feeling dicky as well because the boat bobbing up and down is playing murder with my shoulder. I get talking to the guide bloke who tells me to have a couple of beers to numb the pain and, fair play to him, it works.

WEDNESDAY 23RD FEBRUARY

My back and shoulder are killing me so I phone Russ Bray to let him know I'm not going to be able to do the exhibition we've booked in for at the weekend near Cork in Ireland. I feel bad because I know Russ has already forked out for the flights for both of us (I'll pay him back) but the worst thing is Russ obviously can't do the gig without a player, so he's going to miss out on two day's pay. But there's nothing I can do about it and although exhibitions are big part of my livelihood, I've got to be fit for the tournaments and I can't risk aggravating the shoulder when there aren't ranking points at stake. Bottom line is, without the ranking points my earning power is going to suffer sooner rather than later.

THURSDAY 24TH FEBRUARY

Keep getting recognised and it's beginning to wear a bit thin. I suppose it's because there's so many ex-pats on the island and there's Sky Sports in all the bars, but I don't know if I can take any more conversations like this:

"You are, aren't you?"

"I'm what?"

"You are... you're that dart player."

"What do you mean, 'that dart player'?"

"The one that wears them shirts."

"We all wear shirts... "

"No-one else has got the bottle to wear them kind of shirts... you know, the Hawaiian shirts."

"Yeah that's me, mate, that's me. How you doing?"

"You'll never be world champion..."

You get the picture.

FRIDAY 25TH FEBRUARY

Going home today. Get to the airport, play a game of cards called Crash to kill time (poker's not a lot of fun when there's only two of you) and win six euros off Donna. Superb, cos I'm winning my own money back really.

Go to check the bags in and meet an old couple—they must be in their eighties—and have an interesting conversation with the old boy, who recognised me, about darts in general, how good Phil Taylor is, that kind of thing. Then suddenly the old girl, who's been as quiet as a mouse up to this point, joins in.

"You shouldn't be in Tenerife for a week."

"Why's that then?"

"You should be at home practising."

"Why?"

"Because you're not playing very well, are you?'

"No, I'm not, to be fair."

"Well then..."

"Well what?"

"Bit more practice and a few less holidays I should think."

Everyone's got an opinion. Funny thing is, the old boy is dying his death with embarrassment, apologising as soon as she turns her back. I didn't catch their names, but if you're reading this, you know who you are.

SUNDAY 27TH FEBRUARY

The Essex Open is on today at Rush Green, just a couple of minutes down the road from my house, so I'm going to go down and hopefully see a few old friends and faces. The last time I was free to play in it in

2000 I won the thing and it's on my patch, so it would be daft not to go down and see what's what. I can't play because my shoulder's still giving me grief but I fancy a drink and a chit-chat.

I sort through my emails and there's plenty of bookings among the junk, so the rest of the year is shaping up nicely. I don't struggle for bookings but it's always better to have them in the bag early doors so you know where you are. I've actually got one on the Isle of Lewis in the Outer Hebrides. To be honest, I accepted it before I realised how far it is, but sod it, it'll be an experience, won't it?

Head off to Rush Green and sure enough, there's plenty of familiar faces the moment I walk through the door. I see a bloke called Bob Taylor, who I used to play with when I was a teenager. I haven't seen him in 18 years but the minute I clap eyes on him, we recognise each other straight away. People don't change that much, do they? We have a chat about the good old days. I also bump into a guy called Trevor Glede who I used to play county darts with. Bless him, Trevor seems to spend his whole life leaving Essex only to move back a few years later but he's a great lad and it's good to see him again.

MONDAY 28TH FEBRUARY

Me and Donna decide if we're going to keep up with a healthier lifestyle (yeah, I know, I've been letting things slip lately but I have lost about a stone since I started) then we need more exercise, so we head out to buy an exercise bike. I've got space in the conservatory for it and I know there's more chance of me peddling away in there than there is of actually going out in the cold and rain on a real bike.

In the shop the woman eyes us both up and you can tell she's thinking, what are these two doing buying an exercise bike? I'm not the most athletic looking specimen on the planet and I know she's thinking, 'He's going to kill himself on that thing.'

It takes me an hour to put the bike up back at home (which doesn't do my shoulder any favours) and then I give it a whirl. Hopefully, it won't be a passing fad.

TUESDAY 1ST MARCH

I've decided to completely change my practice routine. It's a big deal for me because I've been practising pretty much the same way for 20 years, but I really feel it's time to freshen things up. I used to practice for maybe a couple of hours at most in one stretch and, as I said before, I'd always start with the treble 20s for an hour, maybe move on to a particular double that had be giving me problems, then finish up with a few high checkouts and that was that.

So today I decide that's all going to change and I start with the checkouts. First I go for 81, then 82, 83 and so on upwards to 120. I find it really focuses the mind to start like this rather than just going through the motions of hitting the 20s and it really works. I haven't enjoyed practice this much for ages. I feel much more alert and I'm definitely concentrating on what I'm doing rather than pretending to be focused. It's easy to kid yourself sometimes that you're putting the work in when you know deep down you're not.

I suppose I'm still coming to terms with being full-time. It's a big change in your life going from the structure of working for someone else and picking up your wages at the end of the week to being your own boss and all that goes with it. The big difference is I've got more time to practice now and I have to find the best way to use that time.

I've realised it's not just how long you practice—although you do have to put the hours in—it's what's you do that is just as important.

It's a day for changes all round because I also decide to part company with Suzanne in Holland. We've worked together for nearly four years but I've been thinking about it for a while now. Today's the day and I phone her to let her know.

She takes the news okay but it's something I have to do. The problem basically is I don't want to be going away for week-long stretches any more and although to be fair to her Suzanne has always got me plenty of bookings, they always seem to come at the same time and I don't want that anymore. Sorting my own diary out will mean I'll have more control over when and where I work.

FRIDAY 4TH MARCH

The new practice regime is still going well. I'm definitely throwing more aggressively, more positively and I feel like I've got my good head back on. One thing I've realised is that whenever I have a break it takes me time to get back into swing of things, so I reckon I'm better off doing fewer but longer stints on the board.

Treat myself to a game of internet poker. Apologies to those of you who don't know the game but I've got to share this story with all the players out there. I draw a couple of aces (nice hand, Wayne, nice) but someone else goes all in before the flop (which are the three community cards that come out face up). Obviously I know they can't have a better hand than me so I call them and they've got a pair of fives—diamonds and spades. The flop is three spades, so they've got four spades but I'm still in the driving seat. The turn (fourth) card is king of clubs, so nothing changes, but then the river (fifth) card is the ace of fucking spades. My three aces loses to their ace flush. Jammy bastard, I can't believe it. Anyone who knows poker knows I should have won and then I could have just sat back and let all the players knock each other out.

(For the non-players out there, sorry again, that must have sounded like a foreign language.)

SATURDAY 5TH MARCH

Today's the South East Budweiser UK Open Regional and I'm playing in a pub called The Castle, near Swiss Cottage in London. Me and Donna arrive at 10 for a midday start. The pub's a big place on a main road into central London with a wrap-around bar. It's typical of the kind of places we play these kind of tournaments in. You know the kind of place that does steak and chips for a suspiciously low £5.99 or whatever, a few fruit machines, smelly toilets and dirty windows. I'm not knocking it but that's the reality of where we play a lot of our darts. The World Championship at the Tavern and Premier League venues you see on the telly are the exceptions to the rule.

I'm on the practice board straightaway for a warm-up and a chat and laugh with the rest of the lads. Everybody talks rubbish really, but it's the most sociable part of the day and everyone likes to have a bit of banter before things get serious.

I've always said that the best of nine legs format is a bit of a lottery and anyone can beat anyone else if they have a 15-minute purple patch so you've got to be on the money from the start or you could be in trouble.

My first game is against a guy called Wayne Atwood from Wales. Wayne's played in the World Championship a couple of times, which means he's no mug, but I play good enough to beat him 5–2.

Next up is a young kid by the name of Adrian Lewis. He's Phil Taylor's protégé (he comes from somewhere around Stoke as well) and has got a lot of promise but I'm too strong for him and it's 5–3 to Mardle.

Things are getting tense now and I pull Mark Dudbridge in the last 16. Of course, Mark beat me in the semis of the World Championship and it's a repeat performance this time around and I lose 5–3. I have a 66 checkout to make it four apiece. I hit the treble 10 with my first dart to leave my favourite double 18 but fluff the next two darts and it's nighty-night Wayne.

I'm not too gutted. I feel like I'm playing more like me again and even though I threw a few silly shots, it's a decent performance and something to build on.

Anyway, it's no disgrace losing to Mark. He's only been on the circuit for a year or so but he's reached the semis at the Circus Tavern and the World Matchplay Final and he's capable of some really fantastic stuff, believe me. He's got a great attitude and he's going to win loads over the next few years.

SUNDAY 6TH MARCH

Three hours of really focused practice today and although I'd rather be in London for the second day of the Budweiser, I feel tip-top. Starting my routine with finishes might sound like a simple change to make but it has made a massive difference.

People often assume us players must be mathematically gifted to be able to work out all the scores so quickly, what finishes we need and all that, but to be honest, it's not like that. I don't really think in terms of the number. For me it's about the patterns and memory. Say, for whatever reason, I'm on 91 and I'm throwing. I know straightaway that treble 17 and tops is the quickest way to finish but I could go, say, treble 15, 10 to leave myself my favourite double 18. But when I approach the oche, I don't have to work any of this out in my head because I know it already. I've thrown this shot thousands of times in the 20 years I've been playing darts, so it's totally automatic. You know before you think about it which ways you can go to leave yourself on a double. It becomes a reflex action.

Sometimes you see players hesitate on a shot and more often than not it's because they're on a number they're not used to and it throws them. That's when you have to do your sums because you're not familiar with the checkout, and then we do have to use the old grey matter a bit. Personally, I'm not a maths genius but I was always alright at it at school and I'm probably one of the better counters on the circuit.

After practice I have 20 minutes on the exercise bike. It's one of those you sit low down on so it's more like a rowing machine really but it gets the heart rate up and I get that glow of smug satisfaction afterwards because I know I've made the effort. I've not been eating great recently and I haven't lost any weight for weeks, but at least I'm trying.

People always make fun of darts players for being fat, overweight and unfit, but it's not just vanity on my part for wanting to slim down. Of course, I'd rather look like Brad Pitt (some hope!) than Jabba the Hutt when I'm on the telly but it's more than that. For a start, if I feel good physically, I'm more likely to feel good mentally and throw better.

The other reason is a player's weight can affect how they throw. Let me explain: I know how far I can comfortably lean forward over the oche and not feel awkward, but I know if lose a couple of stone, I'd be able to lean further forward and that means I'd be throwing just that little bit closer to the board. If I'm able to slightly adjust my release, then that's an advantage because it's always easier throwing closer to the board.

In contrast, if you pile on the pounds, you're not going to be able to lean as far forward (because your bigger belly is going to be more uncomfortable!) and that can be a problem. So yeah, there are plenty of fat darts players but that doesn't mean your weight isn't important, especially if you lose a bit or put a bit on.

It's Mother's Day today and my sister got mum a pair of tickets for a Tony Christie (he of *Amarillo* fame) concert at the Cliffs Pavilion in Southend tonight. He's one of mum's favourites from the '70s. My contribution is the hire of the limo to take mum and dad to Southend and you should see their faces when it pulls up outside the house. It cost a few quid but it's definitely worth it because mum and dad look well chuffed.

After we see them off I play a bit of poker. I say a bit... I mean two hours, but end up losing again. I think I'm going to play differently from now on. I think I need to be a bit more cautious and hedge my bets rather than going all in.

WEDNESDAY 9TH MARCH

Sky Sports send a crew around the house for an interview and sort of 'at home' piece, which will go out as a plug for tomorrow's Premier League in Norwich. It only takes a couple of hours and they seem to know what they want, so it's no hassle.

Have a couple of hours practice in the afternoon but keep getting interrupted by people ringing up to see if I can get them tickets for tomorrow. Everyone seems to think I can just click my fingers and produce the tickets but it doesn't work like that. If it did, I'd have every mate I have in the crowd but it's not going to happen.

Another 20-minute stint on the bike. I concentrate on endurance rather than a sprint today and my legs feel like jelly when I finish. I think I'm enjoying the exercise because I'm not overdoing it and my target now is to keep it up for the rest of the year.

THURSDAY 10TH MARCH

Travel to Norwich with Donna at the wheel and my mum and dad are coming along too. I know it's a bit sad that a man of my age doesn't drive but there you go.

I did take lessons when I was a teenager but I didn't get on with my instructor. He really put my back up and although I don't think I was the best pupil he'd ever had either, I just never picked it up again. I just didn't like his manner and he kept talking to me like driving was the easiest thing in the world. I kept thinking, 'if it's so easy, what the hell am I doing paying you for then?' He was basically a patronising twat who made me feel like a fool. I really hated the old hill starts as well. Maybe I'll give it a go in the future but I don't want to put Donna out of a job, do I?

We're going to make it a long weekend in Norwich because I've got the Vauxhall Holiday Park Classic after tonight's Premier League, so we're staying four nights in all. We're staying at the park itself but because I'm an international darts superstar we're getting upgraded from a caravan to a chalet. Actually, the chalets are quite plush and will do us nicely.

We get to the venue—the Norwich Sports Village—at about four and just mill about for a while. I'm playing twice tonight against Phil Taylor and Roland Scholten and I've got to admit I'm feeling nervous. I still haven't won a match and it's starting to look embarrassing.

The game against Phil is a nightmare and he turns me over 11–1. I can't really say I deserve more than the one leg and Phil is at his bloody brilliant best as usual. When he plays like that there's no other player who can live with him. I've got two hours to kill before I play Roland and I just try and put the last game out of my mind. There's no point dwelling on losing to Phil, is there?

The match with Roland is, thank god, a different story. The first leg sets the tone as I bang in consecutive 180s and for once it's me racing into an early lead—three legs to nothing to be precise. Roland rallies with a worrying number of maximums of his own to make it 5–3 but I'm not throwing this one away. My finishing holds up under the pressure and in the end it's 8–4 to me. I've won... no, really—I've won a Premier League match!

Roland's as gracious as ever in defeat afterwards and I feel like a weight's been lifted off my shoulders. Mum and dad are sitting in the front row and look delighted and I suppose I'll have to bring them along to the rest of the matches because they're obviously good luck.

SATURDAY 12TH MARCH

Today's the 128-man Classic but to be honest I'm still buzzing from Thursday night. I didn't think losing all these matches in the Premier League was affecting me too much but now I've popped my cherry against Roland, I realise it was really bugging me.

Anyway, things go pretty well and I win my first three games to make the last 16 before I get beat by a fella called John McGowan. I would have beaten John if I could have hit a double but the last 16 here isn't too bad and I'm not going to cry about it.

SUNDAY 13TH MARCH

Have a bit of fun today with Donna in the mixed pairs and mixed triples but we're pretty terrible and don't get far. Maybe we should take it more seriously, but it's not life or death, is it?

MONDAY 14TH MARCH

Back home to sunny Essex.

Bit pissed off this afternoon. Spurs get beat at Newcastle in the FA Cup quarter-finals and I had a really good feeling we'd come away with at least a draw. We've been doing okay this season but I should have known better.

Being a Tottenham fan is not an easy job these days. I started supporting them in 1980. It was the week before the FA Cup final between Arsenal and West Ham at Wembley and my old man had a couple of tickets for the game. I'm not really sure why now, but when he asked me if I wanted to go, I said, "No thanks, I'm a Tottenham fan." I suppose it was my stubborn streak, so my sister went instead and I was officially a Spurs boy. And you've got to stick with your team once you've made your choice, haven't you? To be fair, most of the '80s was a good time to be Tottenham—it's only since the 1991 Cup final that things have gone tits up.

I wouldn't mind the life of a professional footballer though. Talk about loaded. I remember one time seeing Gary Speed and his missus in Nike Town in London. They were looking for trainers for their lad and couldn't decide which pair to buy him, so in the end I hear Speed saying, "Sod it, just buy the lot and he can choose his favourites."

We're talking about hundreds and hundreds pounds worth of gear here. Now I like to have a few quid in my pocket but that's just stupid money if you ask me. You've got to lose touch with reality when you've got that much in the bank.

Saying that, footballers can be a bit off as well. I went to Marshalls Park School in Romford with Ray Parlour. We were in the same class for five years but when I saw him about five years ago in Romford and went up to say hello, he didn't seem to have a clue who I was. I didn't expect him to know I was a darts player but it isn't that long ago we were sitting next to each other in maths. What pissed me off was that he looked at me like I was some crazed fan. Seriously, he gave the impression that he thought he was something special and everyone else was a pleb. Truth is, he's just an Essex boy like me.

But to be fair they're not all like that. I met Neil 'Razor' Ruddock at the World Championship at Purfleet last year and he was a top bloke. We had a beer in the bar together and he was saying he loved his darts and he seemed like a bloke who still had his feet on the ground.

WEDNESDAY 16TH MARCH

The next few weeks are going to be pretty hectic so I try and take things pretty easy today. Cut the grass, practice a little but surprise, surprise, I spend most of the day playing poker.

When I say most of the day, I actually mean 14 hours. I fancy beating my 16-hour record but can't quite manage it. It isn't time well spent either because I enter a $200 tournament by mistake rather than my usual $10 to $50 ones and I don't like to lose £130 in one go, which is what happens.

I don't mean to go on about poker more than I do the darts but I can't help it, especially the way I lose today. Final hand, right, and I'm one of five players left out of the original 99, I've got four 2s and I'm thinking I can't lose, only for some other bloke to pitch in with four 6s. I can't believe it! Wifey has to listen to me moaning on about it for hours afterwards. Sometimes I think the woman deserves a medal.

I can't blame the computer for the cards but I am having problems with my internet access. Someone has tried to hack into my personal details and I'm worried because I do all my banking online. I check all the accounts to be sure and they seem fine, except there's not enough money in them, but that could be Donna spending without telling me.

Seriously, I'm going to have to call someone out to have a look at it. I book all my flights, hotels and the like online and I'd be lost without the internet.

THURSDAY 17TH MARCH

Get up and check the post and find a lovely letter from the Darts Regulation Authority (DRA) telling me they're fining me £50. The DRA are an independent organisation that are there to monitor our behaviour and fine us if they think any of the players have stepped out of line. Just like having a wife really.

The fine's for swearing on stage during my World Championship quarter-final with Colin Lloyd. It was during a break but I was still on stage and I said to myself "fucking come on" to gee myself up. I had no idea the cameras were on me and it was going out live but you try telling the DRA that. I reckon if you farted up there, they'd find some clause or other in their precious handbook and fine you for that. They're good like that, the DRA.

What pisses me off is I only did it in the heat of the moment and they still hit you for it. I know I shouldn't swear but it's not the crime of the century and they keep fining people for nothing basically. A lot of the players have had enough with the DRA and there's been more and more talk about sorting them out. We know we need them but it's ridiculous what they're fining people for these days.

I've had quite a few DRA fines now. I've been fined for swearing before and I also got stung for £25 by them when I failed to score for a game during a 'floor tournament' where all the players have to score for the game immediately before or after their own match. We're all expected to muck in because you just can't find enough good scorers to do 32 games simultaneously. So, I was at a tournament at the Robin Hood pub in Dagenham waiting to score for a game when a fight broke out at the bar. The place went crazy and everything was put on hold for an hour while everyone calmed down, but I just couldn't be bothered to hang around and did one. Cost me £25.

It'd probably be easier if I set up a direct debit to the DRA bank account rather than keep sending them the cheques. I know my mate Kevin Painter is planning to. He's always getting in bother with the DRA because he's got a bit of a short fuse but he's spot on when he says they're starting to take the piss these days.

Kev's a good bloke though and a top player. His nickname is 'The Artist', which he got from Sky a few years ago. Painter. Artist. Geddit? Sky like the players to have a nickname but let's face it, they didn't need their finest minds to come up with that one.

Kevin's an aggressive character to say the least and he's always warning people "I'll rare up in a minute" when he's in a temper. He's incredibly easy to wind up as a result. For example, me, him and Peter Manley were out in China last year for a tournament and got into the hotel lift. Kevin's presses the button for the third floor but there's a panel on both sides of the lift, so when he's not looking, Peter presses the cancel button. Kevin presses for the third floor again and Peter cancels it again on the sly. This goes on for a few minutes and Kevin is effing and blinding like a trooper, threatening to stick one on me and Peter when he realises what's been happening. I thought his head was going to explode. Thankfully, he has mellowed a bit since his daughter Madison was born.

FRIDAY 18TH MARCH

Drive up to Manchester for tomorrow's North West Budweiser UK Open Regional Final (catchy title, isn't it?) Stop off on the way and give into temptation and pick up a Kentucky for me and Donna.

I've got to admit we're both ashamed of ourselves because we go for the bargain bucket—10 pieces of chicken, six portions of chips, chicken strips, popcorn chicken, corn-on-the-cob, beans, coleslaw, fizzy drink, the works—and then tell the guy behind the counter a pack of lies to cover up the fact it's all just for the two of us.

Bloke: "How many cups would you like, sir?"

Me: "Er, four please... yeah, four."

Donna: "Shall we get serviettes for the kids?"

Me: "What? Oh yeah, definitely. Does Dave want ketchup?"

Donna: "Yeah. And get some salt for Steve."

SATURDAY 19TH MARCH

I'm playing in the Royal Oak pub in a place with a top name—Chorlton-cum-Hardy. We get there at quarter to 10 in the morning and the bar's shut so I try and charm the landlord into serving us.

"Alright mate. We couldn't get a drink in, could we?"

"It's too early mate."

"Go on, I need a drink before I play."

"What do you want then?"

"Nice one. Large vodka and orange please."

"There you go."

"Have you got any ice?"

"Are you taking the piss? I've got a whole pub to serve and you want some bloody ice. Forget it mate."

I'm totally gobsmacked and I stand there like a lemon. I can't believe he's just talked to me like that. Usually I'd come back with some witty retort but I'm lost for words. Rude bastard.

I beat a player called Mark Hollioake in the last 64 and then I play my old mate Andy Jenkins in the next round and win 5–2. I enjoy beating Andy because he always gives me grief whenever I see him, calling him me a "showpony" and what have you. He thinks he's hilarious. His favourite gag is to say the circus is in town and they've got a position vacant for a new clown, which he reckons would be the perfect job for me. Like I said, he thinks he's a comedian.

Next up is Ronnie Baxter and even though I have shots at the double in every leg, I lose 5–3. It would have been handy to beat Ronnie because he's sixth in the rankings and I'm seventh, so the points would have been useful, but like I've said before, Ronnie's a tough nut to crack at these events.

Ronnie's known as 'The Rocket'. To be honest, I'm not sure how Ronnie got his nickname but I assume it's because most sportsman called Ronnie end up being called The Rocket. Look at Ronnie O'Sullivan. Anyway, take my advice—never, ever go out for a meal with Ronnie because the man can moan for England. Seriously, he never stops complaining about the food, the service, anything he can whinge about. Compared to Ronnie, Victor Meldrew has a sunny disposition.

SUNDAY 20TH MARCH

We're staying at a Travel Inn and check out early so we can get back to my mum's in time for Sunday lunch. I like Travel Inns. No, that's not right... I love Travel Inns. Me and wifey have had too many bad experiences of crap hotels and B&Bs, so it's Travel Inns for us these days whenever we can. I know it's a bit Alan Partridge of me to go on about them but they're great. Clean. Tidy. Nice menu. You just can't go wrong with a Travel Inn. Only problem is, they don't do a loyalty scheme—you know, something like stay nine nights and get your tenth free—which strikes me as daft. I'd be quids in if they did. Still, you can't beat a Travel Inn... and, no, they aren't paying me to say that.

Found out on the way back home that Alex Roy was the winner at the Budweiser. Hand on heart, I'm never that bothered about following a tournament once I've been knocked out but got a bell today telling me Alex had won it.

I'm glad I'm not around for Alex's acceptance speech because he can talk for England. As someone said in an interview a few years ago, he's a nice bloke but you wouldn't want to sit next to him on a flight to Australia because his favourite topic of conversation is usually himself. He's known as the 'Ace of Herts' because he's from Hertfordshire. He's got the look of a prize fighter about him and he remembers every dart he's ever thrown during his career. He's darts' answer to Statto. He's also a funny guy but funny as in peculiar. I remember we were staying at the same hotel for the UK Open in Bolton a couple of years ago and Alex comes down for breakfast. The waitress comes over to show him to a table near the window but Alex is having none of it and insists on sitting in the middle of the room. Absolutely no idea why.

We make it back in time for lunch at mum's and she does herself proud as usual. Don't get me wrong, there's nothing wrong with wifey's skills in the kitchen, but there's nothing like your mum's cooking.

MONDAY 21ST MARCH

Go and see my accountant today because the tax year is nearly over and I need to know how many pounds of flesh the taxman wants. I know he's got to have his cut but I still hate the taxman's guts.

On the way back, I pop into the pet shop. Donna's brother, Daryl, fell in love with our hamsters Vegas and Chops when he saw them, so we've given them to him. I only buy one to replace the pair and we name it Bubbles.

TUESDAY 22ND MARCH

The computer guy comes around in the morning and sorts me out a treat, so I'm back up and running now.

I do an exhibition tonight in Wickford, which is only 20 minutes down the road from the house. The venue's a place called the Little & Large Club and I know a few people down there, so it's a good night all around. The club's above a kebab shop but it's surprisingly nice inside. It's basically a working men's club but it's not the kind of place where old men sit drinking and smoking all day and you'd be happy enough to take your kids along with you. It's got four snooker tables and 12 dartboards, so it's quite a big place.

Sell quite a bit of merchandise (which me and Donna always take with us to earn some extra dough), which is a bonus, but I have four double vodka and tonics, which is far too many for a work night. Naughty boy, Wayne.

THURSDAY 24TH MARCH

Darts is officially a sport! It's on the news today that Sport England has finally decided to recognise darts as a 'legitimate sporting activity' and I'm sure, like me, most of the players will be chuffed to bits that we've taken another step towards proving darts requires as much skill, dedication and nerve as many other sports that people don't look down their noses at.

The decision means a few things. First, being recognised by Sport England could open up a few more commercial opportunities for us. Darts needs to be seen as more respectable if it wants to attract more sponsorship, and this announcement definitely won't do us any harm. It also means we can ask for Lottery Funding to promote the game at grass roots level.

Second, it'll see drug testing in darts because that comes with the territory as a proper sport, doesn't it? To be fair, it won't worry any of the players unless they're looking for traces of Stella or Smirnoff.

But seriously, it's great news and all part of changing the game's image. It'll also improve our chances of making the Olympic Games in Beijing as a demonstration sport. No, I kid you not, there's been a lot of talk about darts in Beijing in 2008 and maybe we're a step closer now. There's been no final decision yet but fingers crossed.

Apparently, there's already 22 countries willing to send a team if we get the nod, which just goes to prove how healthy the game is worldwide.

Going to the Olympics would create one interesting problem

though—how would the Great Britain team be selected? Don't forget, we're talking PDC and BDO players here and I bet there'd be one or two rows along the way before that one gets sorted out.

Personally, I'd sort it out like this. You set the standard over the season for the players, a three-dart average of 90-ish or whatever, so you get the 100 best British players from the PDC and BDO. Those 100 then play in a straight knockout tournament to find the three or four or however many players you need for the team. I don't think anyone could complain about that.

But we'll have to see whether they want us in Beijing first. It would be just my luck for us to miss out in 2008, get the nod for 2012 and then find out London will be hosting the Games. Don't get me wrong, it'd be great for London to get the Olympics but given the choice of representing Britain thousand of miles away in China or an 18 quid cab ride from my house in Romford, I'd go for the foreign option every time.

There's no doubt the game is expanding globally. I mentioned it earlier that the top eight PDC boys were flown out to China last year for a specially arranged tournament to promote the game and the whole thing was sponsored by the Chinese Government. We were based in a city called Shantou, which is about 300 miles north of Hong Kong, and although the crowds didn't have a clue how to react to us, there were packed houses for every match and it was obvious darts is gaining in popularity fast over there.

China was an eye-opening experience to say the least. For a start our hotel was a swanky five-star affair but the foyer also seemed to double as a brothel. We'd walk in and the entire reception area was full of Oriental women dressed, well, like tarts. They were definitely working girls and they were all sitting around trying to attract the attention of the single men coming in and out of the hotel. Luckily none of them bothered with me because I was with Donna but I noticed at least a couple of old blokes—I swear one must have been 80—disappear off to the rooms with them. None of the locals batted an eye at any of this and to be honest, by the end of the week, it seemed normal to us too.

What I never got used to was the poverty everywhere. It really struck how horrendous the conditions were for the locals working and living there. There were kids as young as eight and nine begging for food and money, old women hauling bags of rice heavier than they were around on their shoulders and men riding bikes with dead cattle over the back wheel—probably on their way to market to see what they could get for the meat—as well as a lot of people scavenging for scraps of food in the bins by the side of the roads.

But there were a few laughs as well. We had an interpreter who claimed his name was Michael (come on...) who was no older than 19. Michael went everywhere with his girlfriend Rita in tow and I noticed that they seemed quite awkward together and asked him how long they've been an item. He told me they'd only been together two weeks and that they had met on the Chinese version of *Blind Date*. Apparently, Rita picked Michael. At first, I was sure he was winding me up but he swore blind it was true.

But the funniest moment had to be during my first round match against a Chinese guy called Tang Jun. During the second set the referee and the two scorers started cracking up on the stage. I was angry at first because I was trying to play serious darts but it turned out they're laughing because one of the scorers had just swallowed a fly!

Anyway, I've got an exhibition in Manchester tonight so we leave at 12 on the dot to leave us plenty of time. It takes four hours door to door (or four-and-a-half if we want to stop off for a Kentucky) but I swear today there must have been a pile-up on every single motorway we use, because it takes just short of six-and-a-half hours to do the journey.

We've got 30 minutes in the hotel before we have to set off again for the venue—Denton West End Working Men's Club—and then Donna suddenly decides she wants to drive back home tonight rather than stay over. So that's £50 I've forked out for a half-hour stay in the hotel then. What a bargain. Still, it's probably not the best time to point this out to Donna, seeing as she has just driven me up here.

I got the gig through John Gwynne, who does commentary for Sky and he'll be doing the MCing tonight. John's a good lad and he writes my monthly column, 'Wayne's World', for the *Darts World* magazine. You should check it out, it's a quality piece of work.

Anyway, we get to the venue at 7.30ish for the eight start. It holds about 120 and there are, give or take, three people in. I'm starting to get worried because it looks like this could be a nightmare. You can't help thinking, I've just driven six-odd hours for this. By 8.20 a few more wander in but by nine the place is rammed. Thank God for that.

The exhibition goes down a storm. There are a load of lads in who play in the Denton 501 League, and they lap it up. There's a party feel and I think everyone's generally in a good mood because it's the Bank Holiday tomorrow.

We meet a young boy called Dominic, who's just nine and terminally ill. It's really heartbreaking to hear about his illness and I try and have a chat with him when his dad approaches me to ask. Bless him though, he's really nervous when I come over and seems a bit embarrassed. I give him a set of darts and a signed photo and at the end of the night his dad tells me he's had a great time. I feel sad because it's such a terrible thing to happen to the kid but I do also feel pleased if he's had a good time tonight. Makes you appreciate what you've got anyway, that's for sure.

FRIDAY 25TH MARCH

We got home at three this morning. Now, I'm not exactly saying Donna broke any speed limits on the way back but we got back in record time and we didn't get flashed or stopped, so sod it. It's a job well done on Donna's part, although I'm sure the coffee and Pro Plus played their part as well.

We get a few hours kip and then we're up and about again to look for a new house. Neither of us really want to move but we both fancy something a little bit bigger so we've got to bite the bullet and find somewhere. We're looking around the Romford area because it's where all our family are and it's handy for the M25 and the main airports, so we don't want to go far.

I'm really not looking forward to the whole house-hunting lark though. I'd say me and Donna get on pretty well most of the time and we talk things over rather than row but that all goes out of the window when it comes to houses. Problem is, I don't give a monkey's what a house looks like from the outside—it's the inside that I've got to be happy with. Donna on the other hand likes a lovely-looking house and doesn't care about the interior. It's all cosmetic to her. I know this is all going to create aggravation.

Sure enough, we see a couple of places today and Donna really fancies one of them. It's one those detached places on a new estate with the garage and back garden. For me, it's just got no character or soul and it looks like every other house around the place. Not for me, I'm afraid. Luckily we don't have a big row about it, but I can see it coming, I really can.

SATURDAY 26TH MARCH

Forget about the house-hunting and decide to have a day out together at the casino. As soon as we get there a bloke I don't recognise pulls me to one side.

"You told me to bet on you to beat Phil Taylor."

"Did I?"

"Yeah, in the Premier League. You told me you'd win."

"Did I?"

"Yeah and you lost 11–1."

"I know—I was there."

"You got stuffed."

"Sorry about that."

He takes it quite well, but I have to laugh. He's right—I didn't just lose, I got slaughtered.

Me and Donna enter a poker tournament but I get knocked out

pretty early. I don't know what it is but I always seem to get crap hands when I play 'live' poker. Don't know why, but I never seem to get anything to work with and I'm always playing with a short stack and end up having to go all in.

Even worse, Donna lasts longer than me and starts giving it some, telling me she's the better player and I'm a waste of space. Women love to rub your nose in it, don't they?

SUNDAY 27TH MARCH

Easter Sunday and we're having Danny and Ellie and Donna's nephew Darcy, who's eight, to stay. Having the kids stay with us only reinforces our decision not to have children of our own. The three of them behave like absolute terrors, screaming like four-year-olds and generally not doing as they're told. The little sods are bloody hard work.

MONDAY 28TH MARCH

All the family come round for a barbie (and to collect the kids) and they get royally looked after, even if I do say so myself. The weather is glorious and I've got trout, salmon, fillet steaks, chicken kebabs, chops, you name it, on the go. I do a fantastic job of cooking everything and it's a top day.

Not that the family appreciate it. They spend most of the day ripping me to shreds, joking about how shit I've been playing recently. Even Donna's dad, Terry, gets in on the act.

"Wayne, son, you're throwing rubbish."

"Alright Terry, leave it will you?"

"Even I could beat you at the moment."

"Don't be daft, Terry."

"No, go on, I'll play you now and beat you."

"You reckon?"

"Yeah, let's go upstairs and I'll beat you right now."

"Alright Terry, I'll give you a game... for a oner."

That shuts him up and he's straight back out into the garden.

Everyone's a comedian these days.

WEDNESDAY 30TH MARCH

Playing in the Premier League in Carlisle tomorrow night so we set off in the car at two. We could have flown up to Newcastle but it's still an hour-and-a-half drive from the airport to Carlisle and we'd have to hire a car, so driving is probably the least hassle.

Get to Carlisle at eight and do some exercise before an early night. I've been really slack recently, out of sheer laziness, really, and I know I'm putting weight on because my chins are starting to stack up like a rack of ribs. Ribs with loads of meat on them, that is. I look well attractive at the moment, I really do.

THURSDAY 31ST MARCH

The venue for tonight is the Sands Centre so we plan to leave at around four. I'm just about to turn the telly off in our room—*Countdown* is just finishing—when I see kid called John O'Neil being introduced to the cameras as the contestant for the next show. He's from near Purfleet, my neck of the woods, but the funny thing is he's sat there wearing an authentic Wayne Mardle Hawaiian shirt! All the audience go "Whoo" when they see the shirt and I have a little chuckle.

Nice bit of free advertising... which reminds me—I really need to get the new batch of yellow shirts sorted out. They're already three months late and I'm running out of blues ones fast. I must remember to chase them up when I get home.

Get to the venue and have a practice and a laugh with the lads. I'm up against Colin Lloyd tonight but we're not first on, so I chill out backstage and take in a bit of the atmosphere. The crowd sound great and are probably the least biased lot we've had so far, giving all the players a chance. Carlisle is Peter Manley's hometown, so he obviously gets a good cheer but they seem happy to shout for anyone.

I'm still not really talking to Peter. We still say hello at the tournaments but we both know we're only going through the motions. He's obviously got some sort of problem with me and you already know why I'm pissed off with him. As I see it, it's down to him to make the first move because I've done nothing wrong, but Peter's stubborn and I really can't see that happening. Fuck it, if he wants to play silly buggers, that's his business.

My match with Colin finishes up six all. I'm 6–5 up and get two darts at the double to win but miss and then Colin pulls out a 144 three-dart finish. I know I should have taken my own chance but honestly, a 144 in those circumstances is just unreal. Fair play to Colin, but you just don't expect him to pull something off like that.

Have to laugh later when Peter plays. Before our fall-out, he was always badgering me, saying I should stop showing off all the time and playing to the crowd. He reckoned I should worry about the darts and let the crowd take care of itself. Even though I told him time and time again it wasn't in my make-up, he didn't stop banging on about it. So anyway, Pete only walks on tonight dancing to Tony Christie's *Amarillo*, giving it the large one to the crowd. Pot, kettle, black... unbelievable!

I'm still bottom of the Premier League but I've got three points on the board and the way I'm throwing now, I'm going to go up that table like a salmon leaps up river. Just you wait and see.

CHAPTER FOUR

Stroppy Eric & nutty John

FRIDAY 1ST APRIL

A six-hour trot back to Romford, most of which Donna spends swearing at other motorists, HGV drivers in the outside lane and anyone else who displeases her. It's amazing how many different nob-based insults that woman knows.

In the afternoon we go and look at a couple more houses and we see one in Romford that we *both* really like. It must be a miracle. I know it's April's Fools Day, so I hope she isn't winding me up. It's a three bedroom semi and it ticks all our boxes. We need three bedrooms—one of for us, one for spare and one, of course, for my practice room—and it's got a nice little garden at the back with a fish pond. It's close to all the family, which is very important, and it's in decent nick. We don't want anywhere that needs a lot of work doing, so it's pretty much perfect for us. I think we're going to put an offer in first thing in the morning.

SATURDAY 2ND APRIL

9.00am: Phone the estate agents and put the offer in.

9.10am: The offer's accepted.

9.20am: Inform our solicitor.

9.22am: Inform financial advisor.

9.25am: I'm well excited.

I really hope it all goes through but I'm feeling optimistic and practice for five hours solid without a single poker break. It's amazing what a bit of good news can do for your concentration.

MONDAY 4TH APRIL

Sort out the mortgage details today, which I find quite stressful. There's no reason why the bank won't lend us a few quid but I hate that feeling of being under scrutiny from people who don't know you.

Strangers are in control of my life and I don't like it. They don't even have to give you reasons these days if they knock you back and I just don't want to be mucked about.

My head's not right for practice so I knock it on the head after 15 minutes and me and Donna go and pick up her Nan, who lives in Tiptree, near Colchester. She's staying with us for a few days and she's a good old girl with a nice line in gags so I'm actually looking forward to her staying.

The poor old dear has got Parkinson's. She's not too bad with it and she's always joking about how her hands are shaking. They don't shake violently but she does struggle sometimes and I remember one visit when we gave her a cuppa and some chocolate biscuits. She kept trying to dunk the biscuit in the tea but her fingers kept going into the tea and most of the chocolate ended up around her mouth rather in it.

"You alright nan?"

"Yes, I'm fine."

"Do you want any help?"

"No, I'm alright. But I might need a shower now."

TUESDAY 5TH APRIL

I'm well pissed off because there's a story in the papers today that really gets my blood boiling. There's this bloke called Justin Irwin who's just jacked in his £50k-a-year job working for a charity or something because he reckons he can be darts world champion within a year. The prat reckons there's not a lot of skill involved in darts and he's going to use his new-found free time to practice until he's good enough to be world champion.

Now I don't normally let people wind me up but this is fucking typical. I don't give a toss about the muppet personally, he can do what he likes, but yet again it's crap publicity for darts because it demeans the sport and us players. It just reinforces the impression we're a load of fat blokes who just throw darts in between pints and anyone can do it. It's taking the piss out of what I do for a living and what I've worked for over the last 20 years of my life.

I'm sure the story's been twisted by the press a bit for the sake of a good headline but it still irritates me. I mean, no-one would write a story that takes the piss out of a dustman for the way he earns a living, so why should darts players always get it in the neck?

I sort of hope this bloke does go through with it because he ain't going to be welcomed with open arms by the lads on the circuit if he ever shows his face. Or maybe the PDC should arrange a special match in 12 months time so one of us can shove his words right down his throat.

WEDNESDAY 6TH APRIL

Bit of bad news today—Ron Russ, who owns my darts sponsors B&W, has had a stroke. Although Ron's son Derek says he's not too bad, it makes you think, doesn't it? Just proves you never know what's around the corner. The weird thing is I was planning to go and see Ron at their shop in Walthamstow tomorrow anyway.

THURSDAY 7TH APRIL

Despite yesterday's news, I decide to go to Walthamstow and see

Derek anyway. I take dad along with me and we're both amazed by the shop, which I've never been in before because they usually send me everything I need. I had been expecting some small place but it's a massive great big lock-up packed with anything and everything from darts to pool cues, punch bags to trophies.

I pick up a few Hawaiian shirts while I'm there but there's still no sign of the new batch of yellow ones. Don't expect they'll be coming anytime soon now, what with Ron being ill and Derek taking over. Derek's struggling to be fair because he doesn't really know what's going on, bless him. The main thing is that Ron's stroke wasn't too bad and he should recover.

FRIDAY 8TH APRIL

Travel up to Sheffield for the Midlands Budweiser UK Open Regional tomorrow. Now, I'm no geographer but I could have sworn Sheffield was in Yorkshire not the Midlands. You work it out, because I can't.

We stop on the way up for our usual Kentucky—you know the 10 pieces of chicken and all the rest of it. I haven't mentioned the fitness regime recently, have I? That's probably because it's gone totally out of the window and I'm starting to feel very, very heavy again. I know I've only got myself to blame, although Colonel bloody Sanders might have something to do with it.

Have a couple of Guinnesses with some of the lads—Colin Monk, Andy Jenkins, Chris Mason—in the evening but don't have a late one because tomorrow's matchday.

You already know Andy, but let me introduce Chris and Colin. I tend to spend a lot of time behind-the-scenes with both of them and we've always seemed to click.

Chris calls himself 'The Ace' because he thinks he is and to be fair on his day he's probably the best player on the circuit. Seriously, if he ever gets it together he could easily be world champion. Problem is, trouble always seems to find Chris and he's had a lot of personal problems. He's been inside for GBH and he's just getting back on his feet in terms of his life and his darts. But he's a good fella really and a real talent. I first met him years ago playing in London SuperLeague. He was only a young lad and when he turned up for his first match the rest of the team ripped him to shreds, taking the piss out of his Bristol accent and asking where he parked the combine harvester. We only found out later that he was so gutted that he threatened not to play the following week because he thought it was like that all the time. Chris is a big softie really, despite the reputation he's got after his problems with the law.

Colin, on the other hand, is a certified lunatic. And a good mate. He's imaginatively known as 'Monky' or sometimes 'Harry', which is rhyming slang for Harry Monk, spunk. Don't ask me why because I've got no idea and I really don't want to know. Monky's the worst speller in the world and he's always sending text messages that no-one can understand. He makes me laugh though and I was in stitches last year when he tripped over the oche and popped a bone in his foot. He was in agony but the next day he still turned up for the tournament we'd entered, a crutch under one arm, the darts in the other hand. I still think the foot's giving him problems now.

SATURDAY 9TH APRIL

This is the last Budweiser before the finals at the Reebok in Bolton in June and I've got to make the quarter-finals today at least to make sure I qualify for the main draw. If I don't, I could have to play a preliminary game on the Friday night before the main finals against one of the little fellas. Now, I don't mean any disrespect but the last thing I want to do is have to play some part-timer who's really up for it, maybe playing his only televised game, and run the risk of getting beat. I'm not the only one of the higher-ranked players in this situation, so there could be quite a few tense games today.

I don't want to make any enemies here but the venue, a place called the Wharncliffe, is what I'd call a typical northern pub—small, smokey and dingy—and there's hardly room to swing a cat around the practice boards.

I get through to the last 32 and then I have to play Mark Dudbridge who beats me yet again. I like Mark but I'm beginning to get sick of the sight of him because he's beaten me three times in the last couple of months. To be fair, he didn't miss a thing and I'll just have to wait and see what happens now with qualification for the Budweiser finals.

SUNDAY 10TH APRIL

Get back home just in time for Sunday roast round me mum's. Poor old girl—I'm not sure if she enjoys cooking all the time but we don't give her much choice.

Danny and Ellie are there and they bring their brown Labrador puppy Toby with them, which really makes me want one of my own but it wouldn't be fair with the amount of time Donna and me spend on the road. Saying that, I could do without all the pissing and pooping they do—just like a baby but worse really. I have a little play fight with the little fella but I think he gets the wrong end of the stick and he rips me to shreds with his teeth.

Get home in the evening and play a bit of poker and lose. I just don't enjoy it at the moment. I've even found myself doing some paperwork rather than playing poker recently and what with all the nonsense I've got to sort out for the mortgage, I just haven't been bothered.

WEDNESDAY 13TH APRIL

Excited about today—I'm doing an exhibition in Wolverhampton with The Crafty Cockney, Eric Bristow. Eric was my idol when I was growing up and I've never done an exhibition with him before, so I'm really looking forward to it.

I first met Eric when I was a teenager. I'd just won the Heywoods Pickle British Youth tournament at the Lakeside, which was shown on the BBC at the time and he said to me he'd see me in ten years when I was on the full circuit. I always loved the way he could always step up to the plate when he was in his heyday and answer any questions the other players asked. He really had the lot in his pomp—the personality, the image and the talent—and I really identified with that as kid. He was cocky but he had the game to back it up and I wanted to be like him.

I get to the pub at about half six for a half eight start. Eric's already at the bar but he's arguing with the landlord, Will, who's booked us both. Eric's apparently not happy that he's expected to buy his own beer and poor old Will doesn't know what to make of him. Eric's banging on about never having to pay for his beer when he's working and Will's got no idea whether he's joking or not.

So I have a chat with Eric about darts and life in general and he seems fine but as soon as the exhibition kicks off and we start throwing, he's like a changed man and the rest of the night goes distinctly tits up.

First of all we have a few legs against some of the local players. Now the whole point of an exhibition is to have a bit of a laugh but Eric just keeps bashing everyone off the board. It's like he's trying to prove something but what the hell does a former world champion have to prove to some amateur players who have only turned up for a good night? I like to try and keep the games close so everyone enjoys themselves and I regularly throw games so the crowd can laugh at me, but Eric is taking this really seriously. I find it embarrassing.

We then have a head-to-head between us, the first to 11 legs, and he gets even stroppier. I'm about 8–1 up or whatever and he's getting annoyed big time, muttering to himself and looking like he's having the worst time of his life. It's not like I'm trying to rub his nose in it or anything but he's acting like a spoilt child and I can see the punters are starting to get pissed off with his attitude. They've paid good money (which is going in our pocket) to come and see us and he's acting like he's doing them a favour.

During the Q&A session afterwards things go from bad to worse with Eric giving surly one-word answers or not even bothering to answer at all:

Punter: "How do I improve my game Eric?"

Bristow: "Practice."

Punter: "What's your favourite ever checkout?"

Bristow: "Can't remember."

Punter: "You've had problems with dartitis. Can you give some advice on overcoming it?"

Bristow: "Not interested mate, I've got enough problems of my own."

We're only half way through but at this point he just gets up and walks off and the crowd boo him. Talk about a chip on his shoulder. He's made me look like an idiot and he's made an even bigger idiot of himself. What really pisses me off is I got him the gig in the first place and I've just earned him £600. If you ask me, the man's bitter because he can't cut it anymore and he takes it out on everyone else. The way I see it, he had a great career, won the World Championship five times, earned himself a few quid and should be happy with his lot.

Maybe he's stilled pissed off with the way his career came to an end. He developed what we call dartitis, which is equivalent to the yips in golf and basically means you struggle to release the dart. It might sound comical—a darts player who can't let go of the dart—but it's something every player really fears. No-one really knows why some players develop dartitis but if you get it, you're completely screwed. Some players who suffer with it literally cannot let go of the dart, while others develop an involuntary stutter in their throwing action, which is almost as bad. And like I said, no-one has come up with any explanations why some players are affected and others aren't.

Having said all that, it's still no excuse for his behaviour tonight.

Maybe I shouldn't have been surprised. Remember I said I met him when I was a kid and he'd see me in the future? Well, I saw him about ten years later in Vegas and the first thing he said to me was: "What the fuck have you ever won?" just like that. It really shook me that did. I think he realised the kid he remembered had become a threat and his 'nice face' suddenly slipped.

It's like they say, sometimes it's better not to meet your heroes because the chances are you'll only be disappointed.

THURSDAY 14TH APRIL

Nearly phone Eric today to tell him what a twat I thought he'd been but think better of it. I just can't be bothered with the tosser. Get a call from Will the landlord to say thanks and I apologise about a hundred times for Eric's behaviour. Will says he won't be having him back.

Have a look at the chat forum on the Phil Taylor website later in the day and you're never going to believe this but Eric's on there too. Someone asks him who he thinks will be the next world champion and quick as a flash he replies, 'Not Mardle'.

What the fuck is that about? I must have upset him in a previous life or something.

SATURDAY 16TH APRIL

I've been booked for an exhibition by a pub in Stornoway, which is on the Isle of Lewis, one of the Western Isles off Scotland. Now that's what I call out of the way. I never imagined they'd have exhibitions way up there but what the hell.

To get there we've got to take a flight from Heathrow to Glasgow and then get a connection to Stornoway airport. Everything's fine until we get to Glasgow and I get a look at the plane to take us to the island.

Now I'm not scared of flying—it's boring more than anything else—but I kid you not the plane we've got to get on is one of those rickety, old 35-seater jobs with propellers. Safe-looking it is not.

Me and Donna get on anyway and the stewardess starts going through the safety instructions. It cracks me up because she uses a microphone but she may as well have just talked to us because the plane's that small.

She finishes by saying, "Someone will be round with the drinks trolley shortly." Seconds later *she* emerges with the drinks trolley!

We get to Stornoway in one piece though, get picked up, check into a lovely hotel and do the exhibition. The island looks really remote and desolate at first and driving though Stornoway, you feel you could walk through the entire town in five minutes flat.

But to be fair, we get treated like royalty and the night is a blinder. The venue is called the Stornoway Angling and Social Club. It's on two floors with a nightclub downstairs and the members' bar, where we are, upstairs. It's not tiny but it's quite a narrow room and feels cosy and intimate. They tell me they booked Bob Anderson last year and they're obviously into their darts, which makes my job a lot easier. I don't always enjoy exhibitions but this one is a cracker. It's obvious that tonight's is one of the big nights on the calendar here and they're treating it like a really special occasion.

They're a friendly bunch and the best thing is they really look after Donna. Sometimes when I'm working Donna just sits in the corner with no-one to talk to while I'm up on the stage but tonight there's always someone sitting with her, chatting away and making sure she's got a drink. A nice touch.

The only thing I can't work out is how they make the night pay. What with my fee and the flights from Heathrow for me and Donna thrown in, they're shelling out nearly a grand but they're only charging three quid on the door. There's about a 100 people in, so surely they're £700 down? Okay, so they will make some back at the bar but it still seems a big outlay.

SUNDAY 17TH APRIL

I'm a bit apprehensive about getting on that plane again but we've got to get off the island and get back, so I just have to deal with it.

When we get home, we go round my mum's to pick up the hamster and then sort through some more paper work. On the new house front, we should be getting the contracts through soon. Fingers crossed, although these things never seem to go smoothly, do they?

WEDNESDAY 20TH APRIL

Drive to Plymouth for the Premier League tomorrow night. It's a long old schlep—over five hours—and we add half-an-hour to the journey time stopping off for something to eat. Any guesses what we had? Kentucky? Of course. I tell you, I've got to stop eating junk—it goes straight to my face and belly.

We're staying in a Travel Inn. Obviously. I wonder if I can buy shares in the company? I bet they're a good investment because everyone loves a Travel Inn, don't they? Or is it just me?

All the other players are staying in the New Continental. Both hotels are the same distance from the venue but me and Donna are paying £26 a night while the rest of them have to fork out £70. I know it's all tax deductible but there's no point blowing dough for no reason. It's hard enough to earn it in the first place. Some people think the top players are millionaires, but we're not. We make a good living, but I hate wasting money.

I want to have a nice early night, but I can't sleep. I've just realised I'm always like this before the Premier League but not before any other tournaments. I don't know if it's nerves or what but it's really annoying lying there staring at the ceiling.

THURSDAY 21ST APRIL

We're playing at the Pavillions in Plymouth and it's a great venue. It holds 1,300 but there's still a feeling of space and I reckon the PDC should definitely be looking to use venues like this for other tournaments.

I'm playing Roland Scholten tonight and I need to win. Now where have you heard that before?

The match with Roland is a cracker, even if I do say so myself. We're both in top form, we hit 13 maximums between us which is some going over 12 legs and the crowd lap it up. I should have gone 5–3 up but miss the double 16 and we finish up six apiece. I know I could have won but I'm not too gutted because Roland never has a dart to beat me, so I was in control really. My form is definitely improving.

After the game, me and wifey head back to the hotel and I spot a couple of fellas sitting at a bus stop wearing Hawaiian shirts, so I decide to have a bit of a chat with them.

"Just been to the darts then have you, fellas?"

"No way, it's Mardle!'

"How you doing? You enjoy it?"

"Yeah, it was top. Will you sign something for us?"

"No problem. Got a pen?"

"Yeah, yeah, will you sign my shirt?"

"I tell you what, why don't you have my shirt and I'll sign that."

"You're having us on."

"Nah, you can have it."

I'd already got changed so my match shirt is in a bag and I sign it and leave the two of them beaming from ear to ear.

Later on, we head out for a healthy Chinese and have one of those shameful greedy moments when you order far too much and then have to tell the waiter that no, no-else will be joining you.

Halfway through the meal John Part and Peter Manley stroll in, which puts paid to our romantic night out together and everything starts getting a bit rowdy and beery.

Me and Peter are still playing silly buggers. We say hello but I know neither of us feels comfortable and I'm glad John's around so we both have someone else to talk to.

Saying that, I get caught in a deep conversation with John, who is determined to tell me exactly how good *Star Wars* really is. I tell him I'm more of a *Will & Grace* fan myself but he won't let up and I'm losing the will to live. John's a good bloke but he just doesn't know when to shut up once he gets going.

Luckily I get an escape route when one of the waitresses comes over to our table.

"Mr Mardle?"

"Yes"

"There's a phone call for you."

"For me?"

"You, Mr Mardle?"

"Yes but no-one knows I'm here."

"Someone wants to talk to you."

I'm sure it's Party having a laugh but I decide to play along anyway and pick up the phone.

"Hello, Wayne?"

"Yeah, who's that?"

"You don't know me but you just gave me your shirt."

"You what?"

"At the bus stop, you just gave me your shirt."

"Yeah."

"I saw you walk into the Chinese."

"Right. What's up?"

"I'm in my local and the guv'nor doesn't believe it's really your shirt. Can you come in and prove it?"

I say I might pop in but, got to be honest, I don't. I think Donna would have killed me.

FRIDAY 22ND APRIL

A five-hour journey home (including Kentucky stop, obviously). I've got one of those route planner gizmos in the car but I'm not sure if I trust it. It takes us a very funny way home but we get there eventually.

I'm off to Holland in the morning for the Open Holland tournament, so a nice early night.

SATURDAY 23RD APRIL

Fly from Stansted to Rotterdam and hook up with Dennis Priestley, Colin Lloyd's other half (and Donna's mate), Deta, Cliff Lazarenko, Keith Deller and a young player called Michael Barnard, who darts fans will be hearing a lot more about in the future. We get talking about the rights and wrongs of the game. I always enjoy chatting to the old guard like Keith and Cliff because they've been in the game a lot longer than me and you can learn a lot from listening to them.

Keith's in his 40s now but still plays on the circuit. The highlight of what's been a good career was in 1983 when he famously beat Bristow to win the World Championship in a classic match. His nickname is 'Del Boy', which is a reference to *Only Fools and Horses.* To my mind, it's a bit tenuous because he comes from Ipswich, not Peckham, but each to his own. He's a top bloke but he does go on about golf a lot. All day, every day to be precise. He's always rabbiting on about golf and name-dropping people he's played with in celebrity or charity matches. The problem is, Keith hasn't really played with anyone particularly famous, so it always comes back around to his story of the day he played with Stan Boardman.

I think Keith made his money when he was on the top of his game but he earns a few extras these days from the tour and from 'spotting' for Sky at televised tournaments. Spotting involves predicting what shot a player is going to go for next and then quickly telling the cameraman so he doesn't miss the throw. It's easy enough for the camera to focus on the treble 20 because that's the bread and butter throw during a leg but Sky need experienced players to tell them where to point the camera when they start moving around the board. People like Keith instinctively know how a player is going to approach any given checkout or switch to 19s from 20 and he'll make sure the camera gets the shot.

Cliff's known as 'Big Cliff' because he's 20-stone plus and the fella is a man mountain. Like Keith, he still plays on the circuit even though his heyday was in the '80s. He's been a pro for 30-odd years now and anything he doesn't know about the game probably isn't worth knowing. He still does a lot of exhibitions and it's amazing the number of places I've worked and they tell me they had Cliff in last month or last year or whatever. The bloke must have one of the biggest contact books in the game.

Cliff's got a reputation as one of the biggest drinkers in darts, which is saying something. I've heard he can drink 60 cans of Strongbow in a single day and I do know he likes his cider. I remember seeing him at the bar at a tournament in Great Yarmouth, so I went up to have a chat. He was holding two pints of cider and I asked him who he was with. He looked at me like I was being stupid and said they were both for him.

Cliff is one of the names from darts' golden era in the '80s when there was Bristow, John Lowe and Jocky Wilson and it's good to see he's done well for himself and not suffered once he started slipping down the rankings. You already know my feelings about Bristow, which just goes to prove success doesn't always bring you happiness. I don't know John Lowe that well but he still plays and I think he's got a few business interests that keep him busy. The saddest story is Jocky Wilson, who was world champion twice in the '80s. He's got liver problems and by all accounts lives like a virtual recluse now in Kirkcaldy in Scotland. Bristow tried to organise a benefit night for him a couple of years ago but Jocky didn't want to know. Just goes to prove you've got to earn your money while you can in this game.

I'm looking forward to the tournament, probably because I hit a nine-darter in it last year and, you never know, another one could be just around the corner.

The nine-dart finish, for those of you who don't know, is the holy grail of darts, checking out from 501 all the way to a finish on the double with just three throws (or nine darts). It's the fastest possible way to win a leg. The usual route is 180, 180 and then treble 20, treble 15 and double 18, although there are other possible combinations. They're still rare in tournaments and every player wants to do one. They're the equivalent of a 147 clearance in snooker, only rarer.

I've hit two nine-darters in tournaments in my career. Like I said, one last year in the Open Holland and one in 2001 in the Dutch Open. Plenty of people get close to them but never quite pull it off. It's because there's no margin for error that they're so uncommon—one dart just off and you're buggered—but I reckon most of the pros hit maybe one a year in practice. There's not the same pressure when no-one's watching of course.

I nearly hit two in-a-row once when I was practising but shanked the very last dart. I hit my first nine-darter and was well chuffed, then started another leg, 180, another 180 and I was getting well excited.

I've no idea if anyone has ever hit two on the bounce and I was thinking, even if there's no-one here to see it, this would be really special. So I got the treble 20 and the treble 15 I needed and I've got one dart to do it. You know what happened? I was a million miles away from the double 18. I totally bottled it. No pressure and I cracked, which maybe shows you how special they are.

Even though nine-darters are rare, you don't actually win much if you do get one. Personally, I blame Phil Taylor. Bear in mind that between 1990, when a player called Paul Lim did one on telly, and 2000 there wasn't a single nine-dart finish in tournaments. Then Phil goes and does it twice—in the 2002 Matchplay in Blackpool and the 2004 UK Open Final in Bolton. He picked up a £100,000 bonus for the Matchplay one and I think something like £25,000 for the one in Bolton and I think the sponsors got scared. They'd had over ten years of not having to sign the cheques and then Phil bled them dry and they thought sod this. As far I know, the only tournament with a prize for a nine-darter now is the Grand Prix Double Start in Ireland.

So back to where I started. I hit a nine-darter at the tournament last year and obviously asked what I'd won. One of the organisers looked a bit embarrassed, said she'd go and check and came back with nine beer vouchers!

SUNDAY 24TH APRIL

It's the singles today so I get to the venue at 8.30. I've got no idea what time I'm playing but it could be ten and I want to get warmed up and properly prepared just in case.

Sod's Law, of course, I'm not on until 12 and I beat a couple of decent Dutch players whose names I won't attempt to spell in the first couple of rounds.

Next up is Mark 'Walshie' Walsh, who I beat in the first round of the World Championship last year and is more than a capable player. Walshie has to be the crappest nickname on the circuit. I mean, couldn't he think of anything better? I keep suggesting he should be called 'Slaphead' but he's not keen. I used to play in the London SuperLeague with Mark but it's only in the last three or four years that he's come through the ranks and shown what a good pro he is.

In the match I've got him running this way and that but, in typical Mardle style, my doubles let me down and I get beat. I'm really pissed off because it's a quarter-final game and it's only the semis and final that are being played on the main stage, which is what I'm all about.

Me and Donna hunt high and low for a cab after the game to take us back to the hotel. I've got a headache after being stuck in a smokey, stuffy room all day and when we eventually get back, we crash out at about seven.

I wake up at 11 and order a kebab. I've really got to change my eating habits.

MONDAY 25TH APRIL

We're up at five to catch a 7.15 flight back to Stansted and it's the same old faces at the airport. I'm so glad Donna comes to most of the tournaments with me because I think I'd go mad otherwise, having the same conversations with the same people day-in, day-out.

Although I got beat yesterday, the trip hasn't been a complete waste of time because I patched things up with Suzanne, my booking agent in Holland. I'd said a lot of things about our relationship were bugging me, but we've sorted things out. I've made a few decisions, and we're going to work together again. Basically, the money's gone up, I'll be able to sell my own merchandise over there and I've made it crystal clear she's got to run things by me more than she did. In the past, I've missed tournaments because Suzanne had taken a booking at the wrong time and I've told her I'm having no more of that. Hopefully, it'll all be smooth sailing from now on.

WEDNESDAY 27TH APRIL

A bit of practice today and then I try and sort out some shirt sponsorship. I've got a space going begging and it's a waste not to have some sponsorship. The trick is letting people know it's available, so I'm sending out emails to the marketing departments of a few companies.

I've got the free space because my current deal has just run out. It was with an engineering firm in Romford called G L Reeves and I've been with them for five years but they're not interested in carrying on with the arrangement. They were my first sponsors and covered all my travel and accommodation expenses involved with the circuit in return for the shirt logo and 25 per cent of my winnings. It was a good deal for me then, but, to be honest, I'm looking to get something better this time around.

It's the Premier League tomorrow night in Kidderminster. I'm playing Mark Dudbridge and it's about time I beat him. Mum and dad are coming along for the ride because it's only a two-hour drive, so I've got to put on a good show.

THURSDAY 28TH APRIL

Me and Mark both need a win. We're joint bottom of the league and whoever loses tonight will need a miracle to qualify for the semi-finals.

Everything's going well in the match until the tenth leg. We're both playing pretty good, Mark has his nose in front at 5–4 but I reckon I'm good for at least a share of the points. That is, until he takes out a 164 finish to make it 6–4. A 164 is a fucking unbelievable checkout and it knocks the stuffing right out of me. I can't believe it. A 164? Now that's what I call a good, hard, kick to the nuts. A 170 is the highest finish you can do (two treble 20s and the bullseye) but 164 is still amazing. It's probably the equivalent of a 40-yard screamer into the top corner in football.

I'm all over the place after that, and he wraps it up 8–4. I'm not going to forget that in a hurry, I can tell you, and it looks like I'm out of the Premier League running now. There's always next year I suppose.

SATURDAY 30TH APRIL

The Britannia pub in lovely Truro tonight. It's a cosy little place that feels packed with 40 people and only the locals really drink there. The weird thing about it is the wall where the board hangs is on an angle to the rest of the pub, rather than being square with the other walls, which means the oche has to be at an angle as well.

The night's been organised by a fella called Kevin Dunstall, who works with a lot of the other pros, and I want put on a decent show for him.

Once we get going, I'm like a machine on the doubles. I just keep banging them, one after the other. Sod's Law or what? Thursday night I couldn't hit a double and tonight I can't miss.

It makes me realise that I've got to learn to handle the pressure of the big tournaments better. Tonight proves I don't have any fundamental problems hitting doubles and they only seem to let me down at the big competitions. I honestly don't feel nervous up there at the televised tournaments but it has to be the pressure that's making me miss because when I'm doing these exhibitions, where there's no pressure at all, I am demon for the doubles. How I transfer my 'exhibition finishing' to the big stages consistently is the $64,000 question.

Remember that bloke I mentioned earlier who gave up his job because he reckoned he could become world champion within a year? Well, credit where it's due, I've just read another interview with him and he came across a lot better. I was spitting when I first heard about him but I think what he said was taken out of context and he wasn't as disrespectful about the game as I thought. Basically, he made it crystal clear that he'd never said he could win at Purfleet within a year of jacking his old job in and he was unhappy with the way the media had distorted his quotes. Just goes to show you've got to be careful when you read interviews because they're not always fair and balanced.

SUNDAY 1ST MAY

We decided not to stay overnight in Truro, so Donna drives back and we get home at four in the morning. Travel, travel, travel. It's an easy life, isn't it?

MONDAY 2ND MAY

Nothing much happening on the house front. As far I know, it's still going through but we don't seem to be any further on than we were a month ago. You know the way it is, month after month you wait and all the time you're all keyed up and ready to go. Gets me down, to be honest.

I've got a big couple of weeks ahead with the climax of the Premier League and a lot of exhibitions coming up so I practice hard today to keep me arm in. I'm spending more and more time on the doubles now and it seems to be working, so I'm feeling in a good frame of mind. I don't have any fixed routine for the doubles at the moment other than just spending more time on them really. Sometimes I'll focus on what I consider my stronger doubles like tops and my favourite 18s just to really be on top of them and other times I really concentrate on what I think are my weaker finishes like nines.

Play poker later on but I'm definitely falling out of love with the game. I think I've lost the bug.

TUESDAY 3RD MAY

Call BP about a shirt sponsorship deal. They were one of the companies I contacted and they got back to me, so I chat with one of their bods about an arrangement. I'm not sure why a multinational oil company would be interested, but their money would be as good as anyone else's. I've known some players sell space on their shirts for as little as £100 before but hopefully I'll do better than that, whoever it is.

I can advertise anything I like really as long as there's no conflict of interest with the main sponsors of whatever tournament I'm playing in. So for example I couldn't work with Paddy Power at a Sky Bet event.

Anyway BP are going to get back to me so fingers crossed because that would be a cracker. I'm not desperate but it would be nice, especially with all the cost of moving coming up soon.

A couple of hours practice in the afternoon. It's all doubles again—I don't think I go for a single 60 once in over two hours. I hope that doesn't come back to bite me on the arse.

Speak to Rod Harrington, who is a director of the PDC and the winner of the World Matchplay a couple of times in the '90s, on the phone about the way the tour has been going and how the ranking points are done and he tells me there's going to be a restructure. It's going to be based on a US-style money list like they have in golf and the like. Basically it means the rankings will be decided by how much cash you earn over the course of the season and not by points, as it is now.

I don't really agree with the proposal to be honest because to get points now you have to do well in most tournaments. If it's going to be a money list, then it distorts the whole thing. Say you do well at the World Championship and get beat in the final, then you're going to be straight up in the top two or three because the prize money (it's 100 grand for the winner and 50 for the runner-up this year) is so huge compared to the other events. You'll be ranked high basically on the basis of just one event, even if it is the World Championship, which doesn't seem quite right to me.

THURSDAY 5TH MAY

Wifey drives us up to Widnes today for the Premier League. We don't usually travel up on the same day but I've noticed that when I've been staying in hotels before the other Premier League nights, I end up thinking about the game all night and wind myself up. It's no good really, having too much time to stew on things.

It's a long drive for Donna. She's a good girl, bless her. She says she doesn't mind, but I know she does. I just like having here around. She always settles me down.

I'm playing John Part. Despite being bottom of the table for so long, I'm playing well and I feel very concentrated when I warm up on the practice board. I used to think the warm-up was really just to loosen the arm and I wasn't fussed about what I hit, but I'm starting to realise it's about getting your focus right, about sorting your head out before the match. You only get out what you put in and I'm starting to think you need to be 100 per cent switched on in the warm-up as well for these big matches.

The game goes like a dream and I beat John 8–4. It's a good 8–4 from my point of view, if you know what I mean. I hit all my doubles and I'm not in any real danger at any point. I'd definitely call it a comfortable win.

John seems to take it badly though. I'm chatting off stage with Colin Lloyd after the game and John just sprints up from behind Colin and headbutts me. Quite hard. To be fair, he is only messing about (I think) but the bloke's still a nutter. Colin hasn't got a clue what is going on and I'm thinking it's like some sort of surreal comedy sketch.

"What the fuck, John?"

"What?"

"You just nutted me!'

"That's what you English guys do, isn't it?"

"No, not really, John."

"It's funny over here, right... ?"

"Hilarious, John, hilarious."

After that he rugby tackles me from behind. I think he's annoyed at losing, coming all that way from Canada and then getting beat. He beat me 9–3 in our first Premier League game, so it's only what I owed him anyway.

Later in the night Phil Taylor stuffs Peter Manley 11–1, which takes me off the bottom of the table. Happy days.

I'm watching in the VIP room and when Sky flashes up the new league table, I jump up and start shouting "I'm off the bottom, I'm off the bottom..." Thing is, Peter's standing right behind me and he doesn't look very happy. Who cares? Everyone's been giving me grief for weeks about being bottom so I'm having my little moment of glory. And it's not as if me and Peter have been bosom buddies lately anyway.

CHAPTER FIVE

The bike or the bargain bucket?

SATURDAY 7TH MAY

I should be playing a tournament today in Blackpool called The Bob Anderson QC Leisure Open but it's been postponed due to a lack of entries. I don't know if it's come at an awkward time for everyone or what, but it was announced quite late and they've obviously not pulled it off.

The other problem is it's an Open. Some players want to pay £10 to enter a tournament, beat a couple of muppets and go home with maybe £40 or £50 in their pocket. This one was £60 to enter, there's not going to be any muppets there, so the ones who did put their names down were the hardcore of darts—70 or 80 players—and that's not enough to make it a goer.

Instead, me and Donna go to a BBQ-cum-party in the afternoon. It's at the house of a couple called Dave and Emma Allen. Dave is the PDC's Media Officer and he's a top fella. Colin Lloyd and his missus Deta are there too and it's a good night all round. I've said before, Colin's a fellow Essex boy and I've known him forever. We used to play in the junior leagues in Essex together and what can I say, he's a top fella. His nickname's 'Jaws' because of his lovely set of gnashers and as much as I love Colin, I've got to say he really should get them seen to. His skin's not the best either and he's always coming out in spots, which the other lads take the piss out of. I get heat bumps now and then but poor old Colin really suffers with his complexion.

I take a couple of bottles of wine with us and finish them both off, so I'm quite merry by the time Donna drives us home.

MONDAY 9TH MAY

Lots of practice today because I've had two days off and I don't want to get rusty. I don't know if I am finally growing up but I seem to be taking it all much more seriously at the moment. I've never lacked self-belief but there's a big difference between thinking you've got the ability to do something and actually doing it. I really think the penny has finally dropped.

Recently, I've been focusing on finishes from 81 up to 130 but today I go from 81 to 150 just because I feel good. This game really is all in the head.

Bit of paperwork in the afternoon. I write to Kwik-Fit and Rado watches about that sponsorship deal. I'm still waiting to hear from BP but it doesn't hurt to have a few irons in the fire, does it? Got a Rado myself actually and to be fair they are quality. I've no idea whether they want to get involved with darts, but there's only one way to find out. Got to put yourself out there, haven't you? I don't mind a bit of rejection if you get the result in the end.

Oh and guess what? I'm not getting a new batch of yellow shirts after all. Apparently the fella who was going to sort them out has retired but nobody bothered to tell me. To be fair, it was Ron Russ from B&W who didn't tell me but he's not been well and had other problems to deal with. The good news is Ron's not too bad and there are 300 more blue shirts on the way.

TUESDAY 10TH MAY

It's my birthday today—32-years-old. Jesus, it's unbelievable. I'm still like a kid when I open my prezzies and cards.

When I worked in London I always used to say I wasn't coming in on my birthday, but always bottled it and did. Today I'm going to do exactly what I want... because I can!

Actually, I'm not that big on actually celebrating my birthday but you should be able to do exactly what you feel like. So we go to the casino—me, wifey, mum and dad. I love having such a close family and I'd rather be with them today than anyone else. Family means everything to me.

Spend a few hours in the casino and come out exactly level. Me and Donna were going to play poker, but we realise it's not going to be any fun for mum and dad watching us in the early hours wanting their bed.

Funnily enough, we bump into Ron Russ. He's definitely on the mend and he looks well. I'm in a good mood anyway, but that's the icing on the (birthday) cake.

THURSDAY 12TH MAY

We drive up to Doncaster for tonight's Premier League at the Doncaster Dome and it's another big one. I'm playing Mark Dudbridge again and it's about time I beat him. I think I've played four or five times now and not won, so it's time to put that record straight.

I feel relaxed in the practice room. Mark's in there as well playing golf on his Gameboy and we have a bit of a chat. Some players don't want to talk for whatever reason but Mark is a sociable guy and I'm getting to know him better now. He tells me he's just signed a deal with a supplier called Harrow Darts for all his gear, so he's got a new set of darts. Rather him than me. I've had my arrows all my darting life and it brings me out in a cold sweat just thinking about changing them. It doesn't seem to bother him at all.

It's an intense game all the way but I feel in control and at 6–4 up and I only need one more leg for the two points. Problem is in the eleventh leg I'm on double 20, throwing for the match, when some idiot thinks it'd be a good idea to shout out "Fucking miss" just as I'm pulling my arm back. There's 1,200 people sitting there in silence and then there's this moron, who's obviously had one too many shandies. I miss the double, Mark's back in it at 6–5 and he's got the darts in the final leg.

The last leg is a blinder. I hit three 140s on the trot and take out the 81 in two darts for a 11-dart finish. That's 7–5, two points in the bag, thank you very much.

I'm really pumped up and turn round a give it the two-fingered salute in the direction of the mouthy moron and shout "Up yours". As soon as I do it, I regret it. I know I shouldn't react, but the game means so much to me and I can't help myself.

No doubt that'll be another fine from the DRA. Fair enough, I probably deserve it but what the bloke did in the first place is not right. I'm not playing for fun out there, you know. It's my job. We'll see what happens anyway, but I say you can't take the human element out of the game otherwise you might as well just have a bunch of robots up there.

FRIDAY 13TH MAY

Friday the 13th. Am I superstitious? Nah, can't say I am so I'm not worried about anything going wrong today.

Tonight's exhibition is in Ipswich and I'm looking forward to it. Last night was so tense that it will be good to have a bit if fun and unwind a bit.

The gig is at the Clapgate Lane Conservative Club and has been organised by a bloke called Dave Cook. Everyone's obviously a comedian because there are plenty of comments about my little outburst last night, people copying my little hand gesture, but it's all in good fun and I'm having a good time.

I do my party trick, which is blowing darts into the board with my mouth. I put the barrel of the dart in my mouth so the point is sticking out on the left, the flight on the right and then take a deep breath and sort of spit it out. The dart initially comes out at a right angle to the board but the weight of the point and the barrel pulls the dart round so the flight is at the back and by the time it gets there it's flying point first into the bed. I can be quite accurate at times—hitting double 20 maybe five times out of every 100—but most of them land in the general area I'm aiming for. I learnt I could blow them in when I was a teenager messing about and it always seems to go down well at exhibitions.

As far as I know, I'm the only one on the exhibition circuit who does it. I know a few players who throw nails and things like that, but always from the hand. The nails are special six inch ones, weighted at the front and the tips are filed to make them sharp so they'll stick in the board. They don't have flights or anything like that stuck to them—well, that's the trick isn't it?—and it's always a crowd pleaser. A guy called Joe Hitchcock was the pioneer of it about 30 years ago and I know these days the top BDO player Mervyn King likes to use nails in his exhibitions.

SATURDAY 14TH MAY

A Hawaiian-themed exhibition in Nuneaton tonight. Everyone dresses up in the shirts and hula skirts and it's a scream. It really gives you a buzz when the crowd gets into it like this. The only downer is this young fella behind me, who's constantly barracking me as I'm playing. Funny thing is, he keeps it up for 12 full legs, mouthing off and then he steps up to play me, gets beat and after the game he is as nice as pie. Seriously, suddenly he's a really nice lad after all the abuse he's just been giving me. I don't know if he feels threatened or what. People can be funny creatures sometimes.

We get flashed on the way home doing 35mph in a 30 zone. Hope there isn't any film in the camera...

SUNDAY 15TH MAY

After three long days travelling, it's a day off today so we go round to my mum's for Sunday dinner. Danny and Ellie are there, so I kick a ball around with them in the park. We're not allowed to kick it in the garden because my dad's too worried about his flowers. Dad's garden is like one of those show gardens, bless him, and he spends a fortune on it, so he's not having any football nonsense ruining his pride and joy.

MONDAY 16TH MAY

The people we're buying the house from have got a problem. The house they're buying has fallen through so everything is up in the air. I'm not going to stress about it though. If it happens, it happens.

Anyway, it's a bit of special day today because me and wifey are working together tonight. We're going to the Bonds Club in Sheerness, Kent, which is only an hour down the road. It's a mixed league (men and women) presentation night so they asked for both of us and we're going to play as a mixed pair. Donna's going to wear a little Hawaiian shirt especially for the occasion.

Donna's really nervous when we get there. She's not one for the limelight but she does brilliantly once we get going and I'm really proud of her. It's a bit odd working together, but I think she enjoys it in the end.

WEDNESDAY 18TH MAY

Three-and-a-half hours practice today. Tomorrow night is the last night of the Premier League in Colchester before the top four go through to the semis and there's a lot at stake. I'm playing twice and I know I've got a big chance but I'm also nervous. I'm playing Peter Manley first up and then Colin Lloyd in the final match and with me in fourth place—which would see me through to the semi-finals—my destiny is in my own hands. There's a few permutations about who can still qualify but the smart money is on one win from the two games and I'm safely through. Phil and Colin are already through so there's two more places up for grabs between me, Roland, John, Mark and Peter. John's bottom, I'm fourth like I say and the other three are sandwiched in between us. It's going to be tight whatever happens.

THURSDAY 19TH MAY

Leave the house at around one. It's a six o'clock start tonight and even though Colchester isn't far from us, I want to get there in plenty of time. We arrive at half past two and behind the scenes it's obvious that there's more than the normal amount of tension going around. I suppose it's only natural because this is the business end of the tournament and there's a lot at stake.

I'm feeling the pressure. There are a few people with too much to say for themselves and I'm getting uptight. I don't know why because I'm the one in the driving seat. There's always banter before a tournament but I think today people are talking so much because it helps to distract them from what's coming.

Peter comes up to me to wish me good luck but he couldn't sound more insincere if he tried. Or maybe I'm just being paranoid. No, sod it. I'm sure he's trying to wind me up. I wouldn't put it past him because he's a wily old campaigner and he's well known for using every trick in the book to get an advantage over his opponent. He's not shy that one.

There are loads of things you can do to try and break the rhythm of your opponent. Obviously you can try and get under his skin before you even get up on the stage and once you're up there, it's not hard to break up the flow of the game. Taking your darts out off the board excessively slowly, walking back in front of your opponent when they want to throw and pausing all the time for a drink are all ways to disrupt your opponent's rhythm (especially if they want a faster game) and while they're not exactly illegal, I don't think they're in the spirit of the game. To be fair, I'm not expecting Peter to do any of that today but I wouldn't put it past him either.

I lose 7–5 to Peter. I'm 5–1 down before I really wake up and I play terrible. The most frustrating thing is I know if I play my A-game, I'm going to beat him but I just don't turn up. Peter does a good job on me (and without any funny business, it has to be said) but I'm disgusted with myself and I'm all over the place while I wait to play

Colin Lloyd. Luckily for me, the way the other results have gone, I know I now only need a draw to qualify for the semi-final, but I can't seem to get focused.

Like I said, we're the last match on, and we don't get going until late. The first few legs are a nightmare and I fall 3–0 behind in what seems like a flash. I pull myself together to tighten things up, but Colin pulls away again and it's 7–5 to him.

I haven't coped with the situation very well. Even though I was playing the world number one, which is never easy, I was just not able to get my head right. I swear I can't explain why.

So I've thrown it away. I had a place in the last four in my own hands and I'm going home with nothing. Phil, Colin, Roland and Peter all go through to the semis while I'm £8,000 poorer—I've earned £10,000 but it's a guaranteed £18,000 for getting to the semis—and I'm not a happy bunny.

At least, I think I learnt something about myself tonight. I've got to learn to deal with bad situations, when my head goes, and keep playing my darts. I've got to learn to be in control all the time. Next time hopefully things will be different. I don't think I need a sports psychologist or anything but I do need to learn how to shut out the unimportant, trivial things when I'm playing.

After the match me and Donna go for a beer with Colin at his local called the Spinnaker in Colchester. It's nice to get away from the stresses at the venue and talk to someone who I know is a real mate. Colin says he makes a conscious effort to distance himself from the other players at tournaments because it avoids all the shit and I can't help thinking he might have a point.

The behind-the-scenes atmosphere on the circuit is a bit of a weird one. The lads do genuinely get on but there are rifts. You have to try to get on because you spend a lot of time together at tournaments, away from home and often bored to tears. There's also a sort of unspoken understanding that we're all just trying to make a living, which is something we all have in common, but it can sometimes spill over into one-upmanship and that's when there can be problems because some people take that kind of banter the wrong way. You know the kind of thing: a player talking about his new sponsorship deal or what he's just bought with his prize money and someone else getting their back up about it. I suppose we're just like one big family—there's the good times and then there's the inevitable rows.

Get a call from Derek at B&W. He tells me that Justin Hawkins, the lead singer of The Darkness, wants to meet me for a game and a few beers. Apparently, Justin's a darts nut and he gets his arrows from B&W as well. I reckon it could be a good laugh so I'm up for it. I hope Justin doesn't sing though because his voice is a bit too high for me. I'm more of a Stones man myself.

FRIDAY 20TH MAY

I had too many Guinesses at Colin's pub last night so I feel ragged but I manage to drag myself out in the evening for an exhibition at the Inland Revenue Sports and Social Club in Worthing. I'll get paid by cheque, obviously.

MONDAY 23RD MAY

I've been away lot recently and the grass at the front and back of the house is horrendous. It's got to be two-foot high, no lie. My dad comes round to help me chop it down but I'm worrying because Donna's gone down Romford market with her mates and I know I'll be £300 poorer by the end of the day.

TUESDAY 24TH MAY

I'm playing in the Rod Harrington Golf Day in Chelmsford today with mate of mine called Dave, so I'm up nice and early for breakfast and the off. I haven't played for ages, so I've got no great expectations but hopefully it'll be a good day out.

Unsurprisingly, I play crap but I don't care and I think most people are only there for the beers afterwards anyway. Anyway I get speaking to a fella in the bar later on and yet again I manage to attract one of those nutters who don't care what they say while everyone else in the room is cringing.

Bloke: "I own a pub in Birmingham."

Me: "Right."

Bloke: "Can you do an exhibition for me?"

Me: "What's the date?"

Bloke: "July 15?"

Me: "Yeah, I can do that actually because I know for a fact I'm doing something the day after in Manchester."

Bloke: "You can?"

Me: "Yeah."

Bloke: "Nice one because I wanted to get Colin Lloyd, but he can't do it. Let me just phone the pub and see if my regulars reckon you're worth it."

Charming. Bang goes my ego. Later in the evening, he comes back to me and says he's phoned the missus, who's asked about and apparently I've got the seal of approval.

WEDNESDAY 25TH MAY

My emailing has paid off—I've got the shirt sponsorship all sorted. It's a deal with an electronics firm called Kasdon, who are based in Wolverhampton. They've agreed to pay all my expenses while I'm on the circuit for the next year—hotels, flights, KFC bills and the rest of it—and they get 10 per cent of my winnings and a logo on the shirt, which suits me. I reckon it costs about 12 grand a year on the circuit when you add up all the accommodation and travel costs, so it's a good deal.

There's a few other players with similar deals and I'm more than happy with 90 per cent of what I earn going into my old sky rocket, especially since they're paying for the flights to Vegas for the Desert Classic in July. Result.

The deal came about after I did an exhibition in a pub called the Cleveland Arms in Wolverhampton last month. The organiser Will introduced me to a bloke called Steve Stockley, who's a director at Kasdon.

We got chatting about loads of stuff, including sponsorship, but I didn't give it a second thought until Will phoned me up a few days later and put me in touch with Steve and we took things from there.

Get an email from *FHM* magazine, who want to do a bit on me so I get back to them to sort things out. I think they want to do a 'bloke test', which is fine by me. As long as they don't want me to do any topless shots...

THURSDAY 26TH MAY

North London tonight for a gig at a place called the St Joseph's Hall in Highgate, which is a strange village hall-type place tucked away in the back of a churchyard.

Me, Donna and mum get there at a quarter to eight and we're the first ones there, which is always a bit worrying. Mum's come along to keep Donna company and make sure she doesn't get accosted by some drunk. And I don't mean me.

The place fills up nicely in the end and I present a few trophies and play some of the locals, the usual gig. To be honest, I'm a bit surprised because I had been thinking they might be cocky tonight because we're in London but they're a friendly bunch. I always find down south generally that the crowds are pretty good but you can get some nights up north in Yorkshire and Lancashire when you feel they want to rip your head off. I thought the Londoners might have been a bit funny, like I said, but the night goes well.

I see a few old darts mates in there as well, especially a bloke called little Eddie Villa, who I haven't seen for six or seven years. I used to play in the London SuperLeague with Eddie and bumping into old friends like him who I might not have ever seen again is a bonus of doing so many exhibitions.

Just to explain, SuperLeague is the representative level between pub and County players. A pub player will average around 51 with three darts, a SuperLeague player 72 and a County player will be looking at a 85 average. A PDC professional averages between 90 and 95.

SATURDAY 28TH MAY

I go to the golf range for a bit of a hit. I'm not bothered about improving my swing or anything like that, I'm more interested in getting a bit of exercise. I've been doing nothing recently but the funny thing is I've actually lost some weight because I haven't been feeling too clever the past week.

I can't really put my finger on what it is to be honest. I've been been feeling at death's door or anything like that but I'm not quite myself, you know? I feel a lot more lethargic than I usually do and the best way I could put it is feeling run down. It just sort of crept up on me before I really noticed and now I definitely don't feel 100 per cent in myself.

I play golf for about 20 minutes, but then I feel a blister on my dart thumb coming on so I change my grip. I'm aching like hell when I get home because I've been using neglected muscles and they're not happy about it.

SUNDAY 29TH MAY

Funny one today. I'm doing an exhibition at a holiday park in Lowestoft but the odd thing is it's for over–50s only and it's all part of a London-themed weekend. Now maybe I'm just being thick, but since when has darts been synonymous with London? I've got be missing something. It's not as if the Hawaiian shirt screams London, is it?

Anyway my mate Dave Barnes is setting up the board and everything else for me and another pal of mine, David Harris, is going to be doing the calling.

I'm booked to do a two-hour stint from one in the afternoon. When we get there there's not a soul in our part of the hall but luckily somebody takes pity and announces it all on the loud speakers and about 70 or 80 people pile across.

I think everyone single one of them is an 'exhibition virgin' but they seem to enjoy it. Afterwards I get chatting to one of the old blokes.

"Wayne, would you do a presentation for me?"

"Yeah, no problem, if I'm not working."

"Right. Only thing is, how much do you charge?"

"Standard rate is £500."

"Right, right. That's bloody cheap!"

"Cheap?"

"Yeah, I asked Andy Fordham but he was a bit too expensive."

"Yeah? How much did Andy want then?"

"He asked for two and a half grand..."

Fucking hell! I'm gobsmacked. I'm mates with Andy but I can't believe that, I really can't. If it's true, it's amazing and ridiculous but I suppose that's what going on *Celebrity Fit Club* does for you. I'm a bit pissed off as well because I know I could have made a couple of hundred quid more there.

MONDAY 30TH MAY

It's the Premier League semi-final tonight which obviously I'm not in because I was so crap the other night. I'm still not feeling that well to be honest, so I just stay in and watch it all on the box.

In the first semi it looks like Roland Scholten is going to beat Phil Taylor because he's 11–7 up and it's the first to 13 but Roland's bum goes as the finishing line approaches. He loses all his composure and Phil rattles off six legs on the bounce to steal it 13–11. To be fair, they both play pretty poor but Roland really goes to pieces, which isn't like him at all.

The second semi is between Colin Lloyd and Peter Manley. Colin plays well as usual and it's a straightforward 13–7 win for him, so he'll play Phil in the final. Good luck Colin, 'cos you're going to need it.

I talk to Peter on the phone later in the night and he tells me the crowd wasn't great tonight at all. Apparently, they were giving tickets away and the place wasn't full. I guess that's what happens when I'm not playing!

Things are starting to warm up between me and Peter again. I think we've both sulked for long enough and hopefully we can put it all behind us. We used to be on the phone to each other all the time before 'the incident' and tonight was like old times, chatting away after a big match, putting the world to rights.

TUESDAY 31ST MAY

The two Ps today—practice and paperwork. Yet again I regret letting the paperwork stack up because it's such a pain when I've got a month's worth of entry forms, bills, bookings, emails and all the rest of it to sort out. It's all part and parcel of the professional life but that doesn't mean I have to like it. I swear blind when I finish it all that I won't let it build up again but if you believe that you'll believe anything.

I watch the Premier League final in the evening and to be fair Colin gets a bit of a hiding and Phil wins a one-sided game 16–4. I've got no idea what Phil's changed from last night, when he was very average and even though Colin is deservedly world number one, he's never really at the races. That's Phil £50,000 the richer.

It might strike some people as funny that Colin's ranked number one—he has been all year—when everyone knows Phil, 13 world titles compared to Colin's none, is the man to beat. Phil doesn't play in every ranking tournament though, which is his choice, while Colin puts the miles in and gets the rewards (and the ranking points). I think it annoys Colin sometimes that he's number one and doesn't get the recognition but for me he's earned the ranking and no-one can argue with that.

THURSDAY 2ND JUNE

More practice but I mix things up a bit today by ignoring the doubles completely for the two-and-a-half hours I'm at the board. Just trying to stimulate the old grey matter. I've been finishing okay recently, no more than that, but I do find if I have a day off from the doubles that when I focus on them again my concentration levels are spot on straightaway.

The only problem is that you feel guilty if you're still crap on the finishes after a day off and start thinking you've messed up your routine without getting the results.

I threw my first arrow at the age of ten and by my teens I was dreaming of becoming a pro.

Young love: Donna fancied my best mate at first, but I managed to win her over after a weekend in Yarmouth!

WAYNE'S PERSONAL PHOTOS

Donna and I finally got married in Las Vegas in 2002. Naturally, the dress code was Hawaiian...

My childhood idol Eric Bristow presented my 1990 British Youth tournament winner's prize. Nowadays, we don't see eye to eye.

Inset: Look, I do hit double nine sometimes! Practising my least favourite double in my 'office' at home.

Above: Where the hell is Sammy The Sturgeon? When we moved into our new house, I got a major fish obsession.

WAYNE'S PERSONAL PHOTOS

Having fun with some well-dressed punters at an exhibition at the Wreckers pub in Newquay. This was one of the last big nights there before they turned the place into a fish and chip shop!

I was thrilled to be involved in the Premier Darts League, but an incident during a defeat by Peter 'One Dart' Manley in Reading (inset) caused me and Peter to fall out for a while.

Some people dismiss me as a show pony, but I just do what comes naturally to me when I'm on stage... and, yes, that includes some very silly dancing!

Meet a few of the regulars on the darts circuit…
Here, I'm keeping a close eye on the up-and-coming Mark 'Flash' Dudbridge.

Colin 'Harry' Monk: Harry Monk… spunk… don't ask.

Adrian 'Jackpot' Lewis: unlucky in Vegas.

John 'Darth Maple' Part: sci-fi nut and the most intelligent player in the game.

Colin 'Jaws' Lloyd:
my good mate and a top player.

Phil 'The Power' Taylor:
quite simply, a darts machine.

Roland 'The Tripod' Scholten:
a big lad all over.

Chris 'Mace The Ace' Mason: trouble seems to find Chris but he's a seriously gifted player.

Lionel 'The Lion' Sams:
I'm sorry for assaulting your toy Lion, Lionel!

Kevin 'The Artist' Painter:
Kev used to be Mr Angry but he's mellowed… a bit.

… and this is gravel-voiced compère Russ 'The Voice' Bray

Big-screen drama: The final of the 2005 Las Vegas Desert Classic in July against Phil Taylor all went to plan… unfortunately, it was Phil's plan.

My Elvis impression in Vegas made the crowd smile and John Part fume.

Dennis 'The Menace' Priestley taught me a lesson at the 2005 Grand Prix in Dublin that I won't forget.

© JUSTIN DOWNING/SKY SPORTS

Who the hell would be stupid enough to agree to pose in shorts on Southend beach in midwinter? Hmm…

"There's only one Wayney Mardle...": I feel like the king when I'm up on stage playing in the World Championship at the Circus Tavern with a thousand fans chanting my name.

The ultimate challenge: waiting for Phil Taylor before our 2006 World Championship semi-final match. It proved to be a thriller...

I'm still not feeling too healthy. I don't know why but I just can't seem to shift it. I feel lethargic and just generally under the weather all the time.

SUNDAY 5TH JUNE

It's the Isle of Sheppey Classic today. It's staged in a kind of nightclub called the Merlins Entertainment Complex, but I've played in worse venues and it shouldn't really affect anyone's chances.

It's my first tournament for a while but I play pretty good and get to the quarters before losing to Andy Belton. Andy's having one of those good days and goes on to beat Ronnie Baxter in the final, so I'm not going to lose any sleep over going out.

I get chatting to the likes of Andy Jenkins and Kevin Painter during the day and it makes me realise how much the Premier League had taken over recently because I haven't seen them for ages. I just haven't been on the circuit much of late but it's obvious talking to the other lads that everyone wants to be involved with it next year. The money's good and it's great for your profile.

The great thing is the race to play next year is going to be really intense for the rest of the season. Players like Andy and Kevin aren't far outside the top six and the likes of John Part and Roland Scholten could be under threat. I think they're only looking at the top five qualifying automatically as opposed to six last time (so there'll be two wildcard entries) and there's not much margin for error for me and a lot of other players. A run of bad results for any of us and someone will come up on the rails and take the place.

The way the ranking system works is you earn points for reaching a semi-final or final or whatever at a tournament and then two years later you have do as well or better in the same tournament or you lose points. John and Roland have big points to defend in the tournaments coming up and if they don't do the business they could slip outside the top six and that means bye-bye Premier League.

I'm sixth on the list at the moment but I could be as high as fourth by the end of the year, which ain't bad seeing as I haven't won a tournament since the PDPA Players Championship in Wales last September.

TUESDAY 7TH JUNE

Go to my doctors today to try and find out what's causing this ongoing feeling of lethargy and he reckons I could have a viral infection, which I suspected anyway. I've got to get some blood tests and see what happens then.

The house still hasn't gone through, which isn't helping my state of mind either. I really want to get it sorted before we got to Vegas for the Desert Classic at the end of the month but it's not looking great.

THURSDAY 9TH JUNE

Me and Donna are in Manchester today, well a district called Moston to be precise, at the Lightdown Social Club.

It's a really weird one this. I'm doing the gig with John Part and John Gywnne is calling, but the odd thing is we're playing on what they call a log-end board, which is nothing like a normal board.

They only use log-end boards in the Manchester area and I think they're usually made out of elm and dyed black and they don't have any trebles, just doubles. But the really bizarre thing is they have to be stored in a bucket of water to stop them drying out and cracking so you only take them out when you want to play. When you hang them up for a game, they drip everywhere and make a right mess. It's a strange concept, if you ask me.

Oh and I forgot to mention the board is five inches lower and a touch over six inches closer than a normal one, which isn't great seeing as it's the UK Open finals in two days time. I really should be playing on a normal board with a big tournament just around the corner but exhibitions are my bread and butter and you've got to earn a living, haven't you?

One of the most popular games on a log-end is going round the board from one to 20. You can either do it in singles or if you hit a double, say four, it counts as eight and you move straight onto nine. If you then hit double nine, that counts as 18 and you move on to 19. The one double you don't want to hit is five because that puts you on 11 and then you've got no choice but to take singles all the way to 20.

I give Party a good hiding and I thoroughly enjoy myself. So much so, I'm coming back in a few months.

SATURDAY 11TH JUNE

The UK Open is being held in Bolton Wanderers' Reebok Stadium, but I'm still not feeling great, so we'll see how it goes. I wish it was at White Hart Lane, but there you go.

Me and Donna leave the car in the stadium car park and walk past the fans queuing up to get in. I suddenly decide it's good PR opportunity so I go back to the car and get a few Hawaiian shirts out of the boot and hand them out. It's over a hundred quid's worth of merchandise but the fans seem happy and it makes me look good, so it's worth it.

My first game is against an up-and-coming lad in his early 20s called James Wade. We're up on the main stage in front of the Sky cameras, which I reckon should work in my favour because I've got a lot more experience of that type of situation than he has.

It's not long before I'm 4–1 up and cruising but then it all goes pear-shaped and once he pulls it back to five apiece, I'm not ever at the races and I lose 8–6. It's like my aggression and confidence just evaporate for no apparent reason. What's more worrying, I can't say I really care about getting beat today. I really don't. Another tournament and another failure, but such is life.

Donna drives us home via KFC. When we get in, I notice the exercise bike in the conservatory sitting there and taunting me. I must have only used it half a dozen times and I reckon the most exercise I've had out of it was when I put it all together in the first place. When (or should that be if?) we move I'm going to put it in the spare room and get the fat boy back in the saddle. Honest.

CHAPTER SIX

Viva Las Vegas!

SUNDAY 12TH JUNE

Mum and dad come round and we all sit together watching the UK Open, dissecting everyone's technique and style. There are almost as many variations of styles on the circuit as there are players. Some players grip the barrel with all five fingers, others just use three. Some players (like me) bring their arm back and throw in one movement, others have two or three practice swings before they release. Some players (like me) have a high arc on their throw which means the dart comes down into the board while others (like Phil Taylor) throw very flat darts that hit the board horizontally. Some rotate the dart in flight a lot, some less so.

The point is everyone does what they feel comfortable with and there essentially isn't a right or wrong way to hold the dart or throw it. If you can hit what you're aiming at then it's the right way.

But there are some styles that stand out from the crowd. Take a fella called Dennis 'Smiffy' Smith who's got the oddest routine you can imagine before he throws. Now every player I've ever known aims with the points facing the board but Smiffy lines up his shot with the flights facing the board and only then spins the dart around in his hand (so the point is at the front) and throws. But it seems to work for him because he's in the top 30 in the world. The only problem is it takes him twice as long as most other players to throw his three darts because he has such an intricate style and the big danger is falling asleep on the stage when he's at the oche. Smiffy used to be called 'Breezer Geezer' because he was known to like a Bacardi Breezer or ten. He's a quiet lad really who I've played a fair bit of doubles with in the past and the most striking thing about him (aside from his bizarre style) is he's in desperate need of a decent haircut.

Anyway, it's no great surprise that Phil Taylor reaches the final. His opponent is Mark Walsh, who I beat in the World Championship last December. Mark was two sets up against me at Purfleet before his game fell apart then, but today he sticks to his guns against Phil and gives him a decent test. Of course, Phil wins (13 legs to seven) but fair play to Walshie, he didn't show any fear.

TUESDAY 14TH JUNE

Blood tests at the docs today, but I'll have to wait two weeks for the results.

I can't believe the state of the waiting room, everyone coughing and spluttering all the time. There must be millions of germs flying around in there and if you don't have a cold or whatever when you get there, you sure as hell will have caught something by the time you leave.

WEDNESDAY 15TH JUNE

I'm supposed to be at RAF Lyneham in Wiltshire today, but I feel rotten and I can't face it. I'm meant to be doing an exhibition with Mark Dudbridge to raise money for the families of the 11 servicemen—ten of them from this base—who died in Iraq. Their plane crashed near Baghdad in February and I'd said I help out with their fund-raising day.

I feel terrible letting anyone down, especially when it's something like this, but I'm just not up to it physically. I send my apologies and I'm keeping my fingers crossed that it all goes well for them.

FRIDAY 17TH JUNE

I get an email from the guy who was organising everything at Lyneham and apparently it all went off without a hitch. They made over a grand for the families, so that's a weight off my mind.

I'm off to the Isle of Wight today for the first Professional Darts Players Association (PDPA) Players Championship of the season. I haven't been to the Isle of Wight since I was about four and I don't know why but I've got it into my head that it's a bit of a run-down place with loads of prisons. I might be wrong but that's the picture I've got of it.

We're aiming to catch the six o'clock ferry from Portsmouth to Fishbourne so we set off at four but the traffic is rotten so we don't arrive until gone seven. We just manage to get the 7.30 ferry—we're the last car on in fact—which is a result. I'm pissed off though because it's costing me £70 to get across, which I think is steep. It's only the Solent we're crossing here, not the Atlantic.

We arrive at the Savoy Holiday Camp at nineish and we dump our bags in our chalet and go to the bar. Colin Monk and his missus Kirsty and a few others are there, so we have a few drinks and a chinwag.

SATURDAY 18TH JUNE

Wake up feeling shit, which is pretty usual these days. I'm not hungover, I just can't shake this feeling of constant tiredness. The problem is it's a vicious circle. Feeling knackered all the time is getting me down, and that then makes me feel worse physically. I haven't got a clue what's causing it all. My diet's no better or worse than usual, it's not as if I've fallen off the fitness bandwagon (was I ever on it?) and I haven't been drinking too much.

There are two PDPA tournaments on over the weekend—one on Saturday, the other on Sunday. It's a one o'clock start today, which means there's plenty of time to relax, so I sit outside the chalet, chill out and read the paper. While I'm sitting out, Dave Whitcombe passes by and he stops to have a chat. Dave was in the top three in the world in the '80s. We've never spoken before but get on like a house on fire. He's one of those blokes with a really dry sense of humour and I like him a lot. To be honest, I've no idea if he has a clue who I am, he doesn't ask, but we talk about darts and this and that.

The matches start on time and the first three rounds are no problem but I come up against Ronnie Baxter in the quarter-final and the Rocket beats me 3–1. Hand on heart, I'm quite happy with that. I know a world number six (Ronnie's number three at the moment) should be aiming beyond the last eight but these days you don't really get any easy games and, like I've said before, Ronnie is a tough nut to crack. Anyway, it's ranking points and a few quid in the bank.

Ronnie goes on to win it, beating Roland Scholten 3–2 in the final. You always feel better when you know you've gone out to the guy who wins it.

The day's play is over by seven and when I get back to our chalet, I crash out straightaway on the bed for a few hours—I'm such a lightweight these days.

Donna wakes me up at gone nine. It's a quick shower and we're out with Colin and Kirsty for a stroll round Yarmouth and something to eat. We end up in a nice pub along the harbour. Very pleasant place. Maybe I've got the Isle of Wight wrong.

Colin tells me that he's been ripped off by a travel agent who was supposed to be helping to sort out the arrangements for the Desert Classic in Las Vegas later this month. Peter Manley, in his role as the chairman of the PDPA, recommended a travel agent called Mike Burr to all the players to sort out the arrangements. So players like Colin have sent this fella Burr cash, he's sent back confirmation but then cancelled it all... without refunding the money. Colin's five grand out of pocket and

I've heard of other players who've been stung by this bloke as well and let's just say he's not a very popular fella at the moment.

Now the PDPA are refusing to accept responsibility for the mess even though they recommended the guy. They've said they'll loan money to any of the players who've been ripped off to help them get to Vegas, but they'll have to pay it back out of their winnings. I suppose it's not a bad solution but I'm glad I never got involved with the bloke. I still think the players have been let down by the PDPA. It's their job to look after our interests, isn't it?

We head back to the Savoy at midnight but the cabaret is only just starting. It looks like some sort of *Rocky Horror Picture Show* act but there's plenty of familiar faces so we sit down and have a few drinks.

The highlight of the night is my old mate Jason Clark. I've known Jason for 15-odd years after playing with him in the London SuperLeague and he's a riot. It's obvious he's had three or four too many and he's up there dancing like an idiot for a couple of hours and everyone is in stitches. At one point, he grabs this girl he knows, picks her up and starts throwing her around in some bizarre, drunken dance routine. She doesn't know what the hell has hit her and Jason seems to think he's John Travolta. You probably had to be there, but I was crying with laughter.

The atmosphere is great tonight. All the players are in, everyone's in a good mood and there's none of the edge or tension we sometimes get when we're all together. It's how it should be all the time.

I get to bed at 2.30 completely knackered.

SUNDAY 19TH JUNE

It's another one o'clock start today and, like yesterday, I'm comfortable enough in the first couple of rounds. I play Mark Dudbridge in the last 16 but I'm never in trouble and it's 3–1 to Mardle. I'm well chuffed because Flash has been my nemesis for a couple of months and even though I got my own back in the Premier League, it's nice to let him know I'm not going anywhere.

I play Dennis 'The Menace' Priestley in the quarter-final. If you've ever read *The Beano*, you'll understand Dennis' nickname and why he always wears a red and black striped shirt. He's one of the elder statesmen of the game these days and he's never afraid to air his views. But when you've won two World Championships, you've got a right to say what you like in my book. He's still a good player and he's got bags of experience, so I know I'm in for a real battle.

Things go well in the early stages and I'm two sets to one up (first to three) without really breaking sweat. The problems start in the fourth set when I get five darts at double 18 to win it 3–1 and miss the lot. There's worse to come when I get another five at double 16 to take it 3–2 and miss again and Dennis cleans up. Like I said, Dennis is still a quality player but to miss that many chances to win the match is inexcusable and I'm furious with myself. I don't know why but I'm on edge all through the match and it's the same old story on the finishes again.

There's no big party tonight so we get the ferry from Fishbourne to Portsmouth and, door-to-door, it takes us four hours to get home which isn't too bad.

When we finally sit down I start thinking to myself that I need to go to the bank in the next couple of days. I feel for my wallet... oh no, I've left it in the bloody chalet. What a prat. It's got all my cards in but I suddenly have a brainwave and ring Pete Manley's mobile. Bless, he's asleep but he's still on the Isle of Wight so I get him to get the keys for our chalet and sure enough, my wallet's lying on the bed. Cheers, Peter, nice one. He's going to give it back to me when we see each other in a few days time.

MONDAY 20TH JUNE

A lazy day. We're off to Vegas in a couple of days for the Desert Classic and I'm like a kid waiting for Christmas. Vegas is a gambler's paradise and I love the place.

Remember when I gave a two-fingered salute to some idiot in the

Premier League crowd in Doncaster in May? I said I'd get fined and sure enough the DRA have decided that'll be £250, thank you very much. I just love the DRA, great fellas.

TUESDAY 21ST JUNE

Off to Vegas today. We're flying from Gatwick and I've booked the door-to-door Gatwick flyer, which picks you up at your house and it saves all the hassle of parking at the airport. It's only 30 quid each and you'd spend that on the car park anyway. It arrives at five in the morning, which is too early really, and we're at the airport by ten past seven.

It's a 10-hour flight, which is boring as usual. Donna has this annoying knack of being able to sleep for nearly the whole journey when we're on a plane while I sit there bored and grumpy. I wish I knew her secret.

We arrive in Vegas at 1.30 in the afternoon their time and we jump in a cab to the Flamingo, where we always stay. I love the way they make such a big deal of providing free rooms for us during the tournament, when they know they get all the money back over the tables in the casino. Nothing's too much trouble but it's all a bit of a sham because you end up paying for the room one way or the other.

Our luck is in when we arrive because we get a free upgrade to a bigger room. Bigger as in four-foot bigger than the one we booked, but every little helps, doesn't it? We're on the 27th floor and there's only 28, so I feel we're on top of the pile. Looking out over the Vegas skyline with all the neon lights is pretty spectacular. I dread to think what the electricity bills are like around here though.

WEDNESDAY 22ND JUNE

The Desert Classic doesn't start for five days, so we've got plenty of time to get acclimatised. And gamble, of course.

Today I play in a poker tournament in the hotel. It's only $55 to enter, so the stakes aren't exactly massive, but I want to get my eye in before I start playing for anything a bit richer.

I get down to the last seven out of 40 players but I'm getting pretty shit cards all the way through and I'm not too surprised when I'm the next one out. It's a reasonable start as far as I'm concerned and there's plenty to build on.

I love some of the little variations and tactics the Americans have to poker. They do this thing called 'straddling', which means they double up the betting on the two blind cards. That means the pot is starting at $100 every time and the kitty builds up much faster that way, which makes for more exciting games.

I haven't completely forgotten darts though and I will try and find a pub where I can have a practice. Just one more hand first...

FRIDAY 24TH JUNE

Another day of gambling and an encounter with a British fella that's weird to say the least.

I'm sitting in the hotel casino playing poker when I see this bloke staring at me. After a while he comes over.

"I know you from somewhere, don't I?"

"Do you? Where are you from?"

"Oxford."

"I think you're confusing me with someone else."

"You play darts, don't you?"

"That's right."

"Do you play around Oxford?"

"No, not really mate."

"I play in the league in Oxford and I've definitely seen you playing darts before."

"Maybe it's because I play on the telly?"

"What's your name?"

"Wayne Mardle."

"Yes, that's right."

And then he just walks off. Not another word. Just turns his back and he's off.

Me, Donna, Peter and Chrissie go to see a show called 'O' by

Cirque du Soleil in the evening. No kidding, we've been trying to book it for years now and finally managed to get some tickets. They did cost us $140 each though, which stings a bit.

I think me and Peter have pretty much patched things up now. There's been no big sitdown or pow-pow about what happened in the Premier League, but it's in the past now and it'd be stupid to let it carry on, especially because Donna and Chrissie are good mates too and it's not fair if they suffer as well. People fall out and then they make up, don't they? I'm not sure if me and Peter will ever be quite as close as we were but I'm glad we're back to talking properly rather than just saying a quick hello.

Anyway, the show is excellent. It's basically a bunch of acrobats doing their stuff on water but I just wish they'd turn the air conditioning down a bit because it's bloody freezing. The Americans are totally obsessed with air conditioning.

MONDAY 27TH JUNE

The qualifiers start today, which means the practice boards are up in the venue—the MGM Grand—so I can have a throw and start focusing on the competition. There are 512 players looking to make it through but only 16 qualify for the main event, so it's going to be intense.

The MGM is called the 'City of Entertainment' and it really isn't an exaggeration. It's hard to describe if you've never been there but the place is just massive. It's got 5,000-odd rooms, miles and miles of fruit machines and even a couple of real life lions in cages in the casino. The Americans don't do anything by halves but they must have decided to really go to town even by their own standards when they built the Grand. I'm sure you could fit the whole of Romford inside the place.

TUESDAY 28TH JUNE

The qualifiers finished today and we're having a PDC banquet tonight to watch the main tournament draw. I think it's to show a bit of unity among the players in a foreign land but I don't care as long as I'm fed and watered.

The banquet is a bit of a disappointment. Being in America, I'm expecting large chunks of barbecued cow—steaks as far as the eye can see—but it's all chicken with spaghetti, chicken omelette and the like. At this rate, I'll be in danger of losing weight.

The draw is made at nine-ish and as soon as Phil Taylor's name is called out, you can sense everyone else praying their name doesn't come up. I'm okay because I can't play Phil yet because of the seedings but I can sympathise with the other lads who can. In the end, Mark Holden pulls the short straw.

I haven't introduced you to Mark yet, have I? I think he's got to be the biggest nutter on the circuit. He really is a certified loony and his nickname (which he came up with himself for no apparent reason) is 'Top Banana', which he's got tattooed on the back of his neck in case anyone forgets. He always screams out "Boosh!" whenever he hits a 180.

Next out is Chris Mason and I can play Chris, which I really don't want to do at this stage of the tournament. I've got no doubt he'll be world champion one day and he's not the kind of player you want early doors. But it's not me—Roland Scholten will play him instead. Happy days.

I finally come up and I'm drawn to play Lionel Sams, one of the few left-handers on the circuit. Am I happy? Well, I'm not unhappy but Lionel is no pushover. His nickname is Lionel 'The Lion' Sams (geddit?) and the symbol of the MGM Grand is a lion. In fact, there's two great big golden lion statues on the stage at the Grand, so I hope that's not some bad omen for me.

Lionel's missus Caroline came up with The Lion moniker but he's not exactly the king of the darts world, though he is in the world top 20. To be fair, he's a trier who never knows when he's beat and there aren't many players on the circuit who have the self-belief that he does. He and Caroline appeared on that *Darts Players' Wives* documentary and Lionel said on camera, "I'm a predator" and his missus turned round and said, "A printer?" He got stick for that for weeks. I heard Caroline was thinking of changing her name to Carolion but I don't know whether she's gone through with it yet.

The game is tomorrow, so I leave the banquet early to get my beauty sleep.

WEDNESDAY 29TH JUNE

The Desert Classic is a weird tournament because we have to play in the morning or early afternoon Las Vegas time so the people back home in the UK can watch it live in the evening and it's hard to adjust to playing at that time of day. For a start, if you're playing at ten in the morning, you've got to be up by, say, five to be properly prepared and that's just bizarre. And unless you're in Finland in February or something, it's dark at five in the morning.

Luckily, I'm not on until three this afternoon—the last match of the day—so I get a few hours grace before I have to be up and getting ready.

All in all, the game goes well. I mean I win, which is all that really matters but I feel pretty good against Lionel and I think I've got a few more gears to go through if I need them. It's the best out of three sets and even though I lose the second, I steamroller him in the third. It's a comfortable 2–1 win. Job done.

The big first round upset is Ronnie Baxter going out to young James Wade. Remember him? He beat me in the UK Open finals. I told you he had a lot of potential.

The draw for the second round is made before the end of the day and I pull Andy Callaby. Andy's a solid player who beat Phil Taylor in the Grand Prix last October, so he's more than capable of knocking me over if I'm off colour. There's no way I'm going to take this one lightly. Andy is known as 'Super Cally' as in supercalifragilisticexpialidocious from the muscial Mary Poppins. He's a bit of a volatile one is Andy but he's always up for a laugh, just as long as it's not as his expense.

THURSDAY 30TH JUNE

I'm on at 11 against Andy so it's the dreaded five o'clock start, which gives me enough time to join the land of the living and have a couple of hours practice. It's best of five sets today, so there's still little room for error and you simply have to start well or it's over before you realise.

And start well is exactly what I do. I hit a 112 finish in the first leg, a 121 in the second and I'm absolutely flying. It's one of those days when everything feels right in my world and I know Andy is on a hiding to nothing. I can just feel it.

In the end, I win 3–0 and Andy wins just the one leg. I pull out an 11-dart finish, hit eight out of nine double 18s, which is a great percentage, and basically blow him away. I'm playing really, really well.

It's always a buzz to win convincingly but after the ups and downs I've been going through in the last few months, this win feels even better. Maybe it's because I feel at home in Vegas, I don't know, but I feel worry free and confident and that's being reflected in the quality of my darts. I'm doing myself justice up there and that's all any player can ask for.

I've got my old mate Colin Lloyd in the quarters tomorrow but I know he's not going to sleep as well as me tonight if he saw that performance. Bring it on.

FRIDAY 1ST JULY

It's Donna's birthday today. Being a gentleman, I couldn't possibly say how old she is but let's just say she can't use her Young Person's Railcard any more. I'll take her out tonight for a meal but first things first. She knows my focus has to be on the match with Colin. We're on at midday.

Colin is out of the blocks like a greyhound and the first set (it's first to three again) is done and dusted before I really wake up. I drag it back to 1–1 by taking the second but I still feel Colin's got the momentum and he's soon 2–1 up, averaging something like 110 in the third set. That's unbelievable form; I'm in trouble and he knows it. He only needs one more set and I don't think there's many out there putting money on me to turn it around.

But then one of those inexplicable things happens. It's 2–2 in legs in the fourth and Colin has the darts. He opens up with 180, 140, 170 and then hits the three to leave double four for the match. I'm miles behind and he has a minimum of five darts at the double four to win it. He misses the lot. Now that's not what you expect in a million years from the world number one (especially the way he's playing today) but pressure can do funny things to you and I take full advantage to take the set and level it up at 2–2 with one to play.

Don't ask me why, but I now know I'm going to win. There's absolutely no doubt about it. Colin's been throwing well, but I'm not going to let him get up from that.

The final set goes two legs apiece and we're into a sudden death leg but I hold my nerve—I've got the darts—and it's game Mardle.

I've got to admit I've had a big slice of luck with Colin missing his big chance but that's the way it goes sometimes. It's all about making the most of the opportunity when it comes along.

I'm playing John Part in the semi-final tomorrow. It's Phil Taylor against Wes Newton in the other match, so who knows, it could be Phil and I in a repeat of last year's final. He beat me six sets to four last year but with the way I'm playing at the moment, I reckon it could be a different story this year. First I've got to get past John though.

We go to a place called Morton's Steak House in the evening to celebrate Donna's birthday with my brother Perry, my sister Donna plus a couple of friends my sister is staying with over here. It's a nice night but we're back at the hotel by 11 because I've got to play tomorrow. There'll be plenty of time for late nights when the tournament's over.

SATURDAY 2ND JULY

Another special day today. As I said, yesterday was Donna's birthday and today's our third wedding anniversary. If you remember, we got married in Vegas and it makes it special to be back here for our anniversary.

Funnily enough, it's Peter and Chrissie Manley's first anniversary today as well, so we're all going out together tonight to celebrate. Peter lost to Mark Walsh yesterday, so I'm left flying the flag for the newly(ish)-weds.

John starts the match like a rocket and takes three legs on the bounce to win the opening set. It's a great start for him but I'm genuinely not too worried because I still feel relaxed at the oche and it's first to four sets today, so I've got time to get back into things.

I throw like a dream in the next two sets, taking six legs in a row to go 2–1 up and give John plenty to think about. Just to rub salt into the wounds I win the third set by taking out a 132 checkout with two bulls and then double 16. It's a flash finish, one for the crowd, and it shows how well I'm playing. I know now I'm going to win. That little light somewhere in the head that flashes 'Game Mardle' is going off like the clappers and I really start to relax. It doesn't happen often but it's a great feeling knowing the result is going to go your way.

There's a break after the third. John leaves the stage so I decide to entertain the crowd a bit. The problem is that even though the crowds have been really supportive and as noisy as they can be, we're talking audiences of maybe 900 to a thousand. Thing is, we're playing in the MGM's Grand Garden Arena, which holds about 19,000. It's the place where Mike Tyson took a bite out of Evander Holyfield's ear and lots of other big fights have been held, so you can imagine that even a thousand-strong crowd could be a little lost in a cavernous place like this.

So to get a bit of atmosphere going, I get the microphone and start singing "Viva Las Vegas". It's just a bit of fun, as much for my benefit as the spectators', but I think John's pissed off about it when he comes back because he's got a face like thunder. We usually get on well (especially when he's not talking about *Star Wars*) but I think he's annoyed with me.

I did the same during the game with Colin, which was fine but John seems to take exception to it. To be clear, I never do that sort of thing if my opponent is still on the stage having a few practice throws or whatever because that would be rude. But John walked off so I thought, why the fuck not?

I'm still not worried when John takes the fourth set to make it two apiece because the next two sets are mine. All mine. Game Mardle (I told you) and a place in the final. Happy, happy days. I'm definitely near my best today. Not quite, but close enough.

The other semi is a familiar story. Wes plays really well but you've to play unbelievably well to stand a chance against Phil and it's 4–0 to the world champion. A repeat of last year's final is on.

SUNDAY 3RD JULY

I'm up at a quarter to five, which is probably as much do with nerves as it's the need to be awake so early. I head off to the bar to get a coke and then make my way to the practice room (I'm the first one in). Even though I'm still buzzing after the way I played yesterday, I'm also nervous. This is a high-profile tournament (if not the best one for prize money) and I know I'm hitting form just at the right time.

Phil walks in 15 minutes later and he's talking to one of his entourage. I look at him and think, that's the man I've got to beat if I want to be the champion. Am I showing him too much respect? Am I psyching myself out? Maybe, I'm not sure.

But before I get too tense, something strange happens to take my mind off things. I go over to Phil to have a chat—mainly to try and prove to myself I'm not going to be intimidated—when this young American guy waltzes in to the practice room and starts throwing a few. No-one is meant to be here without a security pass and neither of us recognise him as a player so I go over to him and say:

"What are you doing here?"

"Just practising."

"You playing in the youth tournament?"

"No."

"How'd you get in here?"

"Just walked in."

I leave him alone then but when me and Phil start chatting again he comes over, sits right next us and starts asking us questions about our conversation. Now we're talking about PDC business that outsiders don't need to know, so I give Phil the 'schtum' look and we get the security guards to throw him out.

Okay, so he's probably just a normal young bloke but it really shouldn't happen. What are the security guards doing? Imagine someone just waltzing onto the pitch when Premiership players are warming up. There'd be hell to pay.

The final goes according to plan. Unfortunately it's Phil's plan and he wins it 6–1. I'm five sets to nil down in pretty quick time and by the end I'm just happy to have won the sixth set to make it less embarrassing. There really isn't a lot I can say. Phil opened up the match with a 180, which is a bad sign. I played well enough and he played out of this world. End of story. There's not a player in the world who can live with him when he plays like that and I'm not sure even the best darts of my life would have been enough today.

Put it this way. Long-term, most players will average in the mid 90s. The best average I've ever produced in a tournament was 104 in the second round of the 2003 World Championship, but that's only one match. Against Phil today, I averaged 98, which is strong, but he comes out with 107, which is phenomenal. He once did 112 to some poor sod, but you see what I'm saying. Sometimes even being at your best against him isn't even close.

"Well done," I say to him as we shake hands. "What could I have done?"

He gives me a little smile: "Nothing." To be honest, it's a privilege just to stand behind him and watch when he's throwing like that. Still, I pocket $10,000 for my troubles (Phil banks $20K), so it's better than a kick in the teeth, isn't it?

I'm not feeling suicidal or anything after the game so me and

Donna decide to go for a meal at Smith & Wollensky, where a few stars go. I have the lamb chops, but start feeling a bit dicky afterwards. I'm not sure whether it's the meat or my mystery virus resurfacing, but, either way, I decide to have an early night.

MONDAY 4TH JULY

Independence Day. The Americans go mad today. They're a patriotic bunch, I'll give them that.

Meet up with my sister Donna in the morning. She flew out earlier in the week to stay with friends of hers. Mum and dad are looking after the kids, so it's a nice break for her and we do some of the touristy things during the day. We check out the gondola ride at the Venetian hotel, which I've always thought was pretty spectacular. It's basically a recreation of the canals of Venice and you even get your own bloke with the long stick to take you around. The funny thing is, all the gondolas are obviously motorised, rolling along on runners or something underneath the water, so who the blokes think they're fooling is anyone's guess.

In the afternoon, I'm in one of the hotel bars having a medicinal vodka when I get chatting to an Aussie bloke. I like to think I'm a sociable kind of guy and I'm always getting into random conversations with complete strangers. So me and this fella are chatting and we get talking about Aussie darts players like Tony David, who was the BDO world champion a couple of years back, when this guy asks if I remember an Australian player called Wayne Weening. It turns out this guy used to live just down the road from him. Now Wayne wasn't exactly what you'd call a household name but I remember him well because me and him had a funny chat about 15 years ago at the British Open. At the bar at the British Open to be precise.

"Jeez mate, this beer is terrible," he said.

"It's Fosters. It's Australian,' I replied.

"Piss off. This is never Foster's."

"Honest, it is. Look at the tap."

"Jesus, what have they done to it?"

"No idea."

We spent the next half hour slagging off the beer and then he was off. I never spoke to him again but here I am in the middle of Vegas talking about him with another Aussie I've just met. Small world.

TUESDAY 5TH JULY

We've still got a few days left in Vegas before we fly home, so, trust me, I'm going to play some serious poker before then.

First I've got a great story for you. It's about Phil Taylor's protégé, Adrian Lewis. I promise it will either make you laugh or cry. Or both.

Adrian was in the MGM the other day playing the fruit machines when security came over and told him to stop. You've got to be 21 to gamble here and Adrian's only 20, so his passport proved he was too young to play. But Adrian wasn't having any of that, so when the guards walked off, he carried on playing regardless and put in another $300 into one of the machines, which is a lot of cash for a kid of his age. Suddenly three lions came up, which is the jackpot (remember the MGM's symbol is a lion), and Adrian's $72,000 richer. Or so he thought.

Problem is, when he went to collect his winnings (you can't have fruit machines coughing up thousands out of the bottom, can you?), the casino management refused to pay up because Adrian's under age. He tried to make out his "older mate" had won the money and he was just helping him collect it, but then they showed him the CCTV tapes of him winning the jackpot. I think the conversation ended along the lines of, "Forget the money and shut up or we could have you arrested for illegal gambling."

He must have been heartbroken.

His new nickname? Adrian 'Jackpot' Lewis, of course.

FRIDAY 8TH JULY

Still in Vegas and still living and breathing poker. In fact, I'm going to watch the World Series of Poker today and there's the *creme de la creme* of players on show. My favourite is an American guy called Phil Hellmuth, who's known as the 'Poker Brat'. I identify with him I suppose because he shows a lot of emotion when he plays and not many of the players are like that.

I actually get to have a quick word with him and I tell him I think he's a genius. He says thanks and wishes me luck and I really think he's sincere. Maybe I'm just star-struck, but he genuinely seems a top bloke.

I also get to meet Howard Lederer and Dave 'The Devilfish' Ulliott, a pawnbroker from Hull, who are top players as well. I'm not sure if Dave recognises me or what but he keeps coming over for a chat with me between hands, which is crazy. How can he concentrate on playing and talk to me at the same time?

He cracks jokes all the time as well. First off, he leans over and tells one of the other players his wife is ugly and then asks the audience if they think the dealer looks like ET. Priceless.

It's a great day and I'll never forget it. I'm learning so much out here about the game and I just hope I don't forget all the lessons and tips.

I've definitely decided not to play on the internet anymore. Playing online pales into insignificance compared to the real thing. You can't see the other players online and the more I think about it, the more I realise how rubbish it is.

SATURDAY 9TH JULY

I'm in a bar having a quite drink today when I get talking to a American guy from Florida. He's really friendly, like every single American seems to be, so we get chatting and I ask him a few things.

"So what do you do for a living?"

"I'm a professional gambler. I make my money betting on sports like baseball and ice hockey."

"Right, that's interesting. I'm a darts player."

"No kidding. Got any tips?"

"On how to play darts?"

"On how to make money betting on darts."

"No, not really mate. Phil Taylor's usually a good bet."

"Can I bet on darts on the internet?"

"Yeah, I suppose."

"Can you tell me when someone's going to lose?"

"No, I can't do that."

"Can you tell me when you're going to lose?"

"You what?"

"If you tell me when you're going to lose we could both make a lot of money."

"No, no way."

"NFL and baseball stars do it over here all the time. We can do a deal."

"No mate, it's not on, no way. We've got rules about all this. I'm not interested."

"You sure?"

I'm now thinking I really shouldn't be talking to this fella, so I drink up and leave.

MONDAY 11TH JULY

It dawns on me today that I haven't got much of a tan for a bloke who's spent two weeks in the desert. Fact is, I've spent hardly any time outside—I've been too busy playing poker.

But there's no point changing the habit of a lifetime now, so I decide to head to a hotel called The Aladdin today for a change while Donna and Chrissie Manley opt to stay back and sunbathe by the hotel pool. We've been playing a lot in the casino in the Flamingo, entering the $50 tournaments. My best finish is fifth so far and I've made the final table three times, which isn't too shabby, but there's nothing much on here today.

When we get there we change up $200 into chips and get involved in a cash game. I sit there for two-and-half hours without getting a single decent hand but manage to bluff my way to a few pots and I'm $120 up, which isn't bad.

The next hand things get really interesting.

I pull the queen of clubs and the queen of spades and the community cards are queen of hearts, queen of diamonds and the jack of spades. There's three of us left in, $200 in the kitty and I'm sitting on four queens.

Now, I don't want to go over the top with my next bet because the other two blokes might fold and I won't make the most out of a blinding hand, so I play it cool. The turn card is the 10 of diamonds and one of the other guys goes all in. I'm thinking, okay, they've got a flush but it's going to have to be a running flush to beat my four queens, so I'm still laughing.

I call. There's $900 in the pot.

The river card is the king of diamonds. I can't be beaten, can I? Yes, I bloody can. The guy who's gone all in turns over a running flush, nine, 10, jack, queen and king of diamonds. It's like someone has just slapped me in the face. Hard. I cannot believe it.

I'm completely gutted. We're flying home tomorrow and I don't want to go out like that.

TUESDAY 12TH JULY

Donna doesn't want to go home but now the moment is here, so to speak, I realise I've had enough. It's been great, but I'm definitely ready to go home. Maybe one day we will move to the States like we talk about sometimes, but for now Essex is still where the heart is.

We have a few last hands of poker before the flight, which is in the afternoon, but neither of us win or lose really. At least I'm not flying back on the back of another big defeat.

The flight isn't too busy but it's a long haul home and my heart sinks when a family sit in the seats behind us and the kids start kicking the backs of our chairs. Luckily for us, they want to watch TV and the monitors in the back of our chairs don't work so they soon move to another part of the plane. Result.

Quick as a flash me and Donna recline our seats as far back as possible to "discourage" anyone else from sitting behind us and it works a treat. We're left in peace for the whole journey.

We watch the Clint Eastwood film *Million Dollar Baby*, the one about the female boxer, and I have to admit I cry like a baby. I know I'm a grown man but I've always been in touch with my feminine side. I think Donna's a bit ashamed of me though.

We're well and truly knackered when we get home, but the great news is we're definitely moving into the new house. There's a message on the answer phone saying we can pick the keys up next week. Finally, all the waiting is over.

CHAPTER SEVEN

Lion-taming and other summer adventures

FRIDAY 15TH JULY

Had a couple of days off after getting back from Vegas but I'm back on the exhibition circuit tonight in Ringwood, Hampshire. Donna and mum are coming along but the traffic is horrendous and it takes us four-and-a-half hours to get there. Sod's Law, we can't find the venue when we get there either. It's quarter past eight and I'm getting stressed. I like to be nice and early for these gigs.

When we find the place it's straight to the bar for a little calmer and on with the show. They only expect me to play six games, which is below par for a typical evening, but what they haven't told me until now is that I've got two seasons worth of presentations. On a normal night I might give 200 trophies out, which is no problem, but tonight it's more like 400.

It's a nightmare. Half the people aren't even there to collect the trophies and the whole thing takes forever. There's only so many hands you can shake without a break. I know I shouldn't moan, but I will.

MONDAY 18TH JULY

Check my emails this morning and there's one from that bloke I met in Vegas asking me to help him fix matches. I'd told him I had a website before I knew what he was after, so he must have got my email address from that. He's persistent, I'll give him that, because he's still trying to persuade me to 'help him out'. No thanks, mate, I'll pass.

Truth is, it would be pretty easy to fix a match. Any decent player could lose (probably by a specific scoreline) and not make it look too obvious but thankfully we've never had any problems like that in darts.

I'm in South Woodham Ferrers tonight, which is near Chelmsford in Essex. Turns out to be a really good night, actually, because I bump into my brother-in-law's brother Derek, who I haven't seen for 15 years and a old mate of mine, Ray Chater.

I used to play with Ray seven-odd years ago. He always been a good player and he beats me over the best of three legs. Tells me he hasn't picked up his darts for years. Liar!

TUESDAY 19TH JULY

We've got the keys to the house. Thing is, we're not moving in straightaway because there's some painting and bits and bobs we want doing before we move all our stuff in and I'm up in Blackpool soon for the World Matchplay, which is a big tournament. We don't have to be out of the old house just yet, so we can afford to take our time. We've waited this long so another week or so won't hurt.

THURSDAY 21ST JULY

Sampling the delights of Blackpool tonight. I've been booked by the Carlton Bowling Club for an exhibition, which is handy because the Matchplay starts on Sunday.

When we get to the club, we have a drink and relax before the big kick-off. Unluckily there's a woman at the bar—the local drunkard apparently—who decides we're not going to get any peace and quiet.

She's obviously had more than a few and she starts talking, well, slurring, to me.

"What time you start then?"

"Half eight."

"Get on with it then."

"I'm starting soon."

"It's half eight, throw something."

"It's 28 minutes past actually."

"Look, I'm only staying to see you throw three darts and then I'm off."

"Oh, right."

"Get on with it then."

Charming. I get up to get changed but by the time I get back, about 20 to nine, she's already gone. You can't please everyone, can you?

Turns out, it's one of the quietest night I think I've ever done though. There are only 25 people in the whole night and I don't want to sound cocky, but that's unusual. I find it all bit disconcerting to be honest.

On the upside, we get away relatively early and me and Donna head back to the place we're staying during the Matchplay. It's called the Daryyn Flats and we've stayed here before. It's right next to the Winter Gardens, where the Matchplay is being held.

FRIDAY 22ND JULY

The warm-up tournament for the Matchplay starts tomorrow so today is a chance to chill out. I'm feeling pretty good at the moment. Mentally, I'm feeling positive and physically I'm much better than I have been.

I got the results from the blood tests from the doctor before we left and they confirmed I've had a viral infection. There's nothing he can prescribe for it, so I just have to get on with it. That said, I've been feeling much perkier recently, maybe because I've been trying to eat better, and I've lost some weight as well. At this rate, I might even take up the fitness regime again.

The world in general seems a brighter place. I'm throwing as well as I have since the World Championship and the way I played in Vegas was a real boost to my confidence.

It's my nephew's birthday today by the way. He's 13, a teenager now. Happy birthday, Danny.

SATURDAY 23RD JULY

Danny's birthday yesterday, mum's today. She's the big six something, so happy birthday, mum.

Anyway, the pre-Matchplay tournament I mentioned is the Bobby Bourne Players Championship. Bobby was a PDC official who died after a heart attack and they named the tournament after him. I only knew Bobby for a year or so but he was a great lad, bless him.

When I get to the venue everyone is commenting on how much weight I've lost. I lap it all up to be honest, although I wouldn't necessarily recommend being ill as a sensible weight-loss programme.

I've got a bye in the first round, which is weird. Ask any of the players and they'll tell you no-one really wants a bye. Unless you get Phil Taylor out of the hat that is. Seriously though, players want to play because it keeps your arm in. There's no substitute for board time. The bloke I should have been playing had paid his £60 entry fee and then didn't bother to turn up.

I beat Roland Scholten in the quarter-finals, which is a good result, and I've got Chris Mason in the semis. I'm chatting to Chris before our game and he tells me a funny story about the night before. Him, his wife and the Northern Ireland youth captain Jeff Wiley—a top bloke who's put me up a few times—went out for a few drinks and ended up in a kebab shop. For some reason the owner took exception to Chris and came at him with a meat cleaver. Now Chris has been in bother with the law before and doesn't need the hassle and decides to scarper. He's a lovely fella, Chris, but like I said he does seem to attract trouble.

Maybe he's still traumatised by his scrape because when we get to the oche, he's not on top form and I turn him over pretty easily.

Of course, it's Phil in the final and the scene is set nicely. I want to get my own back for losing in the final in Vegas and I'm throwing well. Shame no-one bothers to tell Phil any of this because he does me three sets to nil and I only win two legs in the whole match. To be fair, I average 96, which is more than respectable and would have been enough to beat 98 per cent of the darting world, but Phil averages 107, which is too good. It's the same old story, isn't it? Good players play a good game against Phil and he just steps up to the next level. I'm not waving the white flag or anything but there's not a lot you can do when he does that.

At least I pocket two grand for the day so I take the birthday girl, dad, Donna and our friends Jill and Steve, who's a PDC official, out to the local casino for a meal.

SUNDAY 24TH JULY

The Matchplay starts today but I don't play until tomorrow, so I'm taking it easy. I don't want to risk a little tweak or strain by overdoing it, do I?

The big news from the tournament is Kevin Painter's defeat by Adrian Lewis in the first round. Now Adrian's a good player but Kevin was expected to win, so it's a shock. It just goes to prove you can't afford to be complacent early on. I know how Kevin must be feeling, I went out in the first round here last year to Mark Dudbridge. I'm not planning on a repeat.

MONDAY 25TH JULY

I'm playing Lionel Sams at 10.30 tonight, a repeat of our meeting in Vegas, so I've got plenty of time to kill and have a mooch around Blackpool.

While I'm out and about I get a text from a mate about a dog. I was going to be a part owner of this greyhound. It didn't happen, but they named it after me anyway—Hawaii 501—the poor mutt. It's running today at one-ish and it's got a great chance. It would be disloyal not to put a few quid on it, wouldn't it?

So I find a bookies, put on £40 and, guess what, it only goes and wins. I get £120 back and decide to have another little flutter on the next race since my luck is clearly in. The gods are only obviously looking down on me today because that one comes in as well and that's another hundred quid in my old sky rocket.

I'm beginning to think this isn't exactly the ideal preparation for tonight when I notice they've got the Matchplay odds up and I'm 9/1 on to beat Lionel. Great odds, not. Nine quid to get a quid back, it's really not worth it. As I'm looking at the board, a bloke pipes up.

"Mardle, what's all this nine-to-one on rubbish?"

"Yeah, I know."

"It's a load of rubbish."

"I don't set the odds, do I?"

"Fair point but come on!"

"I know, I know."

"I mean you're not good enough to be nine-to-one on, are you?"

I get to the venue at 5.30 and soak up the atmosphere. The Matchplay is one of the biggest dates on the calendar and you can feel the excitement in the air.

Before the game I have a chat with the guys from Kasdon, my new sponsors. It's good to see them but it does add a little pressure because you want to do well in front of the people who are writing the cheques.

While I'm waiting to play, I see Lionel's other half Caroline sitting in the lounge. She's got a big toy lion, Lionel's mascot, with her. I start messing around with it and end up booting the lion and it sails through the air and across the bar. She gives me daggers from then on.

The game against Lionel, to be perfectly honest, is a bit of a stroll and I beat him ten legs to two. I genuinely think Lionel is really underestimated on the circuit but he seems nervous and makes it easy for me. The only distraction I have is being aware of Caroline sitting at the front of the audience, still giving me daggers and cheering Lionel on. I can hear her clear as a bell but it seems to spur me on. For the record, Caroline, I'm sorry and I hope the lion has recovered from the experience.

WEDNESDAY 27TH JULY

It's Mark Dudbridge in the second round today. I had a good day off yesterday and a bit of practice, so my preparation has been as good as it could be. And I haven't forgotten he beat me here last year.

I get to the Winter Gardens at half two and Mark finally arrives at four. We're on at 6.30 so I'm thinking he's cutting things a bit fine but he looks worried about something and comes over for a chat.

"Wayne."

"Yes, mate. What's up?"

"I've lost me darts."

"No. What? Where?"

"I think they're in the back of the cab that brought me here but I'm not sure."

"You're fucking kidding."

It's no laughing matter to lose your arrows but I'm also thinking, how the fuck can you leave your darts in a cab when you're playing in front of the cameras in a few hours?

I tell him to go and buy some from one of the merchandise stalls in the foyer, which he doesn't find a very helpful suggestion, but luckily the cabbie turns up with them half-an-hour later and it's game on.

It's the first to 13 legs in the second round and I'm never behind. The only thing Flash can do is try and hang on to my coat tails. To be fair, he's a stubborn bugger, but I can feel all the way that at any moment he's going to go or I'm going to step up another gear and that's exactly what happens. It's my game, 13–10 in the end.

Mark's really gracious afterwards, congratulating me and he's really sincere. When he first came onto the circuit we didn't really get on. It was nothing serious or anything like that but we just didn't seem to click. Maybe I felt he lived up to his nickname of Flash too much but he's definitely mellowed and we've definitely got a rapport now. I think he's realised everyone on the circuit is just trying to earn a living.

Me and Donna head off to the casino afterwards but rather than play poker, we decide to have breakfast. At half twelve at night. I know it's not ideal for the old waistline but I've lost a bit recently, so one's not going to hurt, is it? Saying that, there were three eggs each and loads of bacon, so my cholesterol levels will be through the roof.

THURSDAY 28TH JULY

It's quarter-final day today and I'm playing Peter Manley. The match starts at three, so I get up early and head down to breakfast. I bump into Peter and his mate Dave Ansell and we decide to eat together. I told you we were friends again.

So we're all sitting there, chomping away and chatting about this and that when it suddenly occurs to me how surreal this all is. Peter's talking about his daughter, I'm telling him about the new house and in a few short hours time we're going to want to rip each other's heads off (metaphorically, of course) up on the stage. It's the nature of the beast on the circuit because all the players have to spend a lot of time together but it's all a bit weird as well.

There is a real sense of community on the circuit between the players, their families and all the other people associated with the PDC and it would be a shame if we lost that. I'm determined not to get involved in any more silly little spats. It's just not worth it.

The afternoon start means we don't have hours to kill and before I know it, we're both ready to go on stage. I say to Peter, "You play your game and I'll play mine", which means I don't want gamesmanship up there or any of his old shenanigans and he shakes my hand and says pretty much the same to me. Fair play, game on.

It's the first to 16 legs today and it's nip and tuck all the way. The early legs especially seem to go one to me, one to Peter, but the amazing thing is that in the first 15 legs, Peter has eight darts at the doubles and hits every single one to edge in front 8–7. I know his nickname is One Dart, but, believe me, that is some serious finishing.

What happens next is just as crazy though, as I take seven legs on the bounce to make it 14–8. To do that against someone of Peter's quality is almost unheard of. I know I'm not home and hosed yet but I'm feeling relaxed and I'm the clear favourite now.

The next phase of the match is a nightmare and the legs just slip by. Peter wins four on the bounce—14–9, 14–10, 14–11, 14–12—and I can't find a double to save my life. He takes two legs on my throw, I'm well and truly rattled now and before I know it, it's all level at 14–14. I'm just not on the planet for the last two legs, Peter gets stronger and stronger and he takes it 16–14. What a way to lose.

Credit where's it due though. Peter would be entitled to jump and down like a lunatic after a comeback like that but he just shakes my hand and doesn't go mad. I wouldn't have minded because he's earned it, but it's a nice gesture.

Of course, I'm bitterly disappointed. I was in the driving seat and let it slip through my fingers. But it wasn't all down to me throwing it away—Peter hung in there, showed real grit and then delivered the knockout punch. I know I shouldn't have let him get within range after being 14–8 up but sometimes you can't keep a good player down. I let the pressure get to me but he applied it in the first place.

We head off to the casino again afterwards for another late-night breakfast. Pete and Chrissie are there and we have a chat. Chrissie says it meant a lot to her to see the two of us up on stage showing such good sportsmanship and camaraderie, and I know she's right.

SATURDAY 30TH JULY

The day of the final but we're going to head off early for home. I'm not sulking or anything but it's a long haul and the later we leave it, the more chance there is we'll hit traffic. It's been a good week all in all, so I'm happy enough.

The final's between John Part and Colin Lloyd, which is unusual because there's no Phil Taylor. John did him in the quarter-final—which just goes to prove Phil is beatable—and then went on to beat Peter in the semis.

Luckily, we get back in time to watch the final on the box. Colin produces a darts masterclass and I'm delighted to see him win it 18–12. I call him afterwards to tell him well done and that he thoroughly deserves it. Colin's a mate and I'm genuinely made up for him. Still, feel a bit sorry for John because after beating Phil he must have thought it was his day.

MONDAY 1ST AUGUST

August already! At this rate it'll be the World Championship again before I know it.

It's a quiet month on the tournament front, which suits me fine. We've had the keys to the new house for a while now but we still haven't moved in because there's a little bit more work to be done.

My brother-in-law Perry has been helping us out while we were in Blackpool and he's already painted every wall and skirting board in the place. All we have to do is put the finishing touches to everything.

My practice routine has gone out the window at the moment. I haven't set a board up in my new room yet and with there being no big tournaments coming up soon, my motivation isn't quite what it should be. I'll just have to rely on exhibitions to keep my arm in.

TUESDAY 2ND AUGUST

I've just seen the video for Justin Hawkins' new single... featuring Phil Taylor! The whole video's got a darts theme and Phil's in it all the way through. Guess I won't be having that beer and little game with Justin after all. Never mind, I didn't fancy a career in the music business anyway.

THURSDAY 4TH AUGUST

Head out today to buy filters and pumps for the fishpond that we inherited from the last owners of the house. Everything inside the house is done now, including the floors and we've moved a lot of the furniture and the like in. A couple more days and we'll be officially relocated.

FRIDAY 5TH AUGUST

Up north tonight for work. Whitby, North Yorkshire, to be precise. We leave at 12 and get to the venue, The Stakesby Arms, on the dot of eight. I have a white wine or two before kick-off (I'm on the wine because it doesn't seem to make me as hungry and I'm trying to keep the weight off) and then it's into the fray.

The pub is a real hardcore drinking hole slap bang in the middle of a housing estate. It's definitely not somewhere you'd go for a romantic night out. Not if you wanted to get anywhere that is. The locals are friendly enough but they seem more interested in getting me pissed than they do in seeing me throw some darts and I keep having to turn down free drinks because I'm not in the mood tonight.

Rather than head to a hotel as we'd planned, Donna decides she wants to get home tonight and insists on driving back. I worry about her, but I'm not stupid enough to argue when she's made her mind up. We stop for a coffee and an hour's kip half way back and she seems fine. We get back home safe and sound in the wee hours.

MONDAY 8TH AUGUST

We're finally in the new house. I won't tell you the address because it will only encourage throngs of gorgeous groupies and I'm a married man, you know.

I feel like a weight's been lifted off my shoulders. Moving house is never a lot of fun but when it finally goes through, you feel like you're on cloud nine, don't you? Looking back, maybe the stress of the house contributed to me feeling ill. Well, that's Doctor Mardle's diagnosis anyway.

I put up a brand spanking new board in the practice room in the afternoon. I love throwing at a new board—it's the crispness of it all. I suppose a new board in the new house is symbolic as well.

The new practice room is bigger than my old one, it's maybe 12 foot by nine and there's plenty of room for my board, as well as a desk and chair for the laptop. I didn't bother bringing the coffee maker and fridge from the old place because it's easy enough to nip downstairs to the kitchen and the stairs are good exercise. I put up my dartboard clock and some other pictures and I'm sorted.

WEDNESDAY 10TH AUGUST

Jesus. I've just had another letter from the DRA about that fine I got at the Premier League at Doncaster. I got the first letter just before we set off for Vegas and even though I wrote them a cheque out, I forgot to post it before we left. What with the move and everything, it has completely slipped my mind since. Problem is, I've missed the payment deadline and they've tacked on a 50% fine, so I now owe them £375. It's turning out to be an expensive little outburst. I'll post the cheque this afternoon. There's no way they're squeezing me for another penny.

THURSDAY 11TH AUGUST

Receive a couple of emails for bookings today. One is from a bloke in Germany who wants me to go over for the Oktoberfest beer festival in a couple of months. Now I'm not the biggest beer drinker in the world and I think three days of all that over there would absolutely kill me. I've got to get back to him with an answer by tomorrow. I'm really not sure what to do so I think I'll sleep on it.

FRIDAY 12TH AUGUST

I've decided against the Oktoberfest gig. It's decent money but I know it will be one of those weekends that go on forever, 24 hours a day. I email the guy, his name's Ralf, and tell him I can't do it.

Me and Donna are both still excited about being in the new house, even though we've realised it's crawling with spiders.

SATURDAY 13TH AUGUST

The football season starts today and I'm quietly optimistic about Spurs' chances for once. I know we're not going to win the title but we've made a few decent signings in the summer and we've got a young, exciting squad. Certainly makes a difference from some of the old donkeys we've bought in the past.

I really like the manager Martin Jol. He turned us around last season and we only just missed out on Europe, which is good going for us. Who knows, maybe we can make it into the Uefa Cup this season?

I'm like most Spurs fans. I just want something to cheer about and that's been in short supply in recent seasons. I'm fucking sick of getting shit from Arsenal and now Chelsea fans and just once I want to shove it back down their throats. We'll see but like I said, I've got a good feeling about the season.

We beat Portsmouth 2–0 at Fratton Park. Okay, Pompey are pony but we were away from home and it's exactly the kind of game we've lost in the past. I'm not going to get carried away but it's a decent start. Fingers crossed for more of the same please Martin.

In Southend tonight for what's going to be a bit of a different exhibition. It's a head-to-head challenge with an old mate called Terry Rose, who I used to play youth darts with in Essex when I was 14 and he was 16. We did all the holiday camp circuit and junior tournaments together and he played for England before me. Terry's a top player.

We get to the venue—the American Pool Shack—in plenty of time and it's a nice and relaxed atmosphere. There's plenty of old faces about the place and Terry's there with his mum and dad, Iris and Big Tel, who I haven't seen for what must be ten years. I have a chat with Terry and he's telling me he wants to go pro like I have. He's got the talent but I tell him it takes dedication as well and that's the only reason I've got where I am today.

The challenge is the first to 16 and despite being a little drunk, I go into the break 12–1 up. It's obvious Terry really wants to beat me but I'm not going to make it easy for him. When we come back I have a little wobble, Terry pulls a few legs back but I come out a 16–8 winner.

It's a top night but the thing I can't get out of my head is this bloody great big parrot sat on a perch in the bar. It's a great big African thing, it's probably worth a few quid and it spends the whole night squawking away and crapping everywhere. I just keep thinking, 'What the hell is a parrot doing in a pool hall?'

TUESDAY 16TH AUGUST

It's my last day off before a five-day tour of West Country, so I spend the time getting everything sorted for the trip. I'm looking forward to getting back on the road and it's a nice part of the country.

WEDNESDAY 17TH AUGUST

Me and Donna leave at 10 in the morning. I'm playing at the Wreckers Pub in Newquay tonight, so it's another long journey. The Wreckers is a strange kind of pub because the front of the place is all glass, so everyone can see what's going on from the outside. The interior's all open plan with the bar in the corner. Dark and dingy, it ain't.

We're staying above the pub, which is convenient, and apparently it's one of the last big nights there before they turn the place into a fish and chip shop.

We stop off at a Little Chef on the way (makes a change from Kentucky) but the traffic is horrendous when we get close to Newquay. The Ripcurl World Surfing Championship is on in town at the weekend and it looks like everyone has arrived early. By the time we get to the pub at gone five, the organiser, Pete Lindsay, is looking stressed out. I think he was getting worried I wouldn't turn up.

In the end, we've got plenty of time and have a couple of drinks with some of the locals before the start. I get talking to one fella and it turns out he's got 10 kids. Jesus—the guy deserves a medal.

FRIDAY 19TH AUGUST

A day off yesterday but back to work tonight in Wellington in Somerset. I'm playing at the football club but we're staying at a place called Greenham Hall, outside town. It's one of those big country homes with all the grounds and what not but I've got to say the room we get isn't up too much. It's a bit pokey for my liking and there's no TV either.

We check-in early and head off to country pub for lunch. I order a prawn othello for starters and steak and chips for main. The steak is blinding but trust me, if you ever get the chance to have a prawn othello, which is prawns wrapped in a really thin omelette, try it. You won't regret it.

We get to the football club in the evening nice and early and they've really made an effort. There's a 30-foot by 15-foot Hawaiian-themed backdrop on the stage, which looks great, and everyone is obviously up for it.

After the exhibition I do the usual Q&A session but one woman's questions really worry me.

"You've lost a bit of weight recently, Wayne."

"Cheers. Yeah, thanks for noticing. Yeah, I've shed a few pounds."

"Why have you lost your sense of humour as well?"

"Sorry?"

"People are saying you're not as funny as you used to be."

"Is that what you think?"

"Well, no. But that's what some people are saying."

"I didn't realise."

I really wasn't aware that's what people were thinking. I've got to admit I enjoy the showman reputation. Of course, first and foremost I want to be known for the quality of my darts but the entertainer tag doesn't do me any harm and it's definitely good for exhibition bookings. I'm always true to myself on the stage and it shocks me that some people think I've become dull.

Looking back, I may have been a little more restrained on stage recently but it hasn't been a conscious or deliberate change. I'm surprised no-one on the circuit has mentioned it before. I suppose I was feeling a bit stressed out before Vegas because my form was so poor and I just couldn't seem to turn the corner. Making such a bad start in the Premier League got to me as well and after a good World Championship, everything seemed to go downhill for a few months.

I've always said what you see is what you get with me and I suppose the last few months people have been seeing less of my extrovert side because I haven't been in tip-top form physically or mentally.

SATURDAY 20TH AUGUST

Leave Greenham Hall today to head off to play at the Truro Railway Club. I was there last year, so I know the people, where it is and what kind of night to expect. We're staying in the Brookside Hotel in Truro but before checking in we decide to walk around the town. It's a beautiful place in the summer.

The exhibition itself is really quiet, if I'm telling the truth. The place is busy enough but it's just one of those times when it doesn't quite spark. There's no rhyme or reason to why some nights go with more of a swing than others but tonight is definitely one of the more subdued ones.

SUNDAY 21ST AUGUST

We head off home tomorrow, so tonight's gig at the The Clipper Way Inn in Falmouth is the last of the mini-tour.

It turns out to be one of those strangely serious ones where everyone is more interested in seeing me get beat than having a laugh. There are some good local players on show, fellas who hit a few 180s between them, but it's a disconcerting atmosphere. I've said before, my aim is to entertain but you do sometimes get these nights that have this competitive edge. Still, it's their choice what kind of evening they want it to be.

To be fair, it does get a bit more mellow by the end, especially when one bloke sees one of my posters and rolls over for a chat.

"What part of Hawaii you from then?"

"Romford, mate."

"Romford in Hawaii?"

He's serious. I nearly piss myself.

CHAPTER EIGHT

The life & times of Sammy The Sturgeon

TUESDAY 23RD AUGUST

Remember that exercise bike I bought earlier this year? It's in my new shed now, but I'm going to get it out and set it up. Well, very soon anyway...

I bought four koi carp for the pond this afternoon. They're £50 a pop, which is a lot of dough, but they're beautiful things. You can buy little ones for as little as six quid while the bigger ones can go for £100 or more. One of mine is just under a foot long, silver and red and has this beautiful metallic finish to it.

In the evening I realise the taxman is going to want to see my returns by the end of next month, so I have a crack at the paperwork. Don't you just love doing your tax returns?

WEDNESDAY 24TH AUGUST

The Cleveland Arms in Wolverhampton tonight. Russ Bray is the MC, and it's a kind of round robin tournament with me, Colin Lloyd and two local lads, Darren Williams and Wayne Jones. The top two go through to the final.

It's an important night actually because Steve and Noel from Kasdon and their other halves Donna and Karen are going to be there, so I hope it all goes well.

Despite the best efforts of the M6, we arrive on time and everything goes according to plan. Well, not exactly because Wayne, who is ranked 30-odd in the world, beats Colin to reach the final to play me and then he beats me for good measure. In fact, he beats me off the board. Doesn't he know we're superstar professionals? This kind of thing just isn't on. Seriously though, fair play to Wayne because neither me nor Colin took our foot off the pedal at all. So much for the rankings.

Later on I get chatting to a young bloke who tells me he's interested in the psychology of darts and how players prepare for matches and wants to talk to me about it some other time. Now you know I'm curious about all that stuff as well, so I give him my email and hope he gets in touch. It could be a real eye-opener.

We don't leave the pub until two o'clock, which is usually the sign of a good night, and stop off for breakfast on the way. It's becoming a bit of a habit is this midnight breakfasting.

THURSDAY 25TH AUGUST

I buy *The Da Vinci Code* by Dan Brown today. I usually prefer sports biographies and psychology books but I thought I'd give it a whirl for a change. I think all the hype got to me but we'll see. I've no idea when I'll start it though.

Still haven't got the exercise bike out of the garage.

SATURDAY 27TH AUGUST

Going out tonight for a bit of a social one. Donna and her mates had planned a girl's night out but then decided they all wanted their partners to come along, so we head off to a place called Westlodge for I suppose what you call 'dinner and dancing'. Cabaret and music and not a single dart to be seen, which makes a nice change. Donna drags me onto the dance floor but I'm not a natural mover. The extent of my dancing is the stupid surfing moves I do to the *Hawaii Five–0* music when I'm up on stage. What you see there is my entire routine.

MONDAY 29TH AUGUST

It's the Bank Holiday today and believe it or not it's a beautiful, sunny day so we (me, Donna, mum and dad) head off to get some more fish for the pond. I think I'm getting a bit obsessed by fish.

I had my heart set on koi but I notice a sturgeon and decide I'll have that. Before now, if you'd said to me sturgeon, I'd have thought of caviar but the fish themselves are beautiful, even though they look a bit like little miniature sharks. They're £50 a pop too, but sod it, so I go to talk to one of the staff to check it'll be alight in my pond.

"What size pond you got?"

"Eight foot by 13."

"Yeah, that should be fine."

"Great, I'll have that sturgeon then."

"Have you got a waterfall."

"Oh yeah, no problem."

"A big one?"

"Well no, it's smallish."

"You might need an oxygen stone. Let me go and check."

What I find out is yes, I do need an oxygen stone (what a surprise!), they run off pumps and they're £35 a throw. So that's £85 all in for this one sturgeon. It better not die on me, I can tell you.

I'm going to call him Sammy.

WEDNESDAY 31ST AUGUST

Down near the Oval cricket ground today for the photoshoot for the cover of the book. Not sure having my ugly mug on the front is going to help shift many copies but then what do I know about publishing?

I bring my Hawaiian shirt and shorts with me while Justyn, who first approached me about doing the book last year and is editing the whole thing, brings this massive six-foot-six long replica dart (or the

'Mega Dart' as he calls it) for me to hold. I reckon I could use that as a gimmick at exhibitions, although I'm not sure it'll fit in the Picasso.

"Can I have the dart when we're finished here. Justyn?"

"How much?"

"What do you mean how much?"

"It cost me £600 to get this made up."

"Yeah, but what the fuck are you going to do with it afterwards?"

"Er, I dunno. Keep it in my living room as an ornament?"

"I'll give you £50 for it."

"It cost me £600, but you can have it half price."

The tight bastard won't budge. He's a nice fella is Justyn but he drives a hard bargain. He could talk for England as well. In the end, we agree I can keep it at my house but we're sharing ownership. I'm hoping he'll forget about in a couple of months and I'll get it for nothing.

So we get everything ready for the shoot, with sand on the floor to make it look like I'm on the beach and then I have one of those 'don't-I know-you-from-somewhere?' moments when the photographer walks in.

"Hello, I'm Wayne.

"I'm Paul. Nice to meet you."

"Do you have a blonde wife and two kids?"

"Whaaat?"

He looks a bit startled.

"Yeah, you've got a blonde wife and two kids."

"How the hell do you know that?"

"You live on Jubilee Avenue in Romford."

I used to live with my mum and dad on Jubilee Avenue about eight years ago and still visit regularly so I've seen Paul and his family there. He's a bit freaked out because it's such a coincidence.

FRIDAY 2ND SEPTEMBER

I know I'm getting a bit obsessed by the pond and the fish and what not but I really think there's something in the water like fish lice. I found a dead carp this morning, which is not a good sign, and I'm hoping this isn't the start of something sinister.

Practice for two hours in the afternoon, spending an hour and 40 minutes of it just on the double 16. I don't know why but I just haven't felt comfortable on it recently and the time spent does make me feel better. Hopefully it will pay off in the next tournament.

SATURDAY 3RD SEPTEMBER

Flying from Stansted to Edinburgh today for a gig in St Andrews tonight. The venue, The Stables, is only half and hour from Edinburgh, so even though it sounds like a long haul, it's a pretty easy journey.

A lovely young couple called Martin and Laura pick us from the airport at half two and take us to our hotel. We're staying at the Old Course Hotel at the golf club and it's everything I hoped it would be. Luckily, I'm not paying—it's £450 a night and I'm only a poor darts player—but it's a beautiful place with a real sense of history.

The best thing is that our bedroom window overlooks the famous Road Hole. The funny thing is I was looking at the same scene on my telly back in July as Jack Nicklaus walked up to the 17th at his last Open. It was very emotional and now here I am in person.

Martin and Laura pick us up at half seven. St Andrews is only a small place, so it doesn't take us long to get to The Stables and it's obvious straightaway it's going to be a good night. They're a fun crowd and sure enough everyone, myself included, have a great time. I think we finally leave at about three in the morning but I've had three or four too many by then, so I couldn't swear to the exact time.

SUNDAY 4TH SEPTEMBER

Jesus, my head hurts. I miss breakfast and I'm not feeling too clever at all. I decide to have a quick shower and go for a walk around the course before we leave. Everywhere is covered in thick fog but it's still a buzz to be walking on the hallowed turf. I'll never forget this.

We get a lift from Martin's mum to the airport and we're home by three in the afternoon. My head's still pounding but I have a game of poker while Donna puts the washing on and I lose £40. Not the best hangover cure.

TUESDAY 6TH SEPTEMBER

The kitchen fitters or designers or whatever you want to call them are in today to measure up. It's all going to be a bit more expensive than I thought but since I can't be arsed to shop around, I suppose I can't complain. Once they're finished, we're all done and dusted in the new house.

I try and keep out of their way so I head to my office to write a letter to the PDC about the new rankings system that they're going to implement in January 2007. It's the system PDC director Rod Harrington was talking to me about back in May where your ranking is solely determined by the prize money you earn. So if you're the fifth highest earner on the circuit, you'd be ranked fifth. Hard to understand, it ain't, but my problem with it is that winning the World Championship would all but guarantee someone the number one ranking. Obviously, it is the biggest tournament on the calendar but being number one should not be about winning one tournament.

For me, the number one player should be the guy who's performed the most consistently over the whole season. Colin Lloyd's the top-ranked player now because he does the business week in, week out—even more than Phil Taylor—and his ranking reflects that.

It probably won't make them change their minds but I put in all down in writing to the PDC anyway.

THURSDAY 8TH SEPTEMBER

Speak to a guy called Rob from the Dart Stop in America today about the backboard he's sent me for my practice room. You mount a back-board on the wall behind the board to stop you taking chips out of your plaster if you miss the board completely. Of course, I never miss but the same can't always be said for Donna.

Rob's giving it to me for free, bless him, but I had to get on the phone because UPS turned up with it today and then tried to charge me a £175 import tax. I sent them away because I think that's bang out of order as it's a gift but Rob's agreed to pay it for me. They'll be back round with it this week but I still think it's outrageous people are expected to pay import tax for presents and the like. It's taking the piss, isn't it?

Me, Donna, George Harris, his wife Maria and daughter Kelly head off to the Westcliffe Casino in the evening and for a change I play roulette rather than head for the cards. I win a few hundred quid, which will pay my entrance fees for a few tournaments at least.

FRIDAY 9TH SEPTEMBER

A marathon practice session. I've been letting it slip again recently so I put in a solid five-and-a-half hours today. My treble 19 is a bit off but I really enjoy the session anyway and I feel good about myself when I'm finished. I even resist the temptation to boot up the laptop and play poker.

SATURDAY 10TH SEPTEMBER

Off to Butlins in Minehead today. It's the first time I've worked there and they've booked me for a head-to-head with Ritchie 'The Prince of Wales' Burnett, the 1996 BDO World Champion, and I'm looking forward to it. Phil Jones, the Sky MC, is master of ceremonies and Ritchie's a top bloke to work with, so it should be a good one. It's all part of a sports-themed weekend with various exhibitions and Q&A sessions with the likes of Barry McGuigan, Geoff Hurst, Frank Bruno and Martin Peters.

Ritchie's known as the Prince of Wales because he's from the Rhondda and he's one of the most naturally talented players in the game. He comes across as one of the most intense players around but away from the cameras he's a nutter. He's the kind of fella who won't crack a smile during a match but he'll be the one stripped down to his pants, dancing like a monkey and singing "I'm the king of the swingers" on the karoake machine afterwards.

Takes us five-and-a-half hours to drive there. God knows how we actually manage to arrive on time because I do my level best to get us lost. Remember I've said before we've got a Sat Nav system in the car?

Well, the Minehead Butlins is on Warren Street but I enter Warden Street and neither me or Donna realise the mistake until we're in Somerset and wondering where the hell the camp is. Now, Somerset's a big county and by rights we should be miles off but it turns out Warren Street is only a few minutes down the road from Warden Street. How lucky is that? And how thick am I?

They've laid on a VIP room and while we're waiting to do the exhibition I have a chat with a few of my fellow 'performers'. Barry McGuigan's a nice bloke but he looks like he's made of iron—you can tell immediately he used to be a boxer. I also talk to Scorpio from Gladiators (remember her?), who offers me a slice of pizza. I turn it down of course.

Me and Ritchie are on after Graham Gooch, who finishes his Q&A session a bit early, so we're up on stage and doing the business. We're meant to do four hours but we don't even do two and we're soon back in the VIP room as they clear the stage for Bruno. I'm not complaining though because it means we'll head back tonight now rather than take them up on their offer of a free chalet.

We set off at six but get waylaid by a KFC for half an hour...

Talking of eating (badly), I've got to say I'm the lightest I've been for at least five years –16 stone one—and you can't knock that. I think it's because of being off-colour as well as not pigging out quite as much. I haven't been exercising at all but doing a bit in the garden and around the house recently obviously hasn't hurt.

When we get back at half ten-ish, there's a note on the doormat from our new next-door neighbour John saying he'd had to jump over our garden fence to save Sammy The Sturgeon. Apparently, he'd jumped out of the water and John spotted him flapping about on the grass. I'll have to thank him for that one. Time to put some precautionary, anti-suicide measures in place I think.

TUESDAY 13TH SEPTEMBER

They start the kitchen today and all the banging and drilling plays havoc with my practice routine. I manage 15 minutes before it drives me mad and I give up and go for a walk.

WEDNESDAY 14TH SEPTEMBER

I put some wire mesh around the pond to put a stop to any more of Sammy's tricks. Another couple of koi carp have died in the past couple of days and I'm starting to get really worried now. It's partly the money—two koi is £100 down the drain—but it's also because I don't want the rest of the fish to suffer. I'll see how it goes but if any more die I think I'm going to have to drain the whole thing and clean it.

THURSDAY 15TH SEPTEMBER

I try to put my fish worries out of my head for a while because I'm working tonight. The gig's at the Stafford Court Hotel in Market Drayton, Shropshire, and I want to make sure they get their money's worth.

The place is a tiny venue and there are 60 in, which makes it feel packed. It all goes off well but I have to say I have never heard so much swearing in my life in a venue. Now you may have realised I'm not exactly shy of the odd four-letter outburst myself every now and then but this lot turn the air blue all night, I can tell you. It would have made a sailor blush.

We're staying in a local Travel Inn (of course) tonight because I've got a gig at the Loughborough Students Union tomorrow in Leicestershire, so there's no point going all the way back to Essex. I'm starving after the exhibition but there's nowhere to eat (which is probably for the best) and we're in bed by one.

FRIDAY 16TH SEPTEMBER

Tonight's gig is a blinder. All I've got to do is hand out a few trophies for 20 minutes and that's it. We get there by seven but they don't need me until half ten, so we have a drink and watch the dancers, band and comedian they've laid on. It's not a bad way to earn a living, is it? A Students Union is a bit different to the kind of places

I usually work but I'll say one thing, students can tuck their beer away with the best of them.

The comedian's called Danny Blue and yes, he is. Very. He goes down a storm but he gets his biggest laugh completely unintentionally when he starts taking the piss out of darts players. "All you fucking lot do is drink and smoke before you go up to the hock." He means oche. Everyone is in stitches but I don't think he gets it.

I eventually do my stuff at about quarter to eleven and then me and Donna are back in the car, heading down the motorway and home by three. Nice.

THURSDAY 22ND SEPTEMBER

Working in St Neots in Cambridgeshire tonight with Freddie Williams, one of the Sky Sports callers. Freddie's retiring at the end of the year but he's still got one of those timeless voices that was just made for calling.

St Neots is only an hour-and-a-half away from us and Donna and Freddie's wife Pat both come along. It's the usual thing, 12 legs against some of the locals and a few presentations thrown in.

I've got to mention one of the local players there, a guy called Carl Tokens (as in gift). Now Carl's a rotten player if the truth be told but he's a living, breathing example of a gentle giant. The guy's six foot ten and weighs in at 28 stone but you really couldn't wish to meet a nicer fella. You should have seen the size of his hands though—when I went to shake them after our game I felt like a little schoolboy.

FRIDAY 23RD SEPTEMBER

Heading off to Newport today for a couple of days to play in the UK Open and Players' Championship. I won it last year so my hopes are high of a repeat performance.

We check into a Travel Inn early afternoon and the woman behind reception asks me for my autograph. I ask her if that means we'll get a reduction on the room but knowing my luck she'll probably charge us double.

The good news is there's a McDonald's next door to the hotel, so I'm already looking forward to breakfast tomorrow... oh yes, and to the Players' Championship.

SATURDAY 24TH SEPTEMBER

Up nice and early. Donna has a sausage and egg McMuffin, I have the Big Breakfast. Lovely.

The tournament is being held in the Newport Leisure Centre and I'm playing a lad called Gary Noonan, who I know from playing in the London SuperLeague.

To cut a short story even shorter, it's a disaster. It's my first tournament for four or five weeks and I'm as rusty as hell and I fluff every single big shot that comes my way. Gary plays steady, my concentration is all over the place and I'm out in the first round. I've made a right muppet of myself.

It gets worse because even though I do shake Gary's hand at the end, I then storm off in a huff, which is immature and unprofessional. I'm supposed to hang around and score for the next game on but I just flounce off in a mood. Luckily, Donna steps in for me and scores (she really is a diamond) but I'm already feeling a bit ashamed of myself. I really should know better than to behave like a spoilt brat at my age.

I do calm down eventually and we go out for a curry in the evening with some of the others. I have a madras, which isn't that hot, but another darts player there called Kevin Pearson ordered a vindaloo. Thing is, he doesn't want all his sauce and I offer to help him out with it.

SUNDAY 25TH SEPTEMBER

A bad case of Gandhi's Revenge this morning. I have to make five or six trips to the little boys' room because I'm scared to, ahem, pass wind. That'll teach me to be a greedy guts.

The UK Open today and I'm trying to put yesterday's game out of mind. My first game is against Paul Heston, who I played against donkey's years ago when he represented Lancashire and I was playing for Essex. Representing Lancashire proves you're no mug but I definitely seem to have got yesterday out my system (the game and the vindaloo) because I beat him comfortably.

Next up is Gary Welding. He smacked my arse in the World Grand Prix in Dublin last year and I owe him one. I couldn't hit the proverbial barn door then but today's a different story—five legs to two to me.

So I'm through to the last 16 where a certain Mr Taylor is waiting for me. Truth is, there's never a good time to face Phil and today's no different. I'm not nervous because he's the favourite to beat me but it is time I turned him over, so I'm up for it.

It's the first to five legs and although I take the first one, it's all one-way traffic after that and he wins it 5–1. That's the problem with Phil, if you start well and take the lead, it just makes him angry and he focuses even more. I did miss a few doubles but he's a worthy winner. The only highlight for me was hitting a double 16, which makes a change.

I haven't got any marking duties today, so I say my goodbyes and we hit the road.

Sitting in the car with Donna, I start to worry. Of course, there's no disgrace losing to Phil but I really could have done with picking up more ranking points than I did today. Sky and the PDC are choosing the players for next year's Premier League soon and only the top five in the rankings are guaranteed a place. I'm fifth at the moment but I desperately don't want to miss out on a place at the last minute. The Premier League is big news for darts. Anyway, they announce the five after next month's Grand Prix in Dublin, so I need a good performance there to be sure.

MONDAY 26TH SEPTEMBER

Remember that woman at the exhibition in Somerset last month who asked me while I wasn't being as entertaining on stage these days? I've been thinking a lot about what she said again and it's been bugging me.

Like I said, I don't put on the entertainer thing because I'm just being myself, but I've been thinking why I've been coming across differently recently. I've heard some people suggest it's because I've been trying to take things more seriously, but that's not it. I always take it seriously and it's not been a conscious move on my part to be less extrovert. I'm not deliberately being dull up there or anything like that.

But I can't pretend people haven't got a point about me seeming more subdued. They're not having a go when they mention it, so I've got to accept they are saying what they see.

The question is why I'm behaving differently? I suppose it's because I've been lacking in confidence and subconsciously that's been showing in my manner up on the stage. Maybe I haven't had the confidence in myself to jump around like a lunatic as much. It's not something I've planned, but I think that's it. The happier I am, the more I let myself go, and it's been the other way around lately.

TUESDAY 27TH SEPTEMBER

I've definitely got fish lice in the pond. They're minuscule buggers that stick on the fish and inject poison into them with little pincers. I pull loads of them off Sammy The Sturgeon, a couple more koi have died and I'm going to have to clean the pond from top to bottom. It's only the goldfish that seem fighting fit but then I reckon goldfish would survive a nuclear war.

Dad comes round at 11 to help me start draining the pond. We scoop all the fish into a sort of holding pool, one of those black plastic linings you can get for ponds, and by five it's drained. There's at least four inches of disgusting black gunk at the bottom and I reckon the bloke we bought the house from can't have cleaned it out once in the 17 years he had it.

WEDNESDAY 28TH SEPTEMBER

Wake up and go and check on the fish in the holding pool. Sammy The Sturgeon and a few more of the koi are dead. I feel guilty because I've no idea whether they had enough oxygen overnight but I didn't have a lot of choice. I feel like I killed them.

I fill the pond back up, chuck in a chemical tablet to make the sure the water's the right pH balance (or something) and hope for the best. I'll put the survivors back in tomorrow.

THURSDAY 29TH SEPTEMBER

What's left of the fish are back in. Fingers crossed the clean-up has done the trick but I'll have to wait and see. I'm gutted about all the ones that we've lost. Donna tells me they're only fish but it breaks my heart.

SATURDAY 1ST OCTOBER

I go out and buy two more sturgeons today. I've definitely been getting withdrawal symptoms since Sammy went to the big pond in the sky but I've no idea what to call them. That's it, though—if these two don't make it I'm not spending any more dosh on fish.

I practice in the afternoon and decide to go back to my old routine of concentrating on the treble 20s. I'm not exactly sure why but it just feels right to spend a bit of time on the 20s again. Maybe it's because I'm happy with my doubles (chance would be a fine thing!) or maybe I just need a change. I'm really not sure.

CHAPTER NINE

Missing doubles and hitting rock bottom

SUNDAY 2ND OCTOBER

Practice for four-and-a-half hours today in an attempt to get some more consistency in my game but I'm brilliant then crap, crap then brilliant throughout. If I'm honest, it's more crap than brilliant actually and although I feel loose and positive, I'm very up and down. At least I'm red hot on the double 16 though, which is encouraging.

I've been wrestling with the mental side of the game ever since I turned professional and one thought that comes to me today during practice is it's more important to think about what you're hitting rather than how you hit it. It might sound obvious but it really strikes me today if you don't worry about how you get the dart where you want, provided you hit what you want, then there's nothing to worry about, is there?

A lot of players will tell you that when they're not throwing well, they start to worry about how they are holding the dart. When things aren't going well, the dart doesn't feel quite right in your hand, even though you've held it in exactly the same way for maybe 20 years.

And that's what happens today. I'm throwing crap and I start thinking, am I holding the dart right? And that's the trap. If you're worrying about your grip, you're not concentrating as much as you should on where you're aiming. It's all too easy to be hung up on how you're throwing rather than what you're scoring. I reckon I need to think about that a bit more.

TUESDAY 4TH OCTOBER

Go to Romford dogs today to do a little interview for Sky and take mum over with me for a trip out. The interview doesn't take long, so I have plenty of time to have a couple of drinks and a few bets. Two of them come in, which pays for mum's two vodka and tonics (she can't drink any more than that, bless her) and the rest of the night. I'd also put a few quid on Hawaii 501 earlier, who was running over at Wimbledon. And what do you know? That came in as well, so maybe my luck's changing.

THURSDAY 6TH OCTOBER

Play a bit of poker on the laptop today and can't believe my luck. My bad luck that is. Let me talk you through it, cards fans...

My two hole cards are the ace and four of clubs, which are looking good when the flop comes in with the eight, ten and jack of clubs. Ace flush for Wayne, lovely.

The alarm bells start ringing though when the only other fella left in raises me. I'm still feeling confident but you never know. So he raises me, I raise after the flop and he raises it again after the turn card, which is the seven of spades. So now only a straight flush can beat me and I'm already counting my winnings when the turn card comes up and it's nothing—the two of diamonds. The fella then only goes all in. Obviously, I have to see him because I've come this far and he turns over the seven and nine of clubs. The bastard has got a straight flush! It's just wrong, I tell you. Pacific Poker is all wrong. I cannot believe it.

FRIDAY 7TH OCTOBER

Four-and-a-half hour crawl courtesy of the car park formerly known as the M1 to a place called Wem in Shropshire for an exhibition tonight.

It's a pretty standard night really, expect for one teenage kid in there who's clearly on a mission to piss me off. He's a pain in the arse all night and every time I'm about to throw he makes some noise or another to try and put me off.

"What's your problem, son?", I ask, as jovially as I can.

"Nothing."

"Are you going to shut up then?"

"Dunno."

"Tell you what, keep making that racket and I'll hit a 180 for you."

"Yeah, right."

He made some more noise and I hit the 180.

"How's your luck, brainy boy? How's your luck now?" He went quiet after that.

We head to Blackpool at the end of the night for the Bob Anderson Classic which starts tomorrow. It's no fun for Donna having to drive at this time of night but it's got to be done.

SATURDAY 8TH OCTOBER

I meet up with some of the lads—Andy Jenkins, Kevin Painter and Peter Manley—in the morning at the hotel to find out where today's venue is and catch up. The last 32 go through to the second day's play and I've got a tricky first round game in the shape of Andy Belton, who beat me in the Sheppey Classic this year. Andy's always a threat if you're not playing tip-top but this time around I play to my potential and I beat him 6–3 in legs.

I pull Ritchie Burnett in the second round but I definitely feel like I'm on a Mardle roll now and it's 6–3 to me again. That's me safely through to tomorrow and a job well done.

It's an early finish so me and Chris Mason head off to the pub to watch England's World Cup qualifier against Austria. It's not the best game to be fair but we win 1–0 and we're through to the finals in Germany next summer, so it's turning out to be a good day all round.

By the end of the game, we're a little bit the worse for wear but I'm back in the hotel by nine (via a local Chinese) and tucked up with Donna nice and early.

SUNDAY 9TH OCTOBER

I knew my luck couldn't last because I was just a little bit sick last night. It can't have had anything to do with the drink so it must have been the Chinese. Honest.

Saying that, I don't feel too rough this morning, which is just as well. My first game is against Matt Clark, who's known as 'Superman' because his name's Clark and he's from Kent. I'm really keen to build on a couple of matches yesterday and do well today.

To be fair, Matt has me running all over the board but doesn't hit his doubles, so I sneak past him. It makes a change when it's someone else who struggles with his finishes and I even hit a couple of double 16s. That practice seems to be paying off finally.

It's Roland Scholten in the quarters but he's never at the races and I'm through to the semi-final to face my old mate Colin Lloyd. I've got a good record against Colin but this time it's my doubles that go AWOL and I'm out. You can never be too gutted to lose to the world number one but I just wish I could explain why I can finish with my eyes closed in one game and then go totally to pot in the next one.

MONDAY 10TH OCTOBER

I've been booked for a gig in Manchester tonight, which is only a 50-mile stretch from Blackpool—another clever bit of forward planning on my part. We arrive at the club—the Irlham Steel Recreational Club—at seven and it's dead. By eight, it's heaving with about 200.

It's a top night, especially considering it's a Monday—which is usually a bit quieter than a Friday or Saturday exhibition—but I have to apologise for the way I throw in the first six legs. Embarrassing doesn't even come close and I'm half expecting them to ask for a refund. I do get better after that but really, it's appalling the way I throw at first.

John Gwynne raffles off a dartboard that was signed by all the players at the World Matchplay at Blackpool a couple of months ago. It fetches £430, which is going to the Boxing Day Tsunami appeal.

WEDNESDAY 12TH OCTOBER

Get a phone call from Bob Anderson today asking whether I've cashed my prize money cheque from the weekend yet. I ask why he's bothered and he tells me how the club we used was turned over on the Sunday after the final.

Apparently, the thieves must have known the club wouldn't have had a chance to bank the takings late on Sunday night, turned off the security cameras on the outside of the building and smashed open the metal doors at the back. Bob says they did tens of thousands of pounds worth of damage and nicked about ten grand in takings. He asks me not to cash the cheque for a week or so until everything gets sorted and I tell him no problem. What's the world coming to, eh?

Bob's the kind of fella who has done so much for darts and he's my favourite player because he's such a great ambassador for the game. He never steps out of line, he takes losing with a lot of dignity and basically he's a great role model for any kids taking up darts. He's been a top player for years, winning the World Championship in 1988, and that takes some doing. Bob's called 'The Limestone Cowboy' because he used to wear those cowboy shirts with the metal tips on the collars. I think he likes a bit of country and western as well.

FRIDAY 14TH OCTOBER

I'm flying to Holland today for a tournament called the Open Zwartewater. It's only for the weekend, which is a blessing, but it's a pig of a journey to get there and it goes something like this...

Drive to Stansted—40 minutes

Wait at Stansted—Two hours

Flight—One hour 10 minutes

Wait at Schipol—Two hours

Train from Schipol to Zwolle (no, I haven't made it up)—One hour 45 minutes

Taxi to hotel—45 minutes.

Like I said, a pig of a journey.

SATURDAY 15TH OCTOBER

The tournament starts at ten, so I'm up early and down for breakfast by half eight. I'm the only player down by this time and the others aren't missing anything when they serve up the usual cold boiled eggs and ham. I suppose you've got to go Continental but it's really not my thing.

I'm sat there on my own for 15 minutes when Kevin Painter comes in kitted out in his match shirt, demanding to know where the bar is!

Yeah, it's funny but it does make me think again whether we need to cut the drink out of darts. I've talked about it before and you know I'm not a teetotaller but I think something's got to give one day.

All the players like two or three drinks before they play to steady the nerves and a tournament like this weekend, with early starts, throws everyone out of synch. Drink or no drink, I reckon it's way too early to be playing, personally.

I'm not actually playing until 11.20 but it makes no difference—I lose three legs to one in the last 64 to an English guy called Tony West. He plays alright but I give mediocre a bad name and that's that. I've come all this way to get beat in my first game and pick up a cheque for £30. It's really not worth the effort.

Quite a few big names go out in the first round and there's some grumbling back at the hotel about the early starts and having no time to practice. I've got no sympathy—just get out of bed earlier if you want time to practice.

Anyway, I've got other things to worry about. I could really have done with the ranking points this weekend to make sure of my place in the Premier League and I've blown it. I'm drifting in and out of form again and I'm anxious about everything. I don't have to win the Grand Prix in Dublin to sort it out but I do need to do well.

SUNDAY 16TH OCTOBER

Set off for home in the morning and I can't wait to do that lovely journey in reverse. Me and Donna sit on the train to Schipol with Ronnie Baxter and take all his money at cards. He claims he's not feeling well but it doesn't stop him scoffing a double cheese burger, so I'm not convinced.

We get home at 5.30 and it's straight round me mum's for a roast dinner. None of that Continental nonsense.

WEDNESDAY 19TH OCTOBER

Practice all day from 11 in the morning until half eight in the evening. I have two hours on the board then a half hour off and I find a good rhythm to my throwing.

I go back to the routine where I start on the finishes. I kick off with the 81 to 90 finishes, then have a half hour on the treble 20s before going back to the 91–100 finishes and so on.

I finish up with round the board, going around the doubles in sequence but starting back at one if you miss with three darts. I go round twice without having to restart once, which is a sign of good concentration.

THURSDAY 20TH OCTOBER

The Grand Prix doesn't start until Monday but I've got an exhibition and a UK Open and Players' Championship in Ireland before then, so we're flying out to Cork today. Dad says he'll pop around and give the fish some food and look after Bubbles.

We're getting an early flight from Stansted, so it's pitch dark when we set off from home and Donna's got the right hump. She's not exactly a morning person.

We're in our hotel in Cork by ten in the morning and we have plenty of time before my mate Darryl, who's organised the gig, picks us up for the exhibition. He arrives at seven, tells us we're starting at eight and asks whether we want to have a drink at the hotel bar first. Now I know exactly where this is going because I've done exhibitions in Ireland before and let's just say the Irish aren't a nation of clock watchers.

So sure enough, we don't leave the hotel until gone eight. It's a 20-minute drive to the venue, we get there, have another beer (or dry white wine) and by nine there are still only five people in the whole place. Darryl's not in the least bit worried and sure enough by ten there's over a hundred packed in. We eventually kick off at twenty past ten, nearly two-and-a-half hours after the scheduled start time. But that's Ireland for you!

FRIDAY 21ST OCTOBER

I can't imagine why but I've got a bit of headache this morning. It must be all the fresh Irish air or the pillows in the hotel or something.

We have a lovely breakfast in the hotel—the Irish know a thing or two about a proper breakfast—and Darryl turns up a 11 to take us to Dublin. We're staying at the CityWest Hotel where all the tournaments are being held but luckily we're not in the main hotel but the golf hotel right next door. It's only five minutes walk away but we didn't want to stay in the main bit because it can get a bit rowdy in there of an evening.

SATURDAY 22ND OCTOBER

It's the Players' Championship today and I've got a guy called Steve Coote in the first round. I've beaten Steve at the BDO World Championship in the past so I'm not too fazed and looking forward to the match because I feel my preparation has been good.

Famous last words of course because Steve does me 5–1 and I fall at the first hurdle. It must be boring you to hear it as much as it does me to keep saying it, but I just couldn't buy a double. I had four, five, six darts in every leg at the double and didn't take advantage. It's driving me mad at the moment, it really is.

I retire to the hotel bar afterwards to drown my sorrows in Guinness. The only problem is Guinness gives me bad wind, so my apologies to all those people who I was sitting near.

Later in the night, Peter Manley brings his poker chips around and me and Donna clean him up a treat, coming first and second. I've got to say Donna is a great woman in many ways, but her greatest talent is definitely taking money off people (including me!).

SUNDAY 23RD OCTOBER

The UK Open today and things start badly when I go down for breakfast but commit the terrible crime of forgetting my meal voucher. The waitress in charge is less than impressed and to make matters worse she doesn't seem to speak a word of English. I've no idea what nationality she is, but Irish she ain't.

"Yeah, sorry, I've forgotten my ticket."

Silence.

"Can I get some breakfast?"

She points to the door I've just come through.

"I just want some breakfast."

Finally she replies: "No understand."

"Breakfast? Room 2129."

"Sorry?"

"Breakfast..."

"You got ticket?"

"No, that's what I'm telling you..."

In the end I had to write down my room number before she'd let me anywhere near the bloody sausages.

After a relaxing bite to eat me and Andy Jenkins walk over to the main hotel to get ready. I'm on at 12 against Jimmy Dunlop and I'm nervous as hell. Remember I was saying we should separate darts and drinking recently? Well, I've got to admit I have four cheeky wines before the game but at least it does the trick because I beat him 5–1. I'm still on edge but at least I'm over the first hurdle.

It's a wily old campaigner called Graeme Stoddart in the second round. Graeme's been around for years and he's one of these players who is either really, truly bad or he has a blinder.

Just my luck today's the day he's in great form and he's rattling off tons, 140s, tons all the way through and he beats me 5–4. I'm not terrible but I just can't find the extra gears to get my nose in front. Even then, I get two darts at the double to beat him and fluff them both.

I'm gutted about losing but even more worrying is the fact the Grand Prix, which starts tomorrow, is double start. That means you don't start scoring until you've hit a double and the way I've been finishing lately, I'm not exactly bursting with confidence. Stop thinking so much Wayne, stop thinking!

MONDAY 24TH OCTOBER

The big one. I'm playing Lionel Sams at eight tonight and even though I've beaten him comfortably in the first round of the last two major televised tournaments, my nerves haven't disappeared overnight.

I spend the day just trying to take my mind of the game and stop the nerves jangling. Have a game of cards with Donna, Peter and Chrissie and pitch up at the venue at five to practice and soak up some of the atmosphere.

I've made my mind up that I'm going to try and start with double 18 in every leg. Most players go for tops but I feel most comfortable with 18s, so that's that.

Great decision Wayne. I hardly miss a double 18 all match, score respectably once I get in and before you know it I've won it two sets to nil. Lionel doesn't really do himself justice, but I couldn't care less. The way I've been playing, a win is a win and I'm over the moon. Now that's what I call a stress buster.

TUESDAY 25TH OCTOBER

I'm not playing until Wednesday so it's a day off today and I just do the usual—mooching about, cards and eating too much.

WEDNESDAY 26TH OCTOBER

I've got Alex Roy in the second round tonight and it's going to be a toughie because Alex was very impressive in the first round. I'm even more nervous than I was on Monday and trying to relax is becoming a full-time job.

We're on at ten, so I arrive at six with Steve Beaton and have a couple of drinks and a chat. Steve used to be known as 'The Adonis' but it's 'Magnum' these days because of his striking resemblance to Tom Selleck. It's the 'tash that does it. Funny thing about Steve is he's this six-foot-three bloke with chest hair that would make a gorilla jealous but he's got the girliest laugh on the circuit. Tell him a joke and you'll see what I mean. Anyway, he's a diamond geezer and you'll never hear him saying a bad word about anyone. He won the BDO world title in 1996 but he earns an extra crust these days as part-time driving instructor.

The first two sets against Alex go like a dream. I don't miss a single double 18 and Alex can't compete with my scoring and I go two sets up. The second round is the first to three though and we have a break, which is where it starts going wrong.

When we come back my doubles have deserted me. I don't know whether someone's nicked them at half-time, they're hiding behind the back of the sofa or what but they've gone. Alex picks up his game and it's now 2–1.

I'm starting to get nervous now but I hit a double early on in the first leg of the fourth set, which settles me down and I'm off and running again. It's quite a comfortable 3–1 win in the end but I could certainly have done without that little scare in the middle of the match.

It's only when I get off the stage I remember that that's it. I'm in the quarter-finals and that guarantees me a place in next season's Premier League. You've probably noticed I've been getting stressed out by the whole Premier League thing of late so it's a weight off my shoulders. Nice one, son. I take Donna out for a few celebratory drinks in the evening and I feel great.

THURSDAY 27TH OCTOBER

Another day off today, so I chill out and watch Keith Rooney play

Dennis Priestley in the evening. I face the winner and it never hurts to see who's in a bit of form. Dennis edges it 3–2 in the end and he looks in good nick. Dennis is a fighter whatever kind of form he's in, but he looks confident at the moment. It's going to a battle tomorrow.

FRIDAY 28TH OCTOBER

Spent the day doing nothing much as usual in preparation for a quarter to eight start. I know Dennis is playing well and if he's at his slowest best, I'm in trouble. Dennis plays slow naturally and that can play havoc with my rhythm.

Sure enough the first set (it's first to five) is like watching paint dry and he takes it 3–1. I bounce back in the second to level up but then he goes from slow to full stop and I just can't cope. I reckon it takes him 40 seconds to throw his three darts whereas its taking me about seven and I lose the plot. Dennis wins seven legs out of eight and he's through to the semi-finals as a 4–1 winner.

Now don't misunderstand me, Dennis doesn't do a thing wrong. He's entitled to play how he likes and let's face it, it produced the required result. I don't think it's much of a spectacle for the crowd and it's my job to come up with a solution to that kind of style. He hasn't been world champion twice for no reason.

I say to him when we shake hands at the end that he did a proper job on me and he nods. I think it's called experience.

Me and Donna don't hang about for long after the match. We head back to the hotel, order a pizza and book an earlier flight home. As soon as my head hits the pillow I'm asleep.

SATURDAY 29TH OCTOBER

We get a lift to the airport for a three o'clock flight and decide to go for a McDonald's at the airport to kill some time and also because I'm a greedy pig.

I'm sitting there eating my Big Mac (why do they never really stay in the bun by the way?) when this Irish fella comes over and starts the usual chit chat.

"You're Wayne Mardle, aren't you?"

"Yes, that's me."

"Can I have your autograph?"

"Well, I'm eating at the moment."

"Right, right. Can I shake your hand?"

"I'm eating just now."

"Sure. OK. I'll come back in ten minutes."

Of course, he comes back precisely ten minutes later. I'm on my filet-o-fish by now (well, one Big Mac is never quite enough, is it?) and starts the whole conversation up again without any sorries for interrupting or anything. I just can't believe how rude some people can be sometimes. Or maybe I'm just in a bad mood.

We board the plane a little later and we're sitting there waiting to take off when there's an announcement:

"This is the FR296 Dublin to Stansted flight..."

Suddenly a fella gets up and says "296? I want the 286!" and starts panicking. Now you tell me how can you get on the wrong plane? You've got be fairly thick, that's for sure. But how did he get through all the checkpoints without someone saying, "Sorry, fella, you want that one."

The guy's bag then has to be taken off the plane, which means we're sitting on the tarmac for another 20 minutes. Just when we think we're on our way, there's another announcement...

"I'm sorry ladies and gentlemen but we'll be delayed a little longer because two passengers on 286 have realised they should be on this flight..."

Somebody, somewhere, must be taking the piss. Is this Idiots Day Out or what?

We finally get home to sunny Essex at seven and, after eight nights away, it's lovely to be back.

I start thinking back on the Grand Prix and it makes me realise I've still got a lot to learn. I've been playing darts for donkey's years but I've only been a proper pro for a little while and I don't know it all yet. I'm not going to forget the lessons I learned going out to Dennis that's for certain.

What's annoying me most is I knew he was going to slow it down and I still fell into the trap. It wasn't as if it was a shock. I know other people will try and slow me down in the future and I've got to be able to deal with it. There's no way I can make players like Dennis speed up, so I've got to learn to be patient and kill time between my throws without getting frustrated or annoyed. Maybe I'll take a book up on stage with me next time I play him!

SUNDAY 30TH OCTOBER

I watch the Grand Prix final on the telly tonight. It's Colin Lloyd versus Phil Taylor and because Colin's a mate, I'm sad to report he gets stuffed. Seven sets to one. You can see Colin's head goes down early and if you do that against Phil, you've had it. We've all been there before. Phil sees that and he goes in for the kill. He really is like a predator in that respect. One sign of weakness and he's got you.

Colin looks really down in his interview after the match, which is a shame because he's had another good year. He's got nothing to beat himself up about.

WEDNESDAY 2ND NOVEMBER

A bad day today. It's the second anniversary of the premature death of Donna's sister Dionne. Dionne was at her brother's house when it happened. She fell asleep on the sofa and an hour later they noticed she'd turned a funny colour and called an ambulance. They rushed her to hospital but she never woke up again. She just died in her sleep, bless her. She was only 22. They did all the tests they could think of to determine the cause of death but couldn't come up with an explanation.

It just proves you never know what life is going to throw at you, doesn't it? It doesn't make any sense, that's for sure.

Donna's really going through it today because she was close to Dionne and she's gone to be with her family. The rest of the family get together in the evening to have a drink together. It's everyone's way of showing some respect. It's times like this that make you realise how lucky we all are.

FRIDAY 4TH NOVEMBER

I'm flying up to Irvine in Scotland today for a Players' Championship on Saturday and another regional UK Open on the Sunday. I'm not happy about having to shell out for the flight because it's not like I'm earning much recently from the tournaments. I've got to watch the pennies at the moment.

I'm optimistic even though I know I've been playing in fits and starts lately. I do feel my form's there but it's just that I'm not getting anywhere.

Rod Harrington, Colin Lloyd and Roland Scholten are already playing cards when I get to the airport and obviously it would be rude of me not to have a game or two with the boys. Usually we only play for small stakes, three quid a pot or something like that, but today they're higher and I end up nicking £50 off Roland. Colin and Rod also take money off him, so he's gutted and well out of pocket. I keep telling him the Dutch can't play cards but he won't listen.

We're only in the air for an hour before we land at Glasgow Prestwick and it's straight into a taxi and check in at a trusty Travel Inn. Where would I be without them?

SATURDAY 5TH NOVEMBER

Remember, remember the fifth of November? Hopefully the Scots will see some Mardle fireworks today.

The hotel's only five minutes from the venue—a place called the Magnum Centre—so I get there nice and early to check out the draw for the Players' Championship. I'm playing a lovely fella called Tony Smith from Hertfordshire.

I've played Tony plenty of times before, so I know what to expect, but the way I'm throwing at the moment anything can happen. Which, of course, it does.

It's first to three sets and I don't feel comfortable with myself from the start. It goes two legs apiece in the first but then I have 12 darts at double top for the set and miss the lot. Tony takes it and I've got a horrible feeling it's going to be one of those days.

I take the second set comfortably enough but he steals the third off me. No disrespect to Tony, who's playing well enough, but I'm throwing like a prize loser and suddenly something goes off in my head.

"That's it."

"What?"

"I've had enough."

"What's the matter?"

"Your match, Tony. I can't take any more of this."

"What's the problem?"

"It's your game. I've had it."

And that is it. I shake Tony's hand and walk off. I've never walked away from a game in my life but I do today. Even as I'm walking away, I know it's the wrong thing to do but my head's gone. I just can't handle playing this badly when I know what I'm capable of. It's a nightmare. Why the fuck am I throwing like a wanker? A ten-year-old could beat me at the moment.

I go straight back to the hotel and start brooding. Am I practising too much? Am I practising enough? Why am I going to pieces? I know it's not the end of the world but it feels like it. Maybe I'm just thinking about everything too much? I think you can over analyse things and my head is all over the place at the moment. I just don't know but it's obvious something's not right. It's not going to get fixed today but it needs sorting sooner rather than later.

SUNDAY 6TH NOVEMBER

Wake up feeling miserable, which is Donna's cue to tell me a few home truths; home truths being a bollocking. She never tells me what I want to hear—she tells me what I need to hear.

"Stop being a twat."

"I know, I know."

"You made a right fucking prat out of yourself yesterday."

"I know, I know."

"This is a job. You can't just walk out because you don't fancy it."

"I know, I know."

"I want you in there today with a smile on your face. No excuses."

She's right too. I behaved like a stroppy teenager yesterday. I got the hump because things weren't going my way. Simple as that. If I'm going to sulk every time I play badly, I might as well pack it all in. I've got to be big enough to take it or I'll end up hanging myself.

Donna is a real star. She could do with swearing a bit less but she knows exactly when to be cruel to be kind and when to keep quiet. Today I need both barrels and she knows it. It's easy to lie to yourself when there's no-one around to pull you up but you can't get away with it when you've got someone like her around. Thanks to her, I can safely say my head is firmly out of my backside.

So, back to the darts. I've got Trevor Colin in the first round of the UK Open. I don't know much about him but I'm really not interested in who I'm playing today. Win or lose, it's all about the way I throw.

Turns out to be win. He's decent enough but I finally do a reasonable impression of a competent darts player and beat him five legs to nil. I can't say I'm on fire but it's good enough to go through and after yesterday, I'm happy enough with that. It's all stepping stones, isn't it?

I'm up against Lee Palfreyman in the second round and it's not going to be a walkover because Lee's a solid player. He knocked over Roland in the first round, which tells you he's someone to be respected.

It's nip and tuck all the way and we're locked at four legs apiece. Thing is, he has the throw in the last leg and he makes it count to beat me 5–4.

To be honest, I can't say I'm gutted. I've got no idea what form I'm going to produce in a match right now and the truth is I played okay. Normally I should be beating players like Lee but nothing feels particularly normal at the moment. I'm not happy losing any game but I'm trying to be realistic. Today was better than yesterday and hopefully tomorrow will be better than today. That's the only way I can look at it.

We head off to the airport for the flight home and I've got the keys in the front door by ten, which isn't too bad. All in all, it's been a crap weekend but I'll try not to dwell on it. Look to the future, Wayne, not the past.

CHAPTER TEN

The less I practice, the better I get

TUESDAY 8TH NOVEMBER

Get a phone call this afternoon from a mate of mine called Peter Dillingham. It's bad news. A mutual friend, Jimmy Grannahan, died this morning. They think it was a heart attack.

Before I turned pro, about six years ago, I used to play for the Old Oak in Hampstead in London. Jimmy ran the team and to persuade me to play he always organised a cab to pick me up and take me home and he paid for my beer.

I eventually had to give it up though. I was getting the train to work in the morning, toiling away all day and then going straight out to play. I was getting home at gone two and it was all getting too much. I loved playing for Jimmy and I had a good record for the Old Oak—I think I only lost twice in three years—but something had to give eventually.

Jimmy was the kind of fella who could always lay his hands on what you wanted. So if you walked into the pub and happened to mention you were looking for a Play Station for your boy, he'd pipe up and say he'd get you one at a good price. He always made a few quid for himself in the process but no-one ever minded.

He was only 51 and I'm going to miss him. I dread to think how his family are feeling. Just goes to show that you can plan for tomorrow but sometimes tomorrow never comes.

THURSDAY 10TH NOVEMBER

I've consciously been practising less this week because I haven't felt any real benefit from spending hour after hour at the board lately, but now I've come to a big decision—I'm going to do away with practice altogether!

I really mean it. I'm not going to throw at all unless I'm doing an exhibition or in a tournament between now and the World Championship. Yeah, it's a bit of a gamble relying on exhibitions to keep my arm in but things haven't been going well recently and I've got to do something to break the cycle.

It might sound like a crazy idea but I think it's got to be worth a try. I've been throwing so badly that something's got to give. I've tried to practice through the bad patch but it hasn't worked and the way I see it this is the only other option. At least this way I'm not going to be winding myself all the time, agonising about why I'm in such poor form. I'm hoping a non-practice regime will help me switch off a bit and relax.

FRIDAY 11TH NOVEMBER

I'm going over to Holland this weekend. There are two Players' Championships over the two days and fingers crossed I can do a job.

Donna's not coming with me because she's got the girls coming round to see the new house, so I'm on my own for the weekend. Well, not quite on my own because I'm sharing with Colin Monk to save money. Dear, oh dear, I've swapped my beautiful wife for a bald bloke. I think I've made a mistake.

I fly from Stansted to Schipol as usual. Suzanne picks me up at four and we drive to the Tulip Hotel in Lisse. All the usual suspects are there so I have a few beers and chat. Most of the conversation is about

Jimmy Grannahan, who was well known and liked. Everyone's gutted by the news and we raise a glass or two to him.

SATURDAY 12TH NOVEMBER

I got an early night last night, so I get up for breakfast feeling happy with the world. Ironically, I'm playing Tony Smith again in the first round but I won't be walking off until the end this time. I still feel a bit embarrassed about what happened last week, so I'm psyched up for this one.

It's a bit of a strange match in truth. Like I've said before, Tony's a genuinely nice fella and throughout the game he's saying "nice shot" or "good darts" or whatever when I hit a big score or take out a double. Now if someone else did that, I might think they were playing silly buggers or trying to wind me up but Tony's not like that all. He really means it.

Anyway, the funny thing is that I start to congratulate him when he throws a good shot. I've never done that in my career but suddenly I'm chatting away to Tony as we play. I don't even realise to start with but as the match progresses, I notice I'm talking as much as he is.

It seems to help my concentration and I win it three sets to nil. Now explain that one to, will you? Exactly a week ago I couldn't hit a barn door against Tony and now I've beaten him easily on very little practice. There's just no rhyme or reason to this game sometimes. Maybe I should chat with all my opponents.

I'm down to play a guy called Dave Jowett in the next round but before then there's a bit of a drama in the hall when Raymond van Barneveld turns up. If you remember, Raymond's with the BDO rather than the PDC but this is one of the tournaments on the calendar when they allow 'outsiders' to play as long as they don't mind paying a higher entrance fee. So Raymond's entitled to turn up and it's no surprise really because he is Dutch and we are in Holland.

The problem is he's turned up in jeans and trainers. PDC tournament rules state that players have to wear trousers and shoes, so there's a bit of an argument about whether they'll let him play. In the end, they cave in, Raymond's happy and there's an announcement on the tannoy saying anyone turning up in trainers tomorrow definitely won't be allowed to throw. Talk about one rule for him and another for the rest. Personally, I think the organisers bottled it and should have stuck to their guns. For me, he shouldn't be allowed to play. I don't care who it is.

But back to the darts. I beat Dave Jowett 3–2 and then I knock over Steve Maish 3–1 before Ritchie Burnett turns me over 3–1 in the last 16.

It's a good run to be fair and I'm not going to lose any sleep over getting beat by someone like Ritchie. The guy's a top pro and although I'd expect to beat him if I was on top form, I'm content enough with my day's efforts. I know my world ranking (I'm sixth at the moment) means I should be making the quarter-finals at least of tournaments like this but you settle for less when you know you're not really clicking.

I head back to the hotel bar with Colin Monk and a few of the other lads. There we meet up with Andy Jenkins and things start getting messy. We've all already had a few and we sink more in the bar and start getting a bit loud. Andy and Colin buy a round of local liquors called Jaegermeister, which is a disgusting liquorice flavour. So disgusting, in fact, that I have to spit it back into the glass.

Then me, Colin, Jamie Harvey and a bloke called Raby Bain, who sponsors Alex Roy and Dennis Ovens, decide to head off to Amsterdam for a nose around.

Jamie's Scottish and his nickname is 'Bravedart'. Now I'm not saying everyone from Scotland is mean but Jamie's got to be the tightest man I've ever met. He'll do anything to save a bob or two and he'll always book a hotel for £30 that's 20 miles from a venue if the rooms nearer by cost £45 or whatever. I first realised he was tight about six years ago when we were playing at a UK Open in Newport. Jamie's walking through the bar in his cowboy boots holding two brandy and cokes when he slips on the wooden floor. He falls flat on his back but I swear he didn't spill a drop from either glass.

So we hit a few bars but stay clear of the cafes selling the wacky backy. I'm a good boy after all and I don't smoke anyway. We get a bite to eat and then wander around the city. I've got no idea how it happens, but we end up strolling through the red light district. I'm sure Colin's holding the map upside down.

It's all part of the touristy thing to do when you're in Amsterdam but every time I see it, it reminds me that some people really have no shame. You see blokes doing deals with the girls in the windows and everyone else is stood there watching them. Talk about doing your dirty washing in public. It is fascinating wandering about Amsterdam but it always makes me feel embarrassed and seedy as well. I don't think I'll come back again. But then again I might.

SUNDAY 13TH NOVEMBER

A sore head and the second Players' Championship today. I beat Mark Thompson 3–0 in the first round and a fella called Bob Avenell in the second before Steve Maish demolishes me 3–0 in the last 32. There it is again, that unpredictability of the game. I beat Steve easily yesterday and today the tables are well and truly turned.

Steve goes on to reach the final—he gets beat by some bloke called Taylor, P Taylor I think—so I'm not too disappointed. At least I got beat by someone in good form rather than beating myself.

Overall, it's been a decent weekend and my confidence is a little higher than when I started. I'm still not pulling up any trees but I'm not a soft touch either. It's progress I suppose, although there has to come a time when I stop progressing and actually my hit top form again. Don't ask me when that will be, although some time during the World Championship would be nice.

The tournament's a little over a month away now and I'm thinking about it more and more. It's the ultimate stage for any player and it's the chance to show what you can do to a wider audience than you usually get on the circuit. I'm excited rather than nervous at the moment but the pressure will build when it gets closer.

I'm going home tonight and I can't wait. I can't face the prospect of spending another night with Colin. He hasn't stopped moaning on about how much he misses his missus Kirsty and it's driving me mad. He's like a lovesick puppy.

The flight touches down at Stansted at nine. Donna's there to pick me up and we head home for an Indian and a cuddle on the sofa.

WEDNESDAY 16TH NOVEMBER

Do a nice bit of business today to offload a few of my Hawaiian shirts that aren't selling. Now I'm not saying darts fans are bigger than your average sport fans but I've got 35 small shirts that I just can't seem to shift, so I'm selling them as a job lot at a discount to Pauline Raby, who runs a company called JR Darts. She gets a good price and I'm happy to get them off my hands.

THURSDAY 17TH NOVEMBER

Heading to Great Yarmouth today for the Vauxhall Holiday Park Classic. Donna, mum and dad are coming along, so it should be a good weekend.

It's been a good tournament to me in the past. I've won it five times in eight years beating the likes of Colin Lloyd, John Part and Chris Mason in the finals, so I'm optimistic about my chances.

We stay at the holiday park but now I'm a top 16 player we get to stay in a chalet rather than a caravan, which is a result. The caravans are bloody freezing at this time of year and the chalets are much cosier. They've got TVs (and a TV and video in the main bedroom), microwaves, hot showers, the lot.

FRIDAY 18TH NOVEMBER

The tournament is meant to start at 12 with the draw at half 11 but when we turn up it's all a bit of a shambles. The practice boards don't go up until 11, which is useless, and the draw is late and doesn't finish until quarter to one. Now I know it's a tough job to organise a big tournament like this—there are 128 players entered—but we're meant to be a professional sport these days and it's just not on. How can we expect people to take us seriously when we can't get our own house in order? It's not good enough.

I eventually get drawn against a young kid called Steve Smith in the first round. I used to play with Steve in the Essex Super League and he's been a bit of a bogey player for me in the past. He's only 26 is Steve and he always seems to raise his game when he plays me.

I didn't need to worry though because I beat him five legs to nothing. I'm not going to get carried away because it's only the first round but you can't knock a whitewash, whoever you're playing.

The next round also goes well and I beat a fella by the name of Jim Withers 5–2 to go through to the last 64 and play my old room-mate Colin Monk. This is where it gets serious.

Colin gets off to a good start and it's obvious he means business. It's the first to five legs again and even though I peg him back to 4–2, he's hitting the doubles more consistently than me and he runs out the winner. My form's there but my finishing is back to its erratic worst. Another acceptable but frustrating day.

For the record, Colin Lloyd wins the final, beating James Wade pretty comprehensively to pick up a cheque for £2,400. He really is Mr Consistency on the circuit this season.

SATURDAY 19TH NOVEMBER

Yesterday was the main event but today there's the open singles, first to five legs. It's a bit of a lottery to be honest and anyone can win it.

We play in one of the dingy backrooms on the park and I'm on the worst board in the place. It's a free-standing board mounted on a steel frame with wheels on the bottom and it can be positioned anywhere you like. The one I'm playing on is right next to the door to the gents. Every time someone opens the door, I get a blast of icy, smelly air. There are also kids running around everywhere asking their dads for 10p for sweets and the rest of it, so a darts paradise it is not.

I get through to the last 32 but get beat by a fella I've never heard of in my life, Ryan Something his name is I think, but I'm really not bothered. Today's a bit of fun really and the bloke's on fire. I hit two

180s in one leg and still lose it, which tells its own story, but at least I can go mad with the £20 I make for getting this far. Shall I go for a new car or dream holiday home?

My decision to stop practising doesn't seem to be paying off yet but I'm going to stick with it. I'm happier in myself at least and I want to give it longer to see what happens.

SUNDAY 20TH NOVEMBER

It's the mixed pairs and mixed triples today, which means me and wifey are teaming up. Me and Donna are notoriously bad at the mixed pairs, so let's just say my expectations are not sky high.

To my (and everyone else's) surprise, we actually make it through to the quarters before Wes Newton and Michelle Jackson, who is Peter Manley's step-daughter, put us out of our misery. Donna's happy enough and we haven't had a row so far, which is a bonus.

In the evening we go to the end-of-tournament disco and I have a few vodkas. Just to be sociable. I'm obviously being too sociable because Donna says she's had enough and drags me back to the chalet before midnight.

MONDAY 21ST NOVEMBER

Got a bit of a headache this morning and can't think why. For some reason Donna's not being very sympathetic, so I have to suffer in silence.

We head home and the hangover, I mean headache, eventually feels better.

TUESDAY 22ND NOVEMBER

It's Jimmy Grannahan's funeral today but I've decided not to go. I'm genuinely not feeling the best anyway but the truth is I really don't like funerals. Who does?

THURSDAY 24TH NOVEMBER

The Darts Regulation Authority have announced today that they're introducing drug testing into the game. They've come to an agreement with UK Sport, who'll carry out the tests, and it's all part of the drive to get darts officially recognised as a sport. The tests will be taken randomly during tournaments and the new rules come into effect on 1 January 2006.

To be honest, I don't think it's going to make much difference. Darts has never had a problem with drugs. I've never, ever heard of a player using any illegal drugs to improve their performance and I'll be gobsmacked if they come up with any positive tests. Darts just doesn't have a drugs problem.

The interesting detail in the announcement is the fact they won't be testing the players for alcohol. I've said before, I'm all in favour of reducing the amount players are allowed to drink before a match because I think it would do the image of the game a power of good. You know I like a drink as much as the next man but I'm not being a hypocrite. As things stand, I'm not going to shoot myself in the foot and go on the wagon when everyone else is still drinking before they play. But if the rules changed, I'd support them all the way.

The DRA have missed a trick here. Testing for drugs is a waste of time and they've decided to turn a blind eye to the one substance the game does have a genuine problem with.

FRIDAY 25TH NOVEMBER

I'm off to Holland today for some exhibitions. It's the first time I'll have been over for exhibition work since January and although I can't honestly say I'm looking forward to it, I'm not dreading it either. It's not as if I've got much choice anyway—if I'm going to stick with this no practice experiment I need more exhibitions to keep my eye in.

Donna's not coming with me—she's jetting off to New York for my sister's 40th birthday—so I need to be working to pay for all the shopping she'll be doing. It doesn't bear thinking about really.

I'm flying from Heathrow rather than Stansted for a change but I soon regret it. I get on the plane with no problem, get settled down, and what have you, when the loud speaker comes on:

"Ladies and gentlemen welcome on board. We hope you enjoy your flight today. We have just received our take-off slot and should be leaving Heathrow at 1.15."

Problem is it's only ten past 11! We're stuck in the plane on the tarmac for two bleedin' hours before we even get off the ground and to cap it all it's snowing in Holland when we land. God, I hate travelling.

Suzanne and Russ Bray pick me up at the airport but the weather is so bad that the hour-long drive to a place called Steenwiyk, where I'm working tonight, takes three hours. Have I mentioned I really hate travelling?

The night at least goes down well. I haven't worked with Russ for a while, so it's good to see him again, and the locals seem to enjoy themselves. The organisational skills of the Dutch sometimes leave something to be desired but it runs surprisingly smoothly and everyone's happy.

SATURDAY 26TH NOVEMBER

It's only an hour's drive to tonight's venue. I couldn't tell you where the hell it is—I leave that sort of thing to Suzanne—but the place itself is really a billiards club with a few boards up around the side.

There are about a 100 people in, which isn't too shabby, and again everything's pretty routine. Routine that is except for the obligatory weird conversation with a local. This time it's a mad woman.

"Can I have your shirt?" she asks.

"The one I'm wearing?"

"Yes, I'll swap you mine."

"I don't think so. I'd never get into it. You're tiny."

"I really want your shirt."

"I would but I'll never fit into your shirt. I can't go around topless for the rest of the night, can I?"

It takes me about a quarter of an hour to explain to her it's not a great idea before she finally lets it go. Pink's not really my colour anyway.

SUNDAY 27TH NOVEMBER

Today is going to be the day from hell. I've got to fly back to Liverpool, get across to Manchester for an exhibition, catch a night bus down to London and then jump on a train to Romford. It's going to be a nightmare.

I get up at eight, the driver picks me up at nine and I check in with easyJet at half ten. It would be a lot easier going direct to Manchester but I couldn't get a cheap flight and I'm not shelling out hundreds extra for the sake of it. We take off at half one, land an hour later and then I've got to get a bus from Liverpool to Manchester Piccadilly.

I've got two hours to kill in Manchester, so I grab a sandwich, read seven or eight papers back to front and then head off in a taxi to the venue, which is Frayne's Snooker Club in Hyde. They'd told me it was only three miles but the cab costs me £20, so the day's going from bad to worse. Of course, when I arrive the place is completely deserted and I'm hanging around for half an hour until a fella called Adam shows up.

I do the business, we finish at just gone 11 and John Gwynne gives me a lift back to the bus station. I've got more time to kill because my coach doesn't leave till quarter past one, so I ask some Romanian mother and her son to look after my bag (well, they look trustworthy to me) and I go for a wander. The journey's utter crap because I'm sandwiched between two snorers, so I don't get a wink and we finally get in to London Victoria at sixish. Then, it's the Victoria Line to Liverpool Street, a McDonald's breakfast, the train to Romford and a cab from the station home.

I walk in the front door at half seven, which means I've been on the road in one way or another for 23 hours straight. All for £450.

I'm knackered, pissed off and I fall asleep as soon as my head hits the pillow.

TUESDAY 29TH NOVEMBER

Donna's back later today but before I get to give my wifey a kiss and a cuddle, I'm heading down to the new Ladbrokes bookies shop in

Collier Row, which is only a ten-minute walk. They've asked me to open the shop and it's on my doorstep, so I thought why not?

When I get there, they give me a free £100 bet on the World Championship as a publicity stunt. Players aren't usually allowed to bet on tournaments but this is for charity and I go £50 each-way on Adrian 'Jackpot' Lewis. Adrian was 80/1 a few weeks ago but he's shortened to 20s now and I reckon he could be the dark horse. The kid's raw but he's got all the talent you need and I wouldn't be surprised if he makes a name for himself this year. They've got me at 20s as well, which is a bloody insult considering he's a rookie and I'm in the top ten, but I'm not going to let it bother me.

Donna gets home from America in the afternoon and says she's got a sore throat but had a whale of a time. She can't have missed me that much though because she's back out of the door in the evening to play darts with the girls. So much for absence making the heart grow fonder.

THURSDAY 1ST DECEMBER

John Gwynne's organised an exhibition at the Pendleton British Legion in Salford for tonight and since we're up in Manchester, we're playing on a log-end board again.

The thing with log-ends is that doubles are all important so I'm well chuffed because it will be a good test of my finishing. The log-end doubles are about half the size of the doubles on a normal board, so there's not a lot of margin for error.

In the end, I play like a demon and hit just about every double going. Seriously, it's the best I've ever played on a log-end and my finishing is world class. Of course, I can't help thinking why I can't throw like that all the time. Still, it's World Championship month and I'm made up I'm showing some form.

SATURDAY 3RD DECEMBER

I know I've been moaning about travelling a fair bit recently but it's really getting beyond a joke. We set off for Truro in Cornwall this morning and it took us six-and-a-half hours, which is crazy. The last 60 miles on the A roads were the worst and we spent half the time stuck behind a bloody tractor. I think I'm going to have to invest in a private helicopter at this rate. Second-hand, obviously.

Anyway, I'm in the Britannia pub again. I was here earlier in the year and I know they are a good bunch, so I'm pretty relaxed about the whole thing. The only hiccup is when they ask me to do the draw for the raffle. I get asked all the time to do the draws and me and Donna always buy tickets so as not to look tight. I'm always worried we'll win, which looks bad and sure enough tonight it happens. The prize is only a big tin of Quality Street but as soon as everyone else realises Donna's holding the winning ticket, they start shouting "Fix!". Of course, we insist on a redraw but it does look dodgy, doesn't it? I could have taken them round me mum's for Christmas as well.

SUNDAY 4TH DECEMBER

Still in Truro because I'm working the British Legion tonight, which is only 100 yards down the road from the Britannia, so there's a lot of the same faces in from last night. They're keen this mob, I'll give them that.

I'm definitely in a bit of a purple patch at the moment. I hit 19 180s, which is the most I've ever thrown in an exhibition in my whole life, and I feel tip-top. The World Championship is just around the corner now but things are definitely looking up. Maybe this no-practising lark is starting to pay dividends. At least I feel my confidence is good and I can see no good reason right now to start practising. I know at lot of other pros would think it's crazy to stop practising with the biggest tournament of the year so close but I feel comfortable with my preparation. The proof is in the pudding but feeling relaxed is as important to me as putting the hours in.

MONDAY 5TH DECEMBER

Back home after another nightmare journey. Whenever we get stuck in traffic Donna reminds me it's still got to be better than my old life of working nine to five, but I'm not sure I can agree with her at the moment.

TUESDAY 6TH DECEMBER

The PDC have done the draw for the World Championship. I've got a bloke called Brian Roach from Australia in the first round. I've never heard of him, but I now know I'm playing on the Wednesday before Christmas. The tournament normally starts after Christmas but this year the format has changed. The top 32 in the world qualify automatically as usual, but there are 32 more players this year, 16 qualifiers from the PDC circuit and 16 foreign players, who come from countries like Australia, Barbados, New Zealand, China and Japan. That means there are a lot more games to fit in, so they've decided to bring the start date forward.

I've got mixed feelings about the format change. I can see why the PDC want to get more of an international flavour to the tournament. It's good business because you're probably looking at a bigger television audience with more players from around the world and it can't do the grassroots game any harm either. The PDC want to take the game global and I'm not going to knock them for that. My only worry is whether the foreign qualifiers are up to it. It's the World Championship after all and everyone there should be there on merit. I'm not saying the foreign lads shouldn't play. If they're good enough, bring them on. I just hope they're not lambs to the slaughter because that wouldn't do them or the tournament any favours.

THURSDAY 8TH DECEMBER

Get a very interesting text message today from Matchroom Sport, who run the PDC. They want to know if I'm available next Thursday or Friday for a photo shoot on Southend beach. They want me to wear shorts and stand on a surfboard. I've got no idea what it's all in aid of but they've got no chance of getting me on a beach in shorts in December. I'm not that stupid.

FRIDAY 9TH DECEMBER

I got a call from a fella a couple of months ago booking me for a gig in Llanelli tonight, so we're in Wales. When I turn up I realise it's not going to be a normal night because the bloke starts telling me what he expects.

"Yeah, we've had all the big names down here before."

"Oh right."

"Yeah, I've never seen any of the pros lose a leg here to the locals."

"I'm always losing at exhibitions."

"You're kidding?"

"No, I like to fuck about to make it fun for the punters. There's no point battering everyone off the board, is there?"

"But you're a professional. Aren't you embarrassed?"

"No."

Despite what he says, I throw a couple of games as usual, but try not to make it too obvious just in case he doesn't pay me!

Me and Donna leave at gone 12 and stop off at a Welcome Break for a bite to eat. I want a full fry-up but they won't do me one in the middle of the night, so I have to settle for tomato and basil soup.

MONDAY 12TH DECEMBER

Decide to write a letter to the DRA today to let them know what I think about the new drug testing regulations and ask why they decided not to do anything about alcohol. I don't expect they'll get back to me but I wanted to get it off my chest. There's no point moaning about it in private if you're not prepared to make a stand in public.

TUESDAY 13TH DECEMBER

Play poker online for a couple of hours but it's another tale of outrageous bad luck. To cut a long story short, I'm sitting on four queens, there's only one other player left in and there's about £400 in the pot. And guess what? Yes, he's got four bloody kings.

WEDNESDAY 14TH DECEMBER

Remember I was over in Holland for the Players' Championship last month and had a few too many beers with Colin Monk and Andy

Jenkins? Well, someone's grassed on us and the DRA have now found us guilty of being "probably intoxicated in public at a PDC event" and they're going to fine us. They're meeting today to decide how much and I'm not happy at all.

I've got no idea who squealed but yet again the DRA are throwing their weight around for no reason. They've accused me of being sick over the bar but like I said, all I did was spit a disgusting liquer back into my glass. They're saying we were drunk in public and we've brought darts into disrepute. What a load of bollocks. For a start, we weren't actually 'at the darts'. We were in the hotel bar well away from the playing arena and don't forget we were staying at the hotel anyway. Fair play, we were drunk but when did it become a crime for a few mates to have a drink together? We weren't on PDC duty and we didn't cause any harm.

We'll have to wait and see what the DRA decide but no doubt it'll be something way over the top.

THURSDAY 15TH DECEMBER

Sky want me to record an interview about the World Championship with Sid Waddell at the London Eye. The problem is, it'll be on Christmas Eve and I've got the family coming around, so I knock them back. I know it would be an all-day job and Christmas is a time for the family, isn't it? I'm not trying to keep my head down or anything, it's just bad timing.

It's a shame because a day out with Sid is always an experience. I like to call him 'Bag Of Nerves Sid' because he looks forever on edge and I half expect him to lose the plot at any time. I'm sure Sid's brain doesn't work like the rest of ours. But like everyone else, I like Sid because he's so passionate about his job and there's no arguing he's good for darts.

I've got no idea where he comes up with his mad phrases during commentary. My personal favourite was when he once described Jocky Wilson's throwing action. Jocky had a famously jerky release and I remember Sid said it reminded him of "a Russian Ballerina at the oche". Classic.

FRIDAY 16TH DECEMBER

I've started practising again this morning. I've not been worried at all about not throwing but I woke up today and just fancied a little session. Simple as that. I'm only talking about ten or 15 minutes but that's all I feel I need. As soon as I step up and start throwing, I feel my rhythm is there, so I go round the board quickly, hit a few doubles and that's that. There's no point overdoing it when I feel there's nothing too much wrong with my game at the moment.

I spend the afternoon on Southend beach. I changed my mind about the photo shoot because I found out it's for the *Sunday People* and the truth is it's good publicity for me. They've got me in my Hawaiian shirt standing on the surf board and I must look like a right wally to everyone doing their Christmas shopping wearing their nice warm coats and hats.

CHAPTER ELEVEN

Power struggle in Purfleet

SUNDAY 18TH DECEMBER

The World Championship starts tomorrow and I'm thinking about it all the time now. I don't play until Wednesday but the combination of nerves and anticipation means it's dominating my thoughts. It's always like this just before the tournament starts.

The Premier League earlier in the year was a huge event for our sport, but the Worlds is still the big one. It's the one all the players want to win, the one young darts players dream of winning when they start out. At least I know I did.

Playing the first round before Christmas still seems strange but everyone's in the same boat and I'm not letting it worry me. I've just got to get over the first hurdle and make sure I'm around for the second round, which starts on Boxing Day.

MONDAY 19TH DECEMBER

I don't watch any of today's games on the telly. I'm getting more and more nervous and I think watching the action today will only make me worse. Maybe I'll tune in tomorrow but for now I'd rather give it a miss.

Sort through some old paperwork to kill a bit of time in the afternoon and come across the receipt for the exercise bike, which is still doing a top job collecting dust in the garden shed. Wonder what Argos's returns policy is?

TUESDAY 20TH DECEMBER

Still trying to relax but tomorrow's the big day and the nerves are really kicking in. Like all the big things in life, it's the waiting that's the worst. I just want to be up on stage with my fate in my own hands. At the moment, I just feel in a state of limbo.

Decide to watch Colin Lloyd's first round game on the box tonight because he's a mate. He's up against a qualifier called Gary Welding and in the first two sets—it's first to three—Colin plays like a world champion, really unbelievable darts. It looks like he's going to cruise through, so I get up to make a cuppa and a sandwich and by the time I get back it's two apiece. How the hell did that happen?

I sit down expecting to see Colin pull it out of the fire but Gary isn't having any of it and wins the deciding set three legs to nothing. Bloody hell! The world number one is out already and the tournament's only two days old. I feel for Colin because he must be totally gutted but I'm also thinking about myself. If it can happen to Colin, it can happen to me or any of the other top seeds. I've never felt complacent about tomorrow's game and watching Colin go out proves you can't take anything for granted.

WEDNESDAY 21ST DECEMBER

Wake up at nine. I know I slept well but I feel like I only got two hours kip. That's the nervous tension.

Donna wants to know what I want for breakfast.

"Do you fancy a fry-up?"

"No, not really love."

"How about a bacon and egg sandwich?"

"Yeah, why not."

"Two?"

"No, I couldn't eat two. I'll be stuffed."

"You'll need the energy."

"Oh go on then."

So that's that. If I win today, I'll be eating bacon and egg sandwiches before every game of the tournament. Hopefully I'll be eating a lot of them over the next couple of weeks.

I'm playing at eight tonight, so we leave at quarter to three, which means I'll have my five hours at the Circus Tavern before I'm on.

It's great to be back at the Tavern but I'm nervous because it will be a disaster if I lose today.

There has been talk over the years about taking the tournament to a different venue. The PDC has a rolling one-year contract with the Tavern but I hope we stay where we are. Of course, I'm being selfish because it's just down the road for me, but that's not my only reason for hoping we stay put. I know the Tavern isn't the most luxurious venue you could hope for but it's become the spiritual home of darts and the atmosphere here is unique. I just don't believe the tournament would be the same in some new, shiny and more clinical venue. The Tavern might be a bit shabby but it's got real character and the layout of the place means the crowd are so close to the action. For me, the competition would lose something if we upped sticks to a new, air-conditioned warehouse-type place where the fans would be sitting miles away from the stage.

The people who want to relocate reckon a new venue would broaden the appeal of darts and I can see the logic. But we're taking the game to a new audience all the time in other ways—the Premier League, our trip to China last year—so I just don't see why we can't leave the World Championship well alone.

I head to the practice room at five and do ten minutes on the board and then ten off. It's still three hours before we play and I don't want to get too intense too soon because that can take too much out of you.

I want to be nicely warmed up not worn out.

I ask after my opponent Brian Roach and I find him in the players' bar. As I said before, we don't know each other from Adam, so I want to say hello. It's his first time at the World Championship, he's in a foreign country and I want to do the right thing and check he's alright.

"Brian? I'm Wayne Mardle."

"Hello mate. Good to meet you."

"You too. You alright? You know what you're doing?"

"Think so mate. I've found the bar."

"Anything you need to know just give me a shout."

"Will do Wayne. Cheers."

He seems like a nice fella and I can tell he's well chuffed to be here. He's the Australian champion but the World Championship is another level again and he knows it. He's 70 or 80 places below me in the world rankings and this is definitely the biggest match of his career.

I go back for some more practice, have a few medicinal vodkas and before I know it, we're being called down to get ready for the walk-ons. I can hear the crowd beyond the doors and the hairs are standing up on the back of my neck. The nerves are giving way to excitement now and I'm chomping at the bit to get up on stage and do the business. The doors open, my music comes on and I'm off. Showtime.

The noise is defeaning. It's great being an Essex lad because I get all the local support and it puts a spring in my step. I clock some fans wearing Hawaiian shirts and I know I'm going to have the crowd behind me. I'm playing in my own backyard and it just feels right. I belong here.

It's the first to three sets in the first round and the first set is all way one-way traffic. Brian's nervous and obviously struggling to come to terms with the atmosphere up here and all I have to do is throw steady darts to take it three legs to nothing.

The second set is a lot tighter. Brian looks happier on the stage now and is starting to find his rhythm and he's throwing first. I take out at 160 finish in the fourth leg to make it 2–2 but he holds his throw in the next leg and it's one set apiece.

I'm not panicking but losing the set is a jolt. Brian was so bad in the first set that he lulled me into a false sense of security but he's just shown he can play. I know I can beat him with something to spare but I need to improve my focus. Come on Wayne, put this one to bed.

The third and fourth sets go according to plan. I score heavily, hit my doubles and in the end it's a nice and comfortable 3–1 victory. I'm safely through to the second round after Christmas and I can relax for a few days.

There's no dressing room at the Tavern, so I get changed out my Hawaiian shirt in the players' bar. It's either that or the toilets. I don't hang around for long and we're back home by 10.30. Donna orders a chicken chow mein; we scoff that down and then off to bed.

THURSDAY 22ND DECEMBER

Had a terrible night's sleep. I had a migraine all night which I reckon was brought on by the tension of yesterday, so I feel rotten this morning.

My mood's not improved when the postman arrives with a letter from my good friends at the DRA. They've hit with me a £750 fine for what went on in Holland last month. Andy Jenkins got the same and Colin Monk has been stung for £500. I mean, it was the crime of the century, wasn't it? I'm not going to argue with them though because knowing the DRA they'll probably double it. They really are like darts' secret police.

SATURDAY 24TH DECEMBER

Christmas Eve. I haven't practised at all since I played Brian Roach but decide to have 10 minutes on the board today. I'm not playing until Wednesday and with no exhibition work on until after the World Championship, I want to keep my arm in. I really haven't thought about darts once since I played but I feel good today when I throw, so I'm reasonably happy.

SUNDAY 25TH DECEMBER

Donna's bought me a leaf hooverer-up thingy for the garden. It might not be the most sexy present ever but it's what I wanted and should save me a bit of unnecessary graft come next autumn.

I've got her some Kickers boots. Strictly speaking, she got them and I bunged her the money but it makes sense really. Men just aren't natural shoppers, are we?

We always go round mum and dad's for Christmas dinner and this year's no different. I suppose it's a bit selfish of me because it means Donna doesn't get to see her family but it's a Mardle family tradition and my mum always puts on a good spread.

Like everyone else in the country I pile my plate as high as Everest when dinner is served. God, do I go over the top but it's not my fault. If my mum wasn't such a good cook I wouldn't be such a pig, would I? She's done us proud as usual with roast pork, beef, lamb and chicken (none of us likes turkey) and all the trimmings and I really go for it. Mum's not too impressed though.

"Wayne, love, do you have to pile it so high?"

"Yes mum."

"You'll never eat all that."

"Watch and learn mum."

"Why don't you just take a little and go back for more."

"I'm happy as I am."

"You always were a pig."

She's right of course and I polish off the lot. After dinner we all play cards—another Mardle family tradition—and honestly it's like taking candy from a baby. I win £30 off mum, Donna and my sister. So much for the spirit of Christmas.

MONDAY 26TH DECEMBER

Go to dog track in Romford today (another festive custom) with George Harris, my best man, and a few other friends. I don't see much of George these days because I'm on the road so much, so it's important to make the effort. I pick the winners of the first two races but my luck runs out after that, so I leave the track roughly evens.

TUESDAY 27TH DECEMBER

Second round day tomorrow. I'm playing the Belgian Erik Clarys, who is number 25 in the world and a handy player. He's a bit of a maverick because he goes for unconventional combinations on his checkouts, finishes that other players wouldn't dream of and he's always an unpredictable opponent.

He's certainly a step up in standard from Brian Roach but I'm a lot less nervous now than I was before Christmas. I think the first match is always the worst because there's so much anticipation. Right now I feel relaxed and confident, even though I haven't thrown a dart in anger since Christmas Eve. Not practising seems to suit me. I'll have a couple of hours on the board at the Tavern before I play tomorrow but I really don't feel the need to throw today.

WEDNESDAY 28TH DECEMBER

Still feeling relaxed. Decide to have just the one bacon and egg sandwich for breakfast. I can feel the pounds piling on, especially just after Christmas, so I'd better go steady or they'll have to winch me onto the stage.

I'm playing at six, so Donna drops me off at one. On the way we notice a building development just off the A13. It's a two-storey place which they're going to spilt into flats and Donna turns round and says to me:

"If that was one house it would be really nice."

"Yeah, it would love."

The thing is, we saw the flats a week ago before the first round and we had exactly the same stupid conversation, so it looks like it's another tournament ritual I'll have to stick to now. She's quite superstitious is my wife.

There's no chit-chat with Erik in the practice room. I'd be happy to have a little chinwag but it's obvious the minute I walk in he's not interested because he doesn't say hello. That's fine by me. It's his prerogative and I'm not going to take it personally.

Do a pre-match interview for Sky with the lovely Helen Chamberlain:

"Did you practice on Christmas Day, Wayne?"

"No chance, Helen."

"I think she's surprised because Phil Taylor said in an earlier interview that he'd put in a few hours, as did John Part. But what the hell? It's working for me.

I've decided I'm not going to have a drink before the match. It hit me this afternoon that I'm always going on about the evils of drink in darts and I wrote that letter to the DRA to ask why alcohol wasn't being included in the new anti-doping measures. So I think I'm going to put my money where my mouth is and play stone-cold sober. It's probably a stupid idea but I'm determined to give it a go. I feel relaxed and ready, so if I can't do it today, when will I? I'm not going to tell anyone (except Donna) and see what happens.

It's first to four sets and I drop the first. I miss my favourite double 18 to take it and Erik hits backs with double eight to get his nose in front. Not the best of starts and I'm beginning to regret the decision not to have a drink. I can really feel the pressure now and I wish I'd had a quick vodka just to steady my nerves. Why the fuck did I choose today to suddenly decide to practice what I preach?

Panic over. The next three sets are a procession and I take nine consecutive legs with some good finishing (taking out a 109 and a 105) to go three sets to one up. Erik's not great but I play good solid darts and it's more than enough to put me in the driving seat. One more set and I'm home and hosed.

There's a break after the fourth set and I nip offstage for a quick vodka and orange cordial—I'd asked one of the officials to leave one there for me just in case. I'm not desperate for a drink, it's not like I'm shaking or anything like that, but I think I've given this little experiment long enough now. I'm in front in the match and I've proved to myself that I can get up on stage without any booze in me.

Erik wins the first leg of the fifth set but after that it's plain sailing again; I hit a 105 finish in the third leg and kill him off in the fourth with a 64 checkout. Game Mardle.

It was a decent game but not a classic but I couldn't care less. I'm through to the next round and I haven't really had to exert myself too much.

I definitely won't be carrying on with the no-alcohol experiment for the rest of the tournament. I got just a little bit panicky after that first set and that was because I was sober. Looking back, I've no idea why I suddenly decided to try it but I only got away with it because Erik didn't put me under any real pressure. I dread to think what would have happened up there if I'd been playing someone like Phil Taylor.

We get home by ten and Donna insists on ordering a chicken chow mein because that's what we had after I beat Brian Roach. I play John Part tomorrow. This is where things get serious.

THURSDAY 29TH DECEMBER

A bacon and egg sandwich and a cup of tea this morning. It's a six o'clock start today, so I mooch about the house, read the papers and watch Sky Sports News to kill time before we set off for the Tavern at one, via a lovely-looking new two-storey development split into flats that Donna thinks would look nice as one house. I have to agree with her.

John's already in the practice room when I show my face at three. Typical of John to beat me to the board. I'm not surprised though and I really admire his professionalism. He works really hard at his game and he gets the rewards. He's slipped down to tenth in the rankings this year but he's a former world champion—he won the BDO title in 1994 and beat Phil Taylor in a classic PDC final in 2003—and that's more than I can say. John beat Chris Mason 4–3 in the last round in a great game, which proves he's in top form. You already know I think Chris is one of the most talented players on the circuit and John edging him out after being two sets to one down tells me all I need to know about his frame of mind.

Basically, he's different gravy to my last two opponents and if I'm not on the money today, he'll murder me. Saying that, I've only lost once to John in a televised tournament (the 2004 Grand Prix in Ireland) and we've played in front of the cameras five times, so I've also got every reason to be confident.

Me and John get chatting, which is no surprise. We've done a lot of exhibitions together this year and aside from the head-butting incident, we get on like a house on fire. John's in typically weird form.

"Do you believe in extraterrestrial life?"

"Not sure John. Yeah, maybe."

"I believe in aliens."

"You surprise me."

"How do you think aliens see us? What do you they make of us?"

"I've absolutely no idea, John."

"Do you want to know what I think?"

"No."

"I think they think we're like dogs driving cars."

It's enough to drive a man to drink, so I head to the bar for a vodka. Like I said, there's no way I'm going out against John stone-cold sober.

The walk-on is bizarre. I do my usual, grinning like an idiot and dancing badly, but John walks on accompanied by the cast of *Star Wars*—Princess Leia, Chewbacca, a Stormtrooper and Boba Fett. Seriously, he walks out with a load of actors dressed up as characters from the films, which is bit tacky if you ask me. To be fair, I don't think it's John's idea but how can we expect people to take us seriously when you put on a pantomime like that? There's no way darts is ever going to be an Olympic sport when you've got antics like that.

The crowd, all 1,200 of them, are in great form. They know this is a big match, two big beasts going head-to-head and they're full of expectation. Again, I know the majority are rooting for me and I lap it up. They're shouting my name and I feel like I can take on the world.

Funny thing is, I'm only ever aware of the crowd in the Tavern. I never give a second thought to the people sat at home watching on the TV. It's not that I block it out, it just never crosses my mind when I'm up on stage. I think it's because the fans at the Tavern are so noisy and so close to you that you're wrapped up in their reactions and don't have time to let your mind wander to how many are tuned in at home. Some players can wilt when they start thinking about the cameras and the fact they're on live television but, hand on heart, it's water off a duck's back to me.

The first set (first to four again) is nip and tuck and it's two legs apiece when I take out a 126 finish to take it. My confidence really surges as I hit it. I'm scoring well and for once it looks like my finishing is going to do me proud. I've got a good feeling about this match now.

The second set is all John and he takes it three nothing. I hold throw to take the third and I've got my nose in front again. John bounces back in the fourth and we're all-square again. I'm still feeling confident but it's definitely game on now.

I whitewash him in the fifth with the darts to go within one set of making the quarter-finals but John's throwing first in the sixth. Sure enough he goes two legs to one ahead but then I pull out a 12-darter to level up and then wrap it up with a double 18 in the final leg. I'm through to the last eight.

I have to say it was a cracking match. The crowd loved it and it was good quality all the way through. The thing is, I was really clinical out there. I took my chances when they came my way, I hit my doubles and I kept John at arm's length all match. It was a good professional performance and I handled the pressure of the situation brilliantly. I'm on cloud nine.

FRIDAY 30TH DECEMBER

A bad night's sleep. I got another migraine before I went to bed last night, which is a hangover from all of yesterday's tension and excitement. It's all worth it when you win though.

Get a call later in the morning from Justyn, the editor of this book.

“Hi Wayne, I’ve had a great idea.”

“Yeah, go on... “

“Are you still looking after the Mega Dart properly?”

“Of course. We polish it every day. Why? Do you want it back?”

“No... well, not yet. No, I was thinking you could use it as part of your walk-on today. It’d look great and it would be great publicity as well.”

“Maybe. It’s a bit heavy though.”

“You’ll manage.”

“I’m not sure about this Justyn to be honest... ”

“Trust me, it will be brilliant.”

“Hmm, maybe. I’ll see what the PDC have to say.”

I get to the Tavern at two (I’m on at seven) and I go through the usual ritual of reading the papers and just generally hanging about. I have a word about the Mega Dart (which we just about managed to squeeze into the Picasso to get it to the Tavern) but the PDC aren’t keen because they reckon it could be a health and safety hazard. They’re worried I could have someone’s eye out with it during the walk-on and they’ve probably got a point. I’m not going to argue the toss but I know Justyn will be heartbroken. He’s obsessed with that dart if you ask me.

I’m playing a fella called Alan Warriner-Little. We all call Alan ‘Wazza’ on the circuit but his official nickname is ‘Iceman’ because he doesn’t show any emotion on the oche. He’s a cool dude and never seems to get rattled by anything. I can’t say much more about Wazza though because he’s a quiet fella and tends to keep himself to himself most of the time.

There’s no chat before the match today because Wazza’s got his Walkman on when he’s warming up. I’ve no idea what he’s listening to (maybe Man United songs because he’s a big Red) but it’s obvious he wants to keep himself to himself and fair play to him.

Before we play there’s controversy in the second quarter-final of the day between Peter Manley and Adrian Lewis. It's a tense match but there's a lot of bad blood as well and Adrian walks off the stage during the fifth set because it looks as if Peter says something behind his back when he's about to throw. I watch a bit of the game on the telly in the practice room and there's no doubt Peter's trying to slow Adrian down (Adrian is a very fluid player) by taking his darts out of the board slowly and walking back very sedately after his shot but I've got no idea if Peter's giving it the verbals as well.

The upshot is that Adrian storms off (he's three sets to one down at this stage) but he's coaxed back on and continues. He's clearly rattled though and Peter wraps it up five sets to three.

All the talk after the match is about Peter's tactics. He plays it all innocent in his post-match interview while Adrian resists the temptation to start slagging Peter off and handles himself with great maturity for a lad of 20. I see Adrian in the players' bar afterwards and tell him I think he handled it brilliantly but he still looks gutted.

The problem for Peter is he's already got previous in this tournament. He was playing Dennis Smith in his third round match and was two sets down when he walked off for an unscheduled break to change his shirt. He kept Smiffy waiting up there for a few minutes and Dennis wasn't happy about it. It did the trick though and Peter won it 4–3 in the end, but a lot of people thought Peter was up to his old tricks again.

So it looks like he's public enemy number one now but that won't bother him one bit. He's not shy, Peter, and he's through to the semi-finals, which is what it's all about.

It's time for me and Wazza to get it on. He's been playing well all week and he's going to fancy his chances. I need to be focused from the start today.

Wazza takes the first leg of the first set but I open up with a 180 in the second. A good sign this early in the match. I hit another 180 with my second throw and the nine-dart finish is on. No-one's ever thrown a nine-darter at the Tavern and I'm three darts away from achieving it.

Come on, Wayne. The first shot on your third throw for a nine-darter is another treble 20. It's there and I'm two darts away from history. Next I need treble 15 to leave double 18. Come on treble 15. It's there. All I need is my favourite double 18, good old double 18 and I'm going down in the record books. I try and compose myself but my heart's going like the clappers. There's no point pretending this is just any other dart because it isn't. This could be really special. This could be the greatest leg of darts of my whole career.

I throw the dart...

... I miss by an inch. Not by a millimetre, by an inch. I pull it badly, very badly. I'm not even close. The nine-darter goes up in a puff of smoke. The crowd sigh and I know I've blown it. My head's spinning with the adrenalin that's built up and the disappointment and for a second I don't really know where I am. I just wish I could have that one dart again. I'm sure I'd hit the double 18 this time. Just let me have it again and I'll show you. Of course, it doesn't work like that. You only get one shot at it and I've blown it. I now start to worry that missing it is going to affect my concentration for the rest of the match. We're only in the second leg and I've got to pull myself together. I can't afford to dwell on what's just happened because the match still has to be won. There's no time to think about what might have been.

My focus is wobbling and Wazza comes back from over 200 points behind to take the leg because I miss my doubles to wrap it up. I've just narrowly missed a nine-darter and still lost the leg. Not good at all. I've got to get myself together.

And I do. I nick the first set 3–2 and after that Wazza just goes to pieces. Second set to Mardle (3–1), third set to me (3–0), fourth set to me (3–1). His form has completely deserted him, I've got the nine-darter out of my system and I'm in complete control. The fifth set is like shelling peas and I take it 3–1 to win take the match five sets to zip and I'm through to the semi-finals again.

After the match I head down to the fans' area rather than the players' bar. I get six tickets for the bar for friends and family every time I play but tonight Donna's family and a few of my mates, including George Harris, are in. I didn't have enough passes to get them in upstairs, so I head down to say hello and thank them for showing their support.

I have to sign a fair few autographs when I'm down there but it's not a problem. It's part of the job and I know if I'm going to show my face downstairs, people are going to want to say hello or whatever. It's all part of the Tavern experience.

I get chatting to George who tells me he had money on the match.

"I bet on you to win five nil."

"Nice one. What odds did you get?"

"Four to one."

"How much did you put on?"

"Just a tenner."

So George reckons he's won £50 but I'm suspicious. George likes a flutter but his missus Maria is with him, so like all gamblers, I reckon he's playing down how much he bet. If he confesses how much he's really won, Maria will be wanting a shopping trip, won't she?

Back home with Donna and the chow mein (does it have more or less calories than a Kentucky?) I reflect on the match. Hand on heart, I'm not worried about the nine-darter now—there's no prize money for it, anyway. I'm through to the semis, which is what really matters and I'd rather be able to say that than I hit a nine-darter if I was out of the competition. It would have been something I'd remember for the rest of my career but I'm sort of planning to remember being crowned world champion for the rest of my career. I've got more important things to worry about now, such as the prospect of facing a certain Phil Taylor in the semi-final. Should be nice and easy.

SATURDAY 31ST DECEMBER

The semi isn't until tomorrow so I treat myself to a lie-in. Unlike last year, Donna's doesn't head off to a party and decides to stay in to see in the New Year with me. I suspect it's only because there's no good parties on.

The family come round at five for a bit of dinner but they're gone by eight, so we watch the telly in the evening.

I'm not really with it though and I can't stop thinking about tomorrow. There's no point pretending—I'm going to have to produce the game of my life to beat Phil. I know I've got the talent to do it but it all has to come together at the same time for me to pull it off. If I'm just one per cent off my very best, he'll have me. That's the challenge of playing Phil and so many players haven't been able to quite manage it before. People have come close in the past but time after time Phil finds something extra and that's what makes him such a great champion.

Do I really, really believe I can do it? Yeah, I do. I'm realistic but I'm not intimidated and I know I'll have the majority of the crowd on my side. Yeah, I can do it. He's not invincible and if anyone's going to knock him off his perch, it's going to be me. I'm going to give him the shock of his life.

I head up to the practice room at 20 past 11 for a throw. I still don't particularly feel like I need the practice but it can't hurt either. I'm only on the board for 20 minutes and then I have a quick game of poker on the laptop before Big Ben starts with the midnight chimes and me and Donna have a cuddle and kiss.

SUNDAY 1ST JANUARY 2006

Wake up at nine but I have to wait for me bacon and egg sandwich because Donna's still in bed and I know she won't show her face today for another couple of hours.

It's probably no bad thing having to wait for breakfast because the moment I'm awake I'm aware I've got terrible gut ache, so make a quick exit to the toilet. I don't want to get too graphic, so let's just say nerves can play havoc with your bowels.

I head off to the local shop, which is only a five-minute walk, grab some milk and newspapers and then it's back home to watch Sky Sports News and twiddle my thumbs. Jesus, it's only ten! Donna's dropping me off at the Tavern at three, so I've still got five hours to kill. I'd go back to bed if I could sleep but I can't and I really don't fancy picking up my darts just yet.

Donna surfaces at 11, cooks the traditional breakfast and by the time I've polished it off, it's nearly midday. Three hours to go. Donna now knows better than to talk to me about the match, so we go through the motions of chatting about the most mundane things to avoid the real conversation.

"Do you want a cup of tea?"

"Yeah, cheers love."

"Anything in the paper?"

"Not really. Just reading the match report for the Spurs game against Newcastle yesterday."

"I'll iron your shirt now."

"Cheers darling."

And so on. Anything as long as it's not about darts.

Finally it's time to get in the car and get going. We pass the housing development off the A13 on the way and Donna says: "If that was one house it would be really nice." I don't have the heart to disagree with her and there's no point tempting fate now. "Yeah, it would love."

It's quiet at the Tavern, so I sit down in the corner of the players' room, have a coffee and read some more newspapers.

At four I head to the practice room. I'm only throwing for ten minutes and then having ten minutes off. I feel terrified but full of anticipation as well. I know it's going to be electric out there tonight and it's occasions like this that I play darts for.

Phil arrives in the practice room just before five, hangs up his match shirt and has a throw. We get chatting immediately.

"Do much for New Year's last night, Phil?"

"Went to the bar of my hotel with the missus and [his daughter] Natalie."

"Oh right. A late one?"

"Nah, I was knackered. I was in bed by 11. How about you?"

"The family came round for a bite."

I can't help wishing he'd had a few jars to be honest, but that's just not Phil.

I get my first vodka and orange cordial at five and head back into the practice room. Phil's got a bottle of something he's mixed up himself on the go, which I reckon is probably vodka-based. We're still both in a chatty mood and we talk a lot about poker and how he's going to build another storey on his house so he can have a gym at home.

The first semi-final starts at six. It's Peter Manley against the surprise package of the tournament, Wayne Jones (remember him? He's the guy who stuffed Colin Lloyd and me at that round-robin exhibition event back in August). Wayne's definitely the crowd's choice for this one because of Peter's antics in the previous rounds. He's also had a hard life has Wayne because his wife died prematurely from cancer leaving him with three kids to look after. He had to put his darts to one side for a long time but he's throwing again and it's great to see him in the World Championship semi-finals.

Personally, I don't know how he manages to bring up three kids and play darts. He lives in Wolverhampton and has been driving down to Purfleet on the morning of every match because he doesn't want to be away from the family. I was talking to him before his quarter-final and asked him if it was difficult getting out of bed to get here on time. He said he'd been up all night because his littlest wasn't well. The bloke deserves a medal.

The game goes Peter's way. Maybe it's one late night too many, but Wayne can't reproduce the darts he did in the earlier rounds and Peter storms into a four-set lead in double-quick time when Phil, who's stood watching it with me in the players' bar, turns round and says:

"He won't be doing that to me or you in the final tomorrow."

"How do you mean?"

"Peter. He won't be whitewashing you or me tomorrow."

"No, I suppose not."

For a second, I'm confused. Is Phil taking the piss or does he really mean he doesn't know who'll be in the final? Nah, Phil's not like that. I take it as a compliment. He knows it's not a foregone conclusion.

Peter wraps up the match six nothing and the clock's really ticking. Half-an-hour to go now.

I go to the bar for another vodka and cordial. I've already had 12 to be perfectly honest but they're doing the trick. I'm nervous for sure but not too bad. I'm as ready as I can be. Donna pops her head around the curtain of the practice room. She says "good luck husbandio" (don't ask me why) and gives me a kiss. Then she leaves me to it and I'm on my own now. The next face I see is the official who's taking us down the stairs and the atmosphere between me and Phil changes like that. There's no more matey chit-chat now. It's time to do the business and all the pleasantries go out of the window. It's dog eat dog now. To be fair, I feel as sick as a dog right now.

The crowd goes mental when I walk through the doors with the *Hawaii Five–0* music blaring out. They go absolutely ballistic and all I can hear are the shouts of "There's only one Wayney Mardle, there's only one Wayney Mardle"' echoing around the place. Fucking brilliant. I know Donna's sitting on the left, half way down, so I give her another kiss as I go past (she says I'll lose otherwise) and then I'm up on stage giving it the stupid dance. I feel like a king now because the crowd are still singing my name. The atmosphere is amazing, different gravy to anything in the previous rounds, and there is a nervous excitement rippling through the Tavern. The crowd are expecting something special tonight and they're already doing their bit. It's a wall of sound up here and I can hardly hear myself think. They're 90 per cent Mardle fans out there and they're letting the world know it. Even the great Phil Taylor is going to struggle to shut out all that support. It could be the edge I need.

Phil's walk-on is delayed because he suddenly decides he needs the toilet but I'm not bothered. I'm loving it up here. I could stay here all day.

I've got the darts in the first set and I throw a 14-darter to win the first leg. Nice start Wayne. The next three legs go with throw to make it two apiece and we're down to the deciding fifth. I get to the double first but miss, Phil's got double tops for the set but misses. I've got double two for the set and miss, then Phil misses another three at tops and I miss another three at twos. The tension is unbearable and we're both missing doubles like it's going out of fashion. Phil finally hits tops at the 11th attempt and the set is his. Bollocks. I had my chances but fluffed them. Phil looks bloody shaky too but he's got the first set under his belt.

Phil leaves the stage at the break but I stay. Despite handing him the set, I'm not feeling negative. He's obviously trying too hard to dominate me and if I can pick up my finishing, he's vulnerable. Come on Wayne, you can do this. It's all about belief.

The second set goes all the way with throw and it's 2–0 Phil. I've got the darts in the third but my game's falling to bits now and although I win the first leg, he eventually nicks it 3–1 with a single break. I'm three sets down now and I know I'm in the shit. Phil can run riot in these kind of situations and if I don't pick it up, he's going to humiliate me. I haven't lost the belief I can beat him but my confidence has taken a pounding.

I know the fourth set's going to be crucial. I'm deliberately walking around the stage with my chest puffed out and trying to stand as tall as possible just to let Phil know I'm not beaten, that I'm not going anywhere. There's plenty of fight left in me. It seems to work. I break him in the third leg to make it 2–1 and then I take out a 76 checkout to win the set. I'm alive and kicking. I turn round to where I know Donna is in the crowd and shout out "I'm not finished yet." It's a release of energy, an expression of relief, and it feels great. Bring it on, bring it on.

I'm the one with the momentum now. I blast through the next two sets to level it up at 3–3 and it's all to play for. He's on the ropes and I'm in control. If I can maintain it, I'm in the final.

It's at this moment that my mind goes back to my match with Phil in the final of the Desert Classic in Vegas in 2004. Phil had raced into a four-set lead and I looked dead and buried. I pegged him back to four apiece with some great darts but I clearly remember I then started playing defensive darts as soon as we were all-square. I was trying not to lose, going for the safe options, rather than looking to win and it cost me. He beat me 6–4 that day and I'm determined not to make the same mistake again. I'm not going to go into my shell. I'll take the game to him.

I consciously speed up my throw in the seventh set. It's a message to Phil that I'm going to play aggressive darts and he's going to have do something special to stop me. I'm not going to quietly let him back into the match. It's working. Standing behind Phil on stage you usually only see his throwing arm move because he's got such a smooth action and the rest of his body is completely still. Now I can see his head dipping when he releases the darts. He's definitely feeling the pressure and trying too hard. I take full advantage to take the set 3–2 in legs. That's four sets to three to Mardle. The crowd are going mental. Four sets on the bounce against the world champion.

The eighth set goes to the deciding fifth leg and I get down to a 56 checkout. Phil's a long way behind; I hit the single 20 to leave my favourite double 18 and miss with two darts. My second dart at the double is my worst of the match. I try to put it in rather than throw it properly and I miss by a mile and hit single 18. Phil gets to within range with his next three darts, so I've got three darts to checkout 18. I haven't felt comfortable with double nines in the tournament so far, so I decide to go single ten and leave myself double four for the set. I miss both and Phil steps up and takes it. Shit. Four sets each. I know I've just missed a great chance to go two sets clear but there's no time to beat myself up about it. I'm still in the match and it's no good worrying about those misses now. Stay positive Wayne, stay positive.

I lose the first leg of the ninth with the darts but I'm not going to crumble now. Sod it, I've not come this far to lose. I pull myself together, produce a 122 checkout and the set is mine. I've got my nose in front again and I'm one set from victory and the final. One more set and it's all over.

The tenth set worries me. The treble 20 deserts me and suddenly my 140s become 85s and Phil is finding better form on the doubles. I'm never really at the races and he takes it three legs to one. Five sets all and one to play. I've got the darts coming up and all I need to do is hold throw and I'm home and dry. The crowd have whipped themselves up into a frenzy and I'm feeling on the edge of my seat too. I've never seen the Tavern rock like this before. All I have to do is give them the result they want.

The first leg of the 11th set is the turning point. I've got the darts but Phil pulls an 11-darter out of the hat to take it. I'm trying to stay positive but there's a little voice in my head now saying game over. I'm the one trying a little too hard and I can feel the match slipping away from me. Phil doesn't let situations like this slip and he's got the darts in the second leg. Sure enough, he holds, I hold in the third to make it 2–1 but he's throwing first in the fourth for the match. The world champion holds and the dream is over. My tournament is over.

Phil celebrates like he's just won the title. He's jumping around like a maniac. The relief is written all over his face and I can see the match has really taken it out of him. I go up to give him a hug and congratulate him.

"Great game, Phil."

"You never fucking go away, do you?"

"Yeah, sorry about that."

Phil gives a quick interview to Sky on stage but legs it pretty quickly because he's already thinking about tomorrow's final. I think I say all the right things about it being a great game and all that when the microphone's shoved my way but I'm still in a state of shock. I really need to get my head together.

I head back up to the players' room and when I walk in everyone stands up and starts clapping me in recognition of a great game. It really means a lot to me. Okay, I've just got beaten but it makes me realise there are worse ways to lose. I'm still a bit numb, but the reception I get is amazing. The world is already starting to look a bit brighter.

I nip down to the portakabin (sorry, press box) to give the lads a few quotes but I'm in and out as quickly as possible. The Mega Dart is propped up in the corner—it's been stored there since I brought it down the other day—but I'll have to pop back to collect it tomorrow because the Mardle family are out in force tonight and there won't be room in the car.

I have a quick pint of cider in the players' bar and then it's time to go home. Dad's doing the driving. He's got a Mondeo Estate but because there's eight of us to fit in—me and Donna, mum and dad, sister Donna, Perry, Danny and Ellie—so the 2006 World Championship semi-finalist exits the Circus Tavern car park squashed up in the boot with the two kids. Pure class.

Epilogue

So that was my 2005. It's now a week since I lost the semi-final to Phil and after a couple of days of feeling a bit sorry for myself, I'm feeling pretty philosophical about the whole thing. It was so close but so far again but I can't mope around forever. There are plenty of World Championships left it me yet.

For the record, Phil thumped Peter Manley 7–0 in the final and it was 13 world titles to The Power. No disrespect to Peter, but I wanted Phil to win because I wanted to have been knocked out by the winner and not the runner-up. I've got to admit I felt better for seeing Phil wipe the floor with Peter because it proved what a scare I gave him, but I was also thinking that I'd have beaten Peter in the final if I could have just held on against Phil. I'll never know now.

The day after the semi-final I felt miserable, but then I realised I was 20 grand richer—my prize money for reaching the last four—and that perked me up no end. Hand on heart, I hadn't given the prize money a single thought all tournament, but remembering a big fat cheque was coming my way put a smile back on my face.

The other thing that cheered me up was an email someone sent me via my website. I don't know the fella who sent it but it certainly made me chuckle. It read:

> *Hello Wayne.*
>
> *Do you know what my missus turned around and said to me after you scared the shit out of Phil 'The Power' Taylor on New Year's Day? "That man has just given the most excitement a man has ever given me." That's what she said! Bloody hell! Says a lot for me.*
>
> *Got to agree though, mate—what a game. I like Phil, but you had us shouting from the rooftops. If you had nailed him in the end, I have no doubt you would be world champ today. And you would have deserved it.*
>
> *Congratulations and good luck for the future. Oh, my missus, Tracey, says thanks for a wonderful night. She has never said that to me yet! I best start trying harder!*

Whoever you are mate, thank you. I nearly wet myself laughing.

Looking back on last year, it was definitely full of highs and lows but the funny thing is it ended exactly as it started—defeat in the semi-finals of the World Championship. There were times during the year I would have laughed if you'd suggested I'd make the semis again because my form was all over the place but I got there again and it was only the freak that is Phil that stopped me reaching my first final (as well as doing me over in the Desert Classic final in Vegas). The man really is a phenomenom and I'm not being at all defeatist when I say there's no disgrace in losing to Phil. Hopefully he'll consider retiring soon. The sooner the better as far as I'm concerned.

But the fact remains that I'm not world champion yet. I've got time on my side but I know as well as anyone there comes a time when potential isn't enough and you have do turn it into results. I haven't won any of darts' major tournaments in my professional career and although I'm not too worried about it yet, I will be in a couple of years if I'm still saying the same thing.

I know I've got to win something soon or people will start writing me off, labelling me an entertainer rather than a winner. They are entitled to their opinion but even though it's been an up and down year, I'm still convinced I've got titles in me.

The funny thing is, I was looking at the PDC statistics for the year and, believe it or not, I was the third highest ranking points winner on the circuit behind Phil and Colin Lloyd, which isn't bad considering my form was so unpredictable. I started the year as world number eight and finished as number six, so that's progress. Not spectacular progress, I admit, it wasn't as bad a year as it might of first seemed.

I've also learnt a lot about myself as a professional player this year, particularly in terms of how I practice. I chopped and changed my routine all year but I felt happiest when I decided to virtually abandon all practice in November, only throwing when I felt like it. I respect my job as a professional and I'm not lazy, but slavishly practising for hours every day just wasn't working for me. I tried hard but in the long run it wasn't producing the results.

The moment I decided to practice as and when, I felt like a weight had been lifted off my shoulders. I said early on in the book that darts is as much a mental game as it is technical or physical and I've realised it's probably more in the head for me than for most of the other players. If I feel happy in myself, I throw well. If I don't, the odds are stacked against me.

Freeing myself from a predetermined practice regime made a big difference and I feel my performances at the World Championship justified the decision. I'm always going to make a big effort not to think too much about my game in the future, which some people will tell you won't be that hard for me. Cheeky bastards. Looking back, the more I complicated things, the worse I got and whenever I was relaxed, I produced the form I know I'm capable of. What I'm saying is I'm an instinctive player and I've now got more confidence in just letting things happen and not trying to force the issue.

I'm definitely not going to become serious on the stage. If people want to dismiss me as a show pony, showman or whatever else, then fair play. I'm not acting up there, it's just me and I'd rather give the game up than become some kind of robot at the oche. Everyone's got their own style and that's mine. I don't think it does darts any harm to see a bit of emotion up there and I get emotional. So what? The crowds love it and they're the ones who keep the game going. So sorry, they'll be lots more silly dancing, inane grinning and showing off in the future. You can take it or leave it.

But I genuinely believe my professional career is on the right track. I'm relatively new to the full-time circuit compared to most of the other players in the top 20 and I've made no secret of the fact I'm still learning. I think I've matured as a professional player this year and as long as I continue to develop, I'll be happy.

I've got one or two regrets from the year. I still cringe when I remember storming off during my game against Tony Smith at the Players' Championship in Scotland in November. It was pathetic and childish and I know I shouldn't have done it. It showed a lack of respect to Tony and the tournament and I can only apologise. It was bang out of order and I'll never do that again.

I also regret snapping at Donna a couple of times when things weren't going well. I really wouldn't be here today if it wasn't for her. She's my biggest fan and my harshest critic and I couldn't do any of it without her. She ferries me the length and breadth of the country without a word of complaint (well, hardly any...) and she's a diamond. Wifey, I love you.

So what else have I learned in 2005? I've definitely realised I'm always going to be a bigger-boned gentleman. The truth is I can't diet to save my life, so I'm going to try and cut out the real excess and accept I'm never going to be a slim Jim, which is great news for Kentucky's profits in 2006. I do, though, have to point out I am a pound lighter now than I was at the start of the year.

I also now know fish are an expensive business but not quite as expensive as playing poker online all the time. I'll still play now and then but I am going to cut down this year. Famous last words!

My other New Year resolutions are as follows:

Number one, I'm going to get the exercise bike out of the garden shed… and sell it on eBay. It's taunting me in there, so I might as well get a few quid back on it while I can.

Number two, I'm not going to keep on lining the DRA's pockets. It's a scandal how much I've had to fork out to them and I can't get the thought out my head that I'm just paying for the drinks at their Christmas party.

Number three, and most important, win the World Championship at the Tavern. I know I've got it in me and after three successive semi-finals, I reckon it's my turn.

Take care,

WAYNE MARDLE
January 2006

Acknowledgements

WAYNE MARDLE

I'd like to thank my family, especially Donna and my mum Barbara and dad Billy, for all your love and encouragement over the years. Without you I'd never have got this far and your support means the world to me. You always believed in me and I can honestly say any success that comes my way would mean nothing if you weren't there to share it with me.

My gratitude goes to Paul Downes and Rosie Meckiff at Objective Image for making me look more or less presentable for the cover of the book.

Finally, I'd like to thank Iain for all your advice over the last year and your mysterious knack of turning my random thoughts and observations into something printable. I apologise for all the times I said I would pick up the phone to discuss the book and never did.

IAIN SPRAGG

Thanks to Justyn Barnes for your tireless enthusiam as the book's editor. Without you, I really wouldn't have been able to see the wood for the trees. Thanks too, of course, to Jim Drewett and Toby Trotman at Vision Sports Publishing for believing in the book in the first place. I'm also indebted to Matthew Porter and Dave Allen at the Professional Darts Corporation for your friendly cooperation throughout the project.

And finally, many, many thanks to my wife Julia for sitting through hours of televised darts when *What Not To Wear* was on the other side. Your patience was as surprising as it was vital.

Lukewarm thanks to my beautiful children, Dylan and Devon, and your incredible knack of deciding it was story time every time I sat down at the computer to type.

Also from **VISION SPORTS PUBLISHING**

ISBN: 1-9053260-7-6

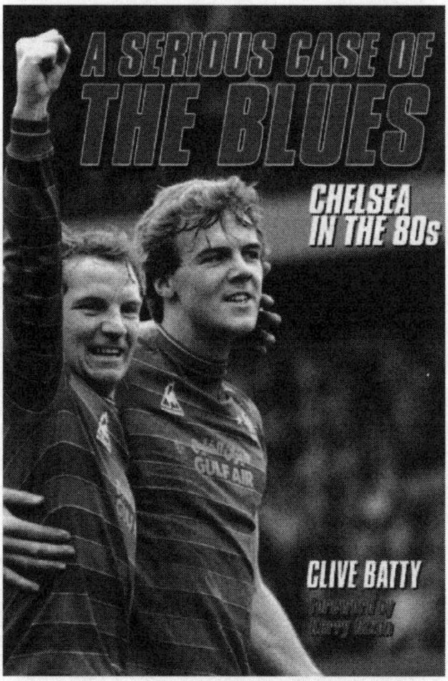

ISBN: 1-9053260-2-5

www.visionsp.co.uk

Also from **VISION SPORTS PUBLISHING**

ISBN: 0-9546428-9-9

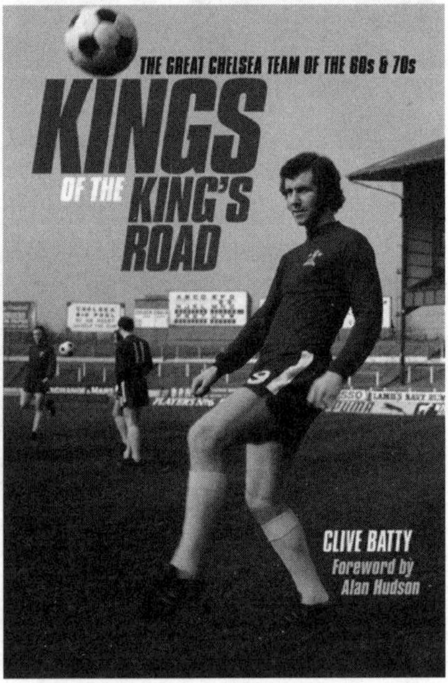

ISBN: 0-9546428-1-3

www.visionsp.co.uk

ISBN: 0-9546428-7-2

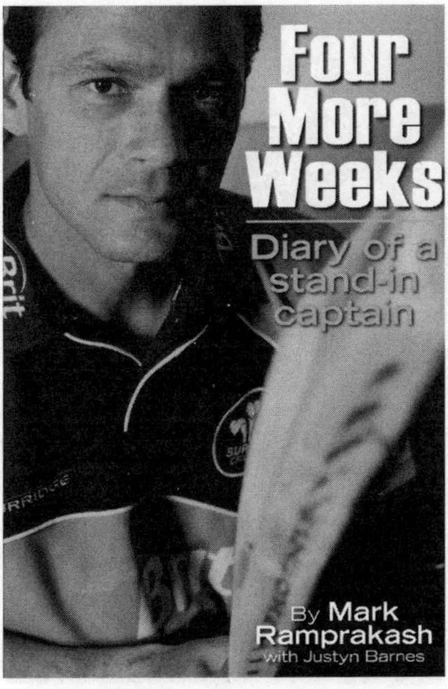

ISBN: 1-9053260-1-7

www.visionsp.co.uk

Also from **Vision Sports Publishing**

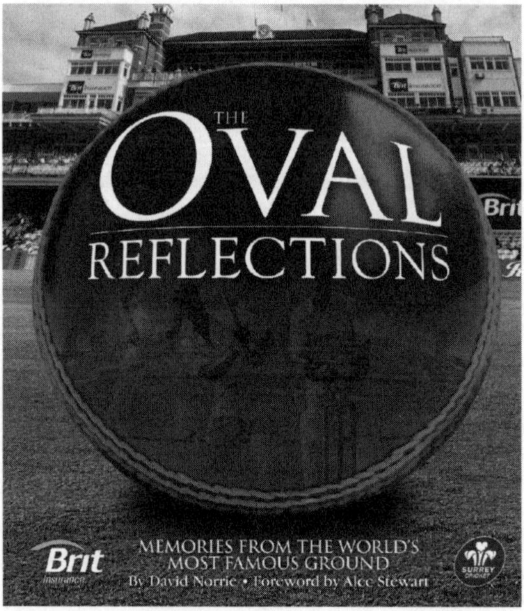

ISBN: 1-9053260-5-X

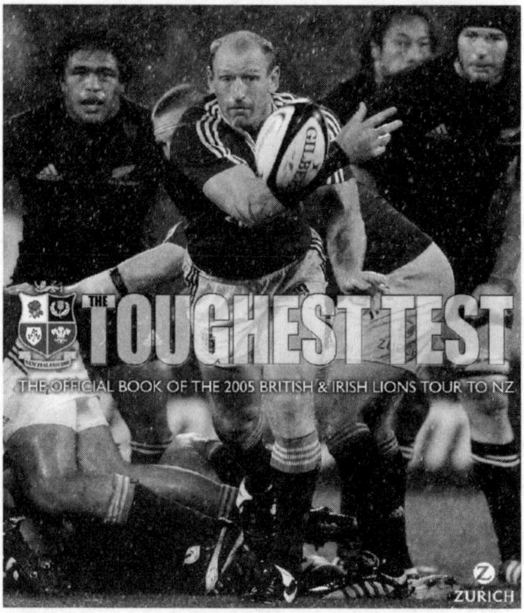

ISBN: 1-9053260-4-1